SCREEN SAVVY

CREATING BALANCE IN A DIGITAL WORLD

ISBN 13: 978-1-4621-2116-8

Published by Plain Sight Publishing, an imprint of Cedar Fort, Inc., 2373 W. 700 S., Springville, UT 84663
Distributed by Cedar Fort, Inc., www.cedarfort.com

Names: Anderson, Ryan J., 1978- author.
Title: Screen savvy : creating balance in a digital world / Ryan J. Anderson.
Description: Springville, UT : Plain Sight Publishing, an imprint of Cedar
   Fort, Inc., [2017] | Includes bibliographical references.
Identifiers: LCCN 2017018716 (print) | LCCN 2017026749 (ebook) | ISBN
   9781462128471 (epub and moby) | ISBN 9781462121168 (perfect bound : alk.
   paper)
Subjects: LCSH: Information technology--Social aspects. | Internet--Social
   aspects. | Internet addiction.
Classification: LCC HM851 (ebook) | LCC HM851 .A646 2017 (print) | DDC
   302.23/1--dc23
LC record available at https://lccn.loc.gov/2017018716

Cover design by M. Shaun McMurdie
Cover design © 2017 by Cedar Fort, Inc.
Edited and typeset by Kimiko Christensen Hammari and Erica Myers

Printed in the United States of America

10 9 8 7 6 5 4 3 2 1

Printed on acid-free paper

SCREEN SAVVY
CREATING BALANCE IN A DIGITAL WORLD

RYAN J. ANDERSON, PhD

PLAIN SIGHT
PUBLISHING

AN IMPRINT OF CEDAR FORT, INC.
SPRINGVILLE, UTAH

In loving memory of Marianne

CONTENTS

INTRODUCTION

PREPARING YOUR MIND:
OUR CONVERSATION

The Right Questions

We tend to have rather odd conversations in my home. In the last year alone, my children have discussed and debated subjects such as the migratory habits of penguins, ways it might be possible to survive entering a black hole, the proper use of the word *apropos*, and tardigrade colonization of Mars. Did I mention my kids are eight and ten years old? Suffice it to say, I am used to my children asking me strange questions, one of which I'd like to share with you.

When my youngest son was five years old, he became a fan of the film *Tron: Legacy* (2010). For those unfamiliar with this movie, it features a master computer programmer named Kevin Flynn who finds a way to enter the digital world inside computers. He uses this digital realm to run experiments in search of creating the perfect system, hoping it will lead to insights that will benefit the real world in a myriad of ways. However, he is betrayed by one of his own creations and trapped in the digital world, leaving his son, Sam, unintentionally abandoned in the real world. Many years later, Sam Flynn is pulled into the digital realm and fights his way through fantastical perils in an effort to rescue his father and return to the physical world.

With the plot of this movie fresh in his mind, my son earnestly asked me, "Dad, if I ever get stuck in a computer, will you come in, fight off the bad programs, and bring me back home?"

The absolute sincerity of his question and the concerned look in his eyes penetrated my heart so much that I choked up a little as I replied, "Of course! I would never leave you stuck in a computer. I would come for you, and I wouldn't leave until I found you and brought you back with me."

He smiled and hugged me, feeling reassured that there was a plan in place. Balance was restored in his young world.

I remember feeling a little silly that I became emotional over a question about something that would never really happen. Then, as I reflected more upon the conversation, it occurred to me that the concern my son had expressed was not merely science fiction: it was a *real* danger. He really could get lost in a digital world. So could I, and so could any of us. This is the danger I want to discuss with you, as well as some ideas about solutions to the problems this danger creates.

It is my hope that in your conversation with me in this book, you won't just rush through it, pick up a few interesting facts, and simply conclude that you either agree or disagree with the points that I make. I invite you to read it thoughtfully and think about it critically. Consider, also, how you may take some piece of our conversation and set it in motion in your own life.

This book is written for a broad audience. It is intended to reach parents concerned about the electronic habits of their child, spouses worried about a husband's or wife's connection to the cyberworld, teens or adults who think they may have a problem with electronics, tech savvy people who are convinced they have no problems with electronics, and clinical professionals seeking to educate themselves on the issue. As such, parts of the book will speak to each one of these groups on their level. Sometimes, what I share may be too technical for some of my audience or too basic. My hope is that you will read through it all and pick out the parts that are most applicable to you. Ultimately, I sincerely hope you will not think this book is just an interesting look into a challenge that *other* people have, but take to heart whatever applies directly to you.

An Invitation to Insight

While it is true that this book will talk about electronics such as smartphones and video games, that's not really what this book is about. This book is about you.

Before you get too much of a big head about that, though, keep in mind that this book isn't just about you; it's about all of us as human beings. A healthy relationship with electronics is just as much about *who* we are as it is about the nature of the electronics themselves. Developing an understanding of challenges inherent to our human nature is an indispensable part of creating a healthy relationship with electronics.

So, here's the million-dollar question: how healthy is your relationship with the cyberworld? Social media? Texting? Gaming? How often is your smartphone out? How often do you turn it off and reconnect with the world around you? How adaptive and functional is your relationship with the cyberworld in relation to the other important areas of your life: work, education, relationships, personal development, healthy physical habits, values, and ethics? Are you giving adequate time, attention, and priority to those things you value most?

This is a hard question to answer, partially due to the fact that defining what is healthy can be problematic. What do we use to measure healthy habits when we cannot directly measure their results with something concrete such as a blood test or an echocardiogram?

One tool people tend to fall back on is looking around and asking themselves, "Is what I am doing normal?" This usually means, "Am I doing what most other people seem to be doing?" They then tend to conclude that if what they are doing largely fits with what other people are doing, then their actions are normal and thus, by questionable logical extension, healthy.

Consider this: *Time* magazine recently reported that Yale University's Prevention Research Center found that half of all deaths in the United States would be preventable by lifestyle changes.[1] Think about that. Half of the people who will die in this country every year don't have to die if they make different lifestyle choices. This tells me that to a large degree, many of the health habits and practices in the US are not healthy. They are so common that they may appear to be normal, but concluding that they are healthy and will not affect us negatively is faulty thinking. In fact, if our physical habits are relatively normal, chances are they are actually unhealthy.

Our insight in this area is demonstrably poor. A recent study found that 60 percent of American women and 75 percent of American men are overweight or obese.[2] However, a recent Gallup Poll revealed that only 45 percent of American adults identified themselves as overweight or obese.[3] The gap between the facts and our perception here is fairly large, partially because the problem is so prolific. We Americans don't know what healthy looks like very well because most of what we see around us in not healthy. With that being the case, what chance does the average American have of evaluating their own degree of physical health? Clearly, the answer is not a very good one.

Some of our habits and approaches to our relationship with the cyberworld are healthy and enriching. However, as we look around ourselves, much of what we see is disruptive or maladaptive to one degree or another. There is ample evidence—which I will discuss throughout this book—that the trend is for our collective relationship with the cyberworld to be unhealthy. Trying to evaluate if our cyber habits are healthy by comparing them to what seems normal is actually using an unreliable measure, and we are deluding ourselves in the process. The issue at hand is not *if* you struggle to have a healthy relationship with electronics, but *when* and *how* you struggle to have a healthy relationship with electronics.

It would be easy to approach the topic of the health of our relationship with the cyberworld with simplistic, black-and-white thinking. Indeed, many people do. Some people are convinced there is nothing wrong with the cyberworld and the way we use it, and other people are convinced there is nothing good that can come of it.

I'll refer to the first group as the Cyborgs. These are the ones who throw themselves headlong into electronic media and the cyberworld and scoff at any concerns someone may raise about it as being old-fashioned, uninformed, intrusive, and infringing upon their rights. Their motto is a revamped version of the classic accusation: *If my music is too loud, it means you're too old.* If you are not on board with the latest technological wave, you are a fossil. At its extremes, you find people who believe that humanity's ultimate evolution will be the "singularity," a condition in which machine mind and human mind will be inextricably joined together, like the concept of evolution if it were a collaborative effort between Charles Darwin and Steve Jobs.

I call the other group the Luddites. They look upon electronic media, the Internet, and all things associated with the Internet with great fear and trepidation. They are very reluctant to have anything to do with it personally, and if they had their way, people would abandon the Internet all together. At their extreme, they see the Internet and the cyberworld as a great evil corrupting and consuming all who dare enter its benighted realm. The cyberworld, to them, is a missing scene from Dante's *Inferno*.

The interesting thing is that neither one of these parties is necessarily wrong. They are both examining the same phenomenon. They are both picking up on some valid points, though they hesitate to grant validity to the other party's observations. It can become like the old story of several blindfolded people examining an elephant. Each person determines that the elephant is like a rope, a fan, a tree, or a spear, depending on which part they happen to be touching. Their conclusion makes total sense to them, and the assertions of someone who is touching a different part of the elephant sound completely absurd. None of these blindfolded people are wrong, but none of them are correct, either.

This would be a good occasion to apply the observation of science fiction author Larry Niven: "There exist minds that think as well as you do, but differently."[4] The fact that someone draws a different conclusion than ours is not evidence of their intellectual inferiority.

If our blindfolded elephant researchers could learn to accept the limitations of their ability to perceive based on their perspective and give some credence to the potential validity of the other blindfolded observers, they would learn that there are parts of an elephant that are indeed like a rope, a fan, a tree, and a spear. The blindfolded people's openness to each other's experiences would help them all come to a greater understanding of what an elephant is. From there, they would be able to better understand the potential benefits and perils of interacting with an elephant, and would be able to determine how to develop a relationship with the elephant that profits from the benefits and helps avoid the downsides.

The Matrix and Self-Justifying Images

The greatest barriers to our own understanding are often inside our own minds. The 1999 film *The Matrix* presented a fictional world in which human beings were enslaved by malevolent machines. In order to keep the humans prisoners to harvest their body heat for energy, the machines plugged the humans into a virtual world that fed information directly into their brains. The brilliant part of this approach was that the humans in this story would never try to escape because they never realized that they were prisoners. They could not distinguish the sensory data the machines fed into their brains from real life experience. Thus, they would never even think to question if they were slaves or if they lived in a real world. Even the very concept that their version of reality might not be real was so astonishingly shocking, few would even consider the possibility when it was presented to them, let alone take the risk of testing the limits of what they had come to consider real. The film is focused around the hero's journey of characters who dared to look outside the Matrix to seek a world of truth and new freedom, even though some of those truths were hard. This journey was not without its challenges, and the most formidable one resided within their own minds and their accustomed ways of thinking.

In a very real sense, each of us faces the challenge of living in a matrix like the one in the film. However, instead of being made up of the carefully calculated cyber-neurological input of machine conquerors, our matrices are made up of our preferred way of seeing ourselves. We usually spin the events in our lives to fit how we like to think of ourselves. This preferred way of thinking about ourselves can be referred to as our self-justifying image.[5] If part of my self-justifying image is that I see myself as responsible and healthy in my relationship with electronics, then when I am being irresponsible and unhealthy with them, I will hide it from myself and spin the situation so it still fits how I tend to think of myself. That's how I can get trapped in the Matrix.

The Point

This book is about the Internet, social media, video games, and our relationship with the cyberworld, so what's the point of these opening philosophical musings?

We live in a physical world that is seemingly intertwined with the cyberworld. It is all around us. It is as common as the air that we breathe. Because it is so ubiquitous, it is easy to not think about it critically, just as it would be easy for a fish to never really stop to think about the water it swims in because the water is a constant part of its experience.

Because of this, we can easily fall into a mindset and a pattern of actions in our relationship with the cyberworld that is similarly mindless, that simply flows with the currents without considering what the currents are and where they may lead, or even the very fact that the currents exist. The irony is, many of us tend to spend a lot of time interacting with the cyberworld without being mindful of it and how it intersects with the real world and with our real lives.

Ask yourself some personal questions about the health of your relationship with electronics. Move beyond the knee-jerk, simple, emotionally gratifying answers we tend to come up with when asked to be introspective. We so easily hide inconvenient truths from ourselves; thus, we must learn to take our own opinions and self-evaluation with a grain of salt. We all too easily feed ourselves comfortably padded reassurances when change is needed. If we quickly conclude, *I'm fine! I don't need to examine my relationship with electronics*, then I would suggest we remember what David Dunning said, "The trouble with ignorance is that it feels so much like expertise," leading him to conclude that by and large, we human beings tend to be "confident idiots."[6]

I hope we can move beyond being such mindless "confident idiots" when it comes to our relationship with the cyberworld. I believe all of us can benefit from moving beyond the answers we obtain through a superficial and noncritical (and thus likely self-deceived) evaluation of our own mindset and behaviors. The answers aren't simple, but when we move beyond dismissive self-assurance, the answers become much less complicated.

My point in this introduction, then, is to encourage you to think—to think carefully, to think deeply, to challenge yourself, to be mindful of your own defenses, to push your comfort zone, to not settle for easy answers. If by the end of this book you haven't questioned yourself at all, you probably haven't really allowed yourself to ponder. Chances are, most of us have something to learn—and very likely many of us have something to change—when it comes to our relationship with the cyberworld.

Endnotes

1. Park, A. (2014, May 1). Nearly half of US deaths can be prevented with lifestyle changes. *Time*. Retrieved on May 22, 2014, from http://time.com/84514/nearly-half-of-us-deaths-can-be-prevented-with-lifestyle-changes/.

2. Murray, J.L., Ng, M., & Mokdad, A. (2014). Global, regional, and national prevalence of overweight and obesity in children and adults during 1980–2013: A systematic analysis for the global burden of disease study 2013. *The Lancet, 377*(9765), 557–567.

3. Wilke, J. (2014). In U.S., majority "not overweight," not trying to lose weight. Gallup. Retrieved June 12, 2014, from http://www.gallup.com/poll/171287/majority-not-overweight-not-trying-lose-weight.aspx.

4. Niven, L.V. (2010). Niven's laws. Retrieved April 4, 2014, from http://www.larryniven.net/stories/nivens_laws.shtml.

5. Arbinger Institute (2000). Leadership and self-deception: Getting out of the box. San Francisco: Berrett-Koehler.

6. Dunning, D. (2014). We are all confident idiots. *Pacific Standard*. Retrieved December 18, 2014, from http://www.psmag.com/navigation/health-and-behavior/confident-idiots-92793/.

CHAPTER 1

THE LOTUS EATERS

To begin the process of critical thinking about the world of computers, let's examine what an ancient Greek tale can teach us about the cyber-world and our complex relationship with it.

One of the most famous and long-lived of the ancient stories is the tale of Odysseus, a Greek hero from the city of Ithaca whose adventures are told in Homer's epic poems *The Iliad* and *The Odyssey*. Odysseus was a reluctant warrior, pressed into military service and forced to leave behind his family and home. While he was loyal to his country, family was his greatest priority, and it was with a heavy heart that he left them to answer the call of duty.

Odysseus and his men had fought in the long and devastating Trojan War. It was Odysseus who made the plan for designing and using the famous Trojan Horse to infiltrate the city of Troy and end the war, thus freeing him to pursue his heart's desire of returning home to his beloved wife, Penelope, and his son, Telemachus. At the war's end, Odysseus and his crew set sail immediately for home, intending to make a speedy journey to be reunited with their families.

However, his journey home became extremely complicated. Men, monsters, and gods conspired against him, and he and his crew faced unimaginable challenges and obstacles to their goal of returning to their homes and families. What should have been a relatively short journey after a decade-long war was stretched out into a ten-year ordeal because of these trials and challenges. Through it all, Odysseus never lost sight of his ultimate goal: to return home to his family.

Some of the challenges Odysseus and his crew faced were obvious dangers, such as their encounter with the giant man-eating Cyclops Polyphemus, or being forced to attempt to navigate their ship between the deadly whirlpool monster Charybdis and the six-headed monster Scylla. These were dangers that anyone would know instinctively and reflexively to avoid, to fight against, and to escape at all costs. The threat of these beasts and monsters was undeniable; each of them could be the reason that Odysseus and his crew would never return home and see their families again.

Among the challenges they faced, however, a few were far more subtle. One of these was their visit to the Island of the Lotus Eaters. After a long time on the sea, Odysseus and his crew found an island. They landed there, hoping to find food and other supplies. Odysseus sent a scouting party of three men to explore the island and report back with what they found.

The three men had not traveled far when they came across a quiet settlement filled with friendly people. The people all seemed extremely relaxed. No one was working. No one was stressed out. In fact, there was nothing much going on at all—a stark contrast to the years of backbreaking labor and fighting that Odysseus and his men had suffered through. The scouting party explained that they were looking for food and supplies. The people of the settlement revealed that they all survived by eating the lotus flowers that grew naturally and abundantly on the island. They offered the lotus to the hungry scouts, who were happy to have something other than fish and preserved rations to eat.

Upon eating the lotus, the scouts became extremely relaxed. Imagine how pronounced that contrast must have felt, going from fending off the desperation of a doomed journey to feeling suddenly, finally, blissfully empty of worry and care. As the effects of the lotus took hold, the scouts' focus on returning home began to fade. They became sleepy and still. They found that they cared less and less about returning home—the home they had been sad to leave and had not seen for a decade's worth of brutal conflict. Their memories of the things and people they loved at home diminished as they experienced the calming and enticing effects of the lotus. Soon, all they cared about was staying on the island and eating the lotus. The thought of home, with fathers, mothers, brothers, sisters, wives, and children that they had not seen in so long was overpowered by the desire to have the lotus and its immediate pleasant effects. After all, why work for happiness later when you can enjoy the hazy glow of immediate pleasure now?

When the scouts did not return, Odysseus went in search of them. He found them lounging in the grass with the other Lotus Eaters, consuming the lotus and deeply enjoying the release and pleasure it gave them. Nothing Odysseus said could motivate them to get up and return to the ship. Odysseus realized that as long as they were under the influence of the lotus, any reminders of their duties and responsibilities were useless to motivate them. Even memories of their loved ones, who they fought so hard to return to, were not enough to spark a recollection of their course. Realizing that he had no other choice, Odysseus decided to take the scouts back to the ship against their will. Even though they could not remember what their priorities were while under the influence of the lotus, Odysseus could, and he knew he had to act to help them do what they would do if they could see clearly.

In the moment that Odysseus tried to take the scouts back, they saw him as a monster and the obstacle to their happiness. They fought back with intense ferocity. Odysseus had to drag them back to the ship literally kicking and screaming. When they arrived at the ship, Odysseus had to tie them to the rudder benches to keep them from throwing themselves into the sea and swimming back to the island. As the ship sailed away from the Island of the Lotus Eaters, the scouts wept in despair. Only days later, when the last effects of the lotus had worn off, did the scouts stop their rage and their mourning as they came to realize what they had almost done under the influence of the lotus. Whereas before they had seen Odysseus as a monster intent on destroying their happiness and taking them away from the one thing they wanted, now they saw him as a hero who knew them well enough to know what they really valued and who helped save them when they could not save themselves, even when they themselves fought against him. Had he listened to their cries or surrendered the fight back on the Island of the Lotus Eaters, the scouts would have never seen their families again, just as surely as if they had been eaten by Polyphemus or Scylla or had drowned in the depths of the sea by Charybdis. The lotus flower was a monster in its own right, just as real as the Cyclops, the six-headed monster, and the demon whirlpool. But instead of inspiring fear, it induced pleasure; instead of scaring away, it lured in. Regardless of its many differences from the other monsters, the end results of its influence were the same: it could destroy what was most important to Odysseus and his men, the ability to return home.

Lotus in Your Life

While there is much potential good that can come from our relationship with the cyberworld, there are many aspects of our relationship with it that can become our own personal "lotus blossom," especially if we are merely riding the tide of social trends. If we rely on determining what is healthy by what is common and normal, we will often be misled. Common sense is not common practice, and the average person tends to sink below what is wise. We can all benefit from learning to think critically about our own society, our own traditions, our own culture, and our own situation, rather than just accepting them on face value and propelling ourselves myopically along the course determined by the crowd.

Self-Examination

To prepare yourself for a deeper examination of the cyberworld, consider completing the following exercise as a pretest of sorts.

1. Identify something in your life in the real, physical world that might be like the lotus flower in *The Odyssey*. Describe it. In what way is it like the lotus flower?
2. Identify something in the cyberworld (Internet, gaming, social media, and so on) that may be like the lotus flower in your life. In what ways is it like the lotus flower?

3. What appeals to you about your personal lotus flowers? What do you like about them?

4. Identify some of the things that are most important to you in your life. To help you think about this, ask yourself what you think will still be important one year, five years, and ten years in the future. What are some things you want to make sure to do with your life?

5. Now, identify ways in which your personal lotus flowers could interfere with the things you identified in question 4. Are there times when your devotion to your lotus flower interrupts any of the priorities and important things you identified in question 4? Describe in as much detail as you can.

6. Like Odysseus's scouts, is it possible that there are people in your life who are trying to help you avoid the dangers of your own personal lotus flower that may look like enemies to you? Who are they? What have their actions been? How have you responded? What do you think you should do now?

7. If you were free of the influence of your own personal lotus flowers, how might you see things differently? Would you feel differently about any of your choices? Would there be any difference in any of your important relationships? What would you be doing differently?

CHAPTER 2

MEET THE CYBER-SCAPE

The Cyber Big Bang

According to current science, the Big Bang, space, and time themselves expanded at a velocity faster than light speed.[1] While I think I understand the concept, it still taxes my mind to actually visualize this event. That being said, a similar, remarkable phenomenon has happened in the last few decades. There has been an expansion of the cyberworld so rapid and so explosive that I have come to call it the *Cyber Big Bang*. A whole new universe—a cyber-universe composed of data—has been created and has expanded at a rate that feels like it is breaking the light barrier. Interestingly enough, if you look at a map of the known universe and a map of the Internet, they look surprisingly similar.

This has resulted in a phenomenon known as *Big Data* and includes information that we each generate *actively* (sending emails, posting on social media, and texting) or *passively* (the digital footprints we leave by using credit cards, being captured on traffic cameras, or even being tagged in someone else's photograph). There has never been anything like it before. It is as if a whole new dimension of reality has sprung into existence and woven itself into the very fiber of the world in which we live.

I have come to call this new part of our world the *cyber-scape*. It has become as ever-present and evolving as the physical landscape around us. The cyber-scape could be thought of as the interface between the digital world and the physical world. It consists of texting, social media, cell phones, electronic surveillance, online games, handheld gaming devices, business networks, news sources, broadcast media, streaming media, and much more. In many ways, this cyber-universe has already expanded to a size that has exceeded our physical world in scope, and it is only continuing to expand.

Cyber Omnipresence and Influence

This cyber-scape surrounds us at all times. Even when we are not actively logged on or plugged in ourselves, we are entrenched. Indiana University professor Mark Deuze has observed that we tend to live our lives *within* our media, rather than *with* our media. He said, "Media are to us as water is to a fish. . . . This does not mean life is determined by media—it just suggests that whether we like it or not, every aspect of our lives takes place in media."[2] The cyber-scape has become a part of our culture. It has altered our language and our perception. It has also had an impact on our priorities, values, and interactions. It affects the way we think and process information. As we will explore later in the book, it is even shaping the very structure and functioning of our brains. It is shaping us; our own creation is molding us like clay. Whether you participate in the cyberworld directly or not, the way it shapes the world around you has a direct impact on you.

Did you know the word *selfie* was elected Word of the Year 2013 by the Oxford English Dictionary? Indeed, the duck-face selfie has become the poster child for the millennial online image. Many of us seem to be in a competition to either copy others in popular trends or one up each other in posting variations of the self-taken photo online as many times as possible. Selfies have become one of the most common forms of communication, but what do they express? In my mind, the duck-face selfie in particular is like an inside joke that everyone repeats because they think they look cool and to appear a part of the in crowd, but nobody understands the punch line.

Selfies are a harmless diversion, right? Perhaps, at worst, we might see them as rather immature or limiting. Yet selfies have also been linked to a rise in narcissism[3] and body dysmorphic disorder, a disorder in which people develop highly distorted views of what their body looks like and how bodies in general actually appear. As much as I love editing my photos, think about how many images we see a day that are filtered, trimmed, and distorted to fit an ideal. In addition, studies have linked selfie photos to addiction and other mental health disorders.[4]

In many ways, these trends and correlations make perfect sense. While image has always been a part of how we form our identity, learning to value ourselves and each other as more than merely our superficial image has always been a challenge in our development.

It is my observation that the one thing the Internet exceeds at above all else is portraying an image divorced from substance. The cyber-scape is filled with attractive, unrealistic, hollow facades masquerading as real identities. We are constantly bombarded by people putting their physical image out there for the world to see. Then we receive a flood of information as people begin to remark on, even vote on, with likes and comments, the quality and caliber of our cyber self. Thus, we have upped the ante with how much our physical appearance is worth in social currency. In doing so, we preach a very loud sermon to the world about the importance of our physical appearance. We tell each other that our sexualized bodies and our sensationalized images are all we really have to offer, and thus the only thing that gives us any value. Growing rates of narcissism and body dysmorphic disorder seem to be a natural extension of this kind of image evangelism.

We see others building virtual shrines to themselves online and being affirmed for it. We are implicitly sold narcissism as a cheap and easy surrogate for self-esteem. Self-promotion is the social skill we substitute for sophistication. All of this happens in hundreds of thousands of ways. Usually, none of this is taught explicitly, but some unabashedly detrimental cyber regions do exist, such as pro-anorexia websites and websites that urge people to post gossip and criticism about other people anonymously.

Many of us who share this subtle cyber self-worth message would feel shocked if someone accused us of any such intent. We would strongly protest that we don't hold those values. But stop and think; how often do our online actions and attitudes send a message contrary to what we believe or value? That is one of the conundrums of being human. We are well aware of what we intend to do, so we tend to judge our actions off of our intentions. This can blind us to the actual results of our actions. We may very well be taking in more of these messages than we know, and in turn, we shift our views subtly and, without realizing it consciously, reinforce those attitudes.

An Ocean of Information: We Can Swallow It, but Can We Digest It?

Obviously it follows that with this Cyber Big Bang, people are communicating more with each other than in any other time in history. This raises some interesting questions:

- What is being said?
- Who is saying it?
- How reliable is the information being shared?
- What is the average person's ability to determine the validity of the information being shared?
- And even more important, what is the average teenager's ability to know what is legitimate and what is not?

To begin exploring the answers to these questions, let's start with two words that strike terror into most people's hearts: pop quiz! Can you answer the following questions correctly without looking them up?

- In statistics, at what sample size does a regression analysis begin to be able to validly show statistical significance?
- In an ANOVA table, what is the proper way to interpret what is implied by the slope?
- What are the criteria that must be met for correlational data to adequately imply a possible causational relationship between two factors?
- How do you evaluate for heteroscedasticity in outcome data, and what implications does this have on the potential validity and reliability of a statistic?

Some of us may take comfort in the fact that although we are not personally equipped with the knowledge necessary to answer these questions, we can turn to many sources for these answers. We can Google them. We assume that these sources are monitored by people with the knowledge and skills necessary to determine if the information we are given is accurate. We feel some confidence turning to advice and interpretation from people considered professionals in their fields. The sad truth is that poor data evaluation is not just a condition confined to the average Google-happy Joe or Jane.

I have asked the questions above to well-educated professionals, consumers of scientific research, many of whom have PhDs. What has surprised and slightly dismayed me is that even in a room with a crowd like that, only a very small number of people can answer even a single one of these questions, let alone all four of them. Yet, these are very basic concepts that are required for someone to understand in order to begin to evaluate the validity of statistics. These people, whom others will look to as professionals and will give greater credence to their opinions, either never learned this information or allowed their knowledge to lapse. What this tells me is that we are in over our heads when it comes to being reasonably informed consumers of the vast amounts of information, research, nonsense, hyperbole, and intellectual pig slop available to us on the Internet.

But wait! You may say that you only trust scholarly journals and the occasional foray onto Wikipedia. You're good, right? Many people feel a much higher degree of confidence in the validity of their information if it has been published in a peer-reviewed journal. There are multiple complications with this, however. Many peer-reviewed journals require expensive subscriptions, either to journals or larger libraries like EBSCO or ERIC. For example, a quick perusal on Google Scholar demonstrated that you may end up paying thirty-five dollars for a single article if you do not have a subscription. Without paying for access, the average layperson or professional reader is confined to merely reading the abstract of the article, which doesn't give enough information for a solid evaluation. This creates a barrier to information, or *pay wall*.

To help combat the pay wall problem, open access journals have emerged. They pay their operating costs by author publishing fees, rather than by subscriptions. They utilize the peer review process and thus purport to be rigorous and efficacious in safeguarding the quality of the information being published and consumed.

However, in a recent sting operation, the journal *Science* put together a spoof article and submitted it to a large number of open access, peer-reviewed journals. The paper was purposefully, openly, and obviously flawed. It was basically doing the literary equivalent of placing a "kick me" sign on its own back. Its author, John Bohannon, stated, "Any reviewer with more than a high-school knowledge of chemistry and the ability to understand a basic data plot should have spotted the paper's shortcomings immediately. Its experiments are so hopelessly flawed that the results are meaningless."[5]

Theoretically, the peer review process of the journals this article was submitted to should have detected the flaws and rejected the paper. That was not the case. This fatally flawed paper managed to pass the peer review process of 157 open access journals, including well respected entities such as Sage and Elsevier.[5]

The peer review process, then, is only as good as both the skill and the intellectual integrity of those doing the review. Degrees and official-sounding titles should not be taken as evidence of competence in and of themselves. Even in reputable and traditional journals, peer reviews should not be seen as a panacea; every piece of research and information—even those from the most reputable of sources—merits careful consideration of its methods, agenda, biases, limitations, and applications. Good consumers of data must evaluate each piece of information on its own merits, regardless of its source. Sadly, most people are not equipped to do so, nor do many people realize they even need to do so.

Scrounging from Digital Dumpsters: A Diet Rich in Mental Junk Food

The attention to detail and careful consideration necessary to be a good consumer of data is a lot of work, and it does not jive very well with the pace of modern life. The *microwave burrito mentality* is common: wanting things fast and convenient, even if it is at the cost of quality and content. Most of us want our information with as little effort on our part as possible and prefer to avoid data that challenges the way we like to think about the world.

As evidenced by the peer review sting experiment, most of us are not very skilled at evaluating our information, and even the professionals may fail to be thorough. We tend to cherry pick. Often, we consider information valid when it agrees with us and invalid when it challenges us. This poor reasoning leads to the false sense of certainty or an ignorance based self-assurance.

The Internet does provide us with a veritable feast of high-quality, useful information, resources, and experiences, but most of us probably spend more time than we would like to believe gorging upon mental junk food from the digital dumpsters of the cyber-scape. Most concerning to me is that we tend to not know the difference between when we are consuming good data and when we are consuming junk data. If we are to truly be a digital culture, we need to get better at making this distinction. If we do not, we run the risk of metaphorically discovering ways to make fire, but having no idea how to extinguish the flames. In our current state of collective competence in data consumption, we are boldly making rash decisions based on junk data.

Big Entities on the Cyber-Scape Continents and Waterways of the Cyber-Scape

All aspects of the cyber-scape are made of data, just as all aspects of the physical world are made of matter and energy. The data of the cyber-scape has forms and functions as diverse as the different geological features that make up the physical world. While there is a tremendous amount of variation to the topography of the cyber-scape, there are several major features that tend to dominate the digital realm. Chances are, if we are interacting with the cyber-scape, then we are engaging with these particular features. Forty percent of the time Americans spend online is spent in just three areas: social media (22.7 percent of online time), email (8.3 percent of online time), and online games (10.2 percent of online time).[6]

Picture these three entities as the major continents of the cyber-scape. They are vast landmasses where the population of the cyber-scape works, plays, and engages in all manner of social interactions.

Streaming medias are the fourth member of the digital pantheon. Try to envision them as the freshwater rivers, lakes, and waterways in the cyber-scape, great surging cascades of constantly flowing information that have become an indispensable part of all aspects of the cyber topography. Just as water is indispensable for organic life in the physical world, streaming is lifeblood for digital media delivery. Streaming media giants Netflix and YouTube account for 51 percent of all Internet download traffic.[6]

Cyber-Nations, Cyber-Citizenship, and Cyber-Leaders

The Internet has opened up unprecedented opportunities for human connection. Historically, people's social networks were limited to a relatively small geographic region. The Internet has broken down many of those barriers, allowing us as individuals to bypass physical boundaries and take part in larger communities. This has allowed social units to form online independent of physical limitations in the real world.

These new communities come with their own populations, cultures, boundaries, and leaders. The magnitude of these cyber communities is astonishing. For example, in October of 2012, Facebook reached one billion users.[7] That's approximately one-seventh of the world's population. This makes Facebook the third most populous nation in the world, coming in behind only to China and India. Granted, the population of Facebook is not united or homogeneous in any way. They are united in a single venue but with no single leader. The dynamics of the cyber-nation of Facebook is like a highly fragmented but overlapping tribal nation, with a dash of anarchy thrown in just to keep things interesting.

Other cyber-nations are much more united. Some form specifically to align with a single leader. Some seem to operate like a totalitarian state whose citizens revere their leader almost as a demigod. For example, in October of 2012, Lady Gaga reached 30 million followers. To put that in perspective, she has slightly fewer followers than the total population of Canada and enjoys essentially a 100 percent approval rate from those followers, something for which the political leaders of a physical nation could only dream.[7] Lady Gaga's followers, who go by the appellation of Little Monsters, are known for being particularly ardent in their allegiance to her.

It's hard to imagine the followers of the Greek goddess Hera being more fiercely devoted than Lady Gaga's loyal fans. When Lady Gaga recently had an online feud with gossip writer Perez Hilton, her followers became militant in their efforts to defend her honor. This actually led some fans to make death threats against Hilton. To her credit, Lady Gaga eventually asked her followers to stand down, and like loyal soldiers they obeyed.[8]

I must admit to serious concerns about what they may have done had she not given that order. They seem to adore her with a crusader's zeal. This passionate loyalty and irrational thinking when challenged is not uncommon for followers of other cyber leaders such as her and can be found in other areas of devotion.

Some people are not so much aligned around cyber leaders as they are aligned with ideas, ideals, or processes, like the free exchange of information or libertarian freedom from governmental or societal regulation. For some people, their online affiliations and loyalties surpass those they have in the physical world. Wikipedia contributors were found to consider their affiliation as *Wikepedians* as a stronger and more important part of their identity than their political affiliations.[9] Many people connect and congregate online based on their political affiliations, thus serving to deepen their ties and loyalties to their physical world political parties. In many cases, this radicalizes their positions, which we will discuss later in greater detail. Other online groups known for the ardor of their followers include Slashdot, Anonymous, CopBlock, and the Open Source movement that believes in the free and collaborative sharing of data in general. YouTube tends to operate as a completely anarchist nation, with no single leader or philosophy but with plenty of people willing to jump up and join a trending mob. Consider the growing trend for YouTube users to make endless variations on a theme of any given viral video, like the fire challenge. This involved people apparently showing off their ability to remove their genetic material from the gene pool by lighting themselves on fire.

Regardless of the specific site or cyber-nation, the cultures and influence of these entities upon the thoughts and actions of those who walk within their borders is considerable. Traveling through or joining these cyber-nations can have a powerful effect upon our thoughts and actions. If we are not cautious, we can be rapidly caught up by the contextual factors of the cyber-scape without even recognizing that the changes in our thoughts are occurring.

The Power of Context

Context has its own magnetic pull. I have had a number of experiences that have taught me the power of context firsthand. A memorable example occurred while I was in graduate school. My wife took a job as a hall advisor in a college dorm for freshman girls. During the summers, while most students were away, the university ran continuing education programs, and our dorm would be filled with a wide variety of people. One of the highlights was a women's conference the university holds each year. Women of varied backgrounds came to learn together and spent their free time in our dorms. Stay-at-home moms, lawyers, professors, scientists, judges, doctors, and businesswomen were all packed together under a single roof. It was fascinating how the setting of a college campus, and a dorm room in particular, would impact everyone's behavior that week, and I felt we had our freshman college girls back. There were late-night ice cream runs, silliness, competitiveness, drama, and even a few midnight makeovers. It was as if each woman had traveled back in time and became freshmen again. I even saw this sort of transformation in women who were in their sixties and seventies. As a student of human behavior, I was oddly fascinated by what I was seeing, and I remember wondering exactly what had led to this social anomaly.

The same phenomenon is also apparent in other situations. One example is high school reunions. A lot changes when people graduate from high school. People go in all different directions: some to college, some to the military, some to technical training, some to menial jobs, and some to heartbreak and sorrow. But when you put these people back together, you will see them transported back in time. Often, participants reproduce some of the attitudes, actions, and social patterns that typified who they were in high school. The difference may be a little harder to observe at a five-year reunion because there has been a relatively short amount of time for people to mature and develop new patterns in their lives. But show up to a ten, fifteen, or twenty-year reunion, and the transformation can be astonishing. Think of the cliques, friendships, rivalries, crushes, and even interests long since forgotten and how they erupt in a chain reaction when people are drawn together again at a reunion. Regardless of how involved an individual may be in the life they have built since high school, in those halls, with those familiar people, they revert.

These are just two examples, but this phenomenon in which people's attitudes and behaviors change based on their situation and surroundings is very common. Why exactly does this happen?

Just as the combination of preceding information can change the exact meaning or feeling behind a single word in a sentence, the circumstances surrounding an event shape our understanding. The people, places, seasons, traditions, culture, chronological time, physical objects, and even abstract things such as thoughts, ideas, and beliefs that are a part of our unique experience make up our personal context.

One of the things we need to realize about context is it isn't just some passive force making up the background scenery of an experience. Context plays a major role in forming an experience and exerts a very powerful influence on human thought and human behavior. You have experienced this on a constant basis, most likely without it crossing your mind.

To get an idea of the power of context, imagine yourself in a football stadium. The energy of the crowd ebbs and flows and changes shape depending on the way the game is going. Imagine that you look to your right and you see that the crowd has started to do the wave. What do you do when the wave gets near you? How do you feel? Do you sit and ponder or worry about whether you should participate? Do you stand up and participate in the wave without really thinking about it? Do you just sit there as if nothing has happened? Do you actively refuse to participate in the wave? How do the people around you react to your actions?

You could ask yourself a lot of questions about why you do what you do in that situation, but a big part of it has to do with your present context at the football game and pieces of your context from the past that influence the way you see the context now.

Now imagine yourself in a courtroom. The atmosphere is somber and a little tense. As you sit and observe the proceedings, the person next to you stands up and tries to get the audience to perform the wave. What do you do? Do you participate in the wave like you would at a football game, or does the different context make you reconsider doing it?

Chances are you would make a different choice about participating in the wave in both of these situations. If you did decide to do the wave in both, the reaction of those around you would be different. You won't get a charge of contempt of court with a fine and likely prison time for doing the wave at the football game, whereas you will if you do it in court. Most people conform to the influence exerted by the surrounding circumstances. The context of the game encourages the wave, and the context of the court does not. Of course, for each person that chooses to conform, the context has increased power to impact on every participant's attitude and behavior.

Contexts function as systems and are therefore exponential in their power to influence. In a system, individual parts are both influenced by every other part while simultaneously influencing all those same parts. Imagine, if you will, the inside of an old wind-up clock. It is made up of a series of cogs with carefully carved teeth, all connected to a spring that provides tension. The cogs connected to the spring keep the tension of the spring from letting go all at once. The cogs turn slowly, letting just a tiny bit of tension out of the spring at a steady pace. The teeth of one cog interface with the teeth of another, which affects the rate and direction of each rotation of those cogs. A change in any part of the system of interacting parts affects all other parts.

We can also see this type of interaction on a much larger scale. Consider our solar system. It is made up of four rocky planets, four gas giant planets, and a large number of asteroids, minor planets, comets, and other phenomenon, each orbiting around the large star at its center, the sun. The movement of every object in the solar system is affected by gravity, not just the gravity of the sun but the gravity of every other object in the solar system. In turn, every object in the solar system exerts a pull on the sun, which helps to determine how it rotates in the local cluster of stars and ultimately its grand rotation around the galactic center. Every part is both affected by every other part and affects every other part, and to change the mass or the trajectory of any one part would change the whole.

When I am part of a system with other people, either in the physical world or on the cyber-scape, their actions influence me, and my actions influence them. We help to create each system we are a part of, and in turn, the system exerts a strong force on us that helps to define our identity, attitudes, and behavior in that system. Ultimately, our influence on the system is always smaller than the influence the system has on us. The total influence of the system is greater than the sum of all its parts. That is one of the properties of a system. We also need to factor in all of the elements of the context around us to fully understand the system in which we function. We influence each of these, but each of these exerts a force on us that has both obvious and subtle effects on defining how we think, feel, and act.

One striking example of how this works is found in what has become known as the Stanford Prison Experiment, one of the most famous and controversial experiments in the history of the social sciences. Philip Zimbardo,[10] a respected researcher at Stanford University, was trying to understand the development of the phenomenon of abusive prison situations. He thought the abuse that developed had to do with the typical personality of the prisoners and the typical personality of people who worked as prison guards. He did a rigorous series of psychological tests to prescreen the 75 potential research subjects, and then selected the 24 most psychologically healthy people in that group to participate in the study. Half of them would randomly be assigned to be prisoners, and half of them would randomly be assigned to be prison guards for a two-week period in a simulated prison. This composed a neat set of parameters to study what commonly led to abusive prison situations.

Based on his hypothesis, Zimbardo did not expect any abuse to develop; after all, the participants were psychologically healthy. He would observe to see the difference between what happened in their simulated prison versus what happens in real prisons. To test whether it was really personality types that led to abuse, he wanted to make sure that the conditions in the simulated prison had the same elements as real prisons. Keep in mind that everyone involved knew this was a research project, that they were not really criminals, and that they were not really in prison. None of them had ever been prisoners or prison guards before. The guards were specifically told they could not do anything to hurt the prisoners.

On the beginning of the first day, both the guards and the prisoners participated but didn't seem to take the situation too seriously.

Things began to develop quickly, and by the second day a riot had broken out. As the experiment progressed, all of the people involved in the research project got sucked in deeper and deeper into their fictional roles, including Zimbardo, the scientist in charge of it all. When he heard rumors of some of the prisoners planning to escape (behaving like real prisoners, instead of just asking to be let out of the experiment like the volunteers that they actually were), he found himself responding with an elaborate plan to thwart the escape.

The guards became increasingly cruel to the prisoners as punishment. By the time the sixth day of the experiment was halfway over, more than one-third of the guards had gone beyond force and were actually demonstrating sadistic behaviors and abusing the prisoners. The experiment was stopped early when the researchers saw that the situation had gotten out of control. They were only able to recognize it had gotten to this point when Zimbardo's girlfriend came to visit him and was appalled at what she saw. By then, Zimbardo had been sucked into it so far that he, himself, did not recognize the abuse.

These people who had been found psychologically healthy and the researcher in charge of it all had devolved in less than a week. Analysis of the experiment showed that the most powerful contributor to the transformation from regular, everyday people to abusers was context. They had gradually started to act in small ways that reflected the context of a prison, and the power of the context was magnified until it sucked them all in and had them all acting and feeling like something they were not. Most of the research participants were shocked and humiliated that they had been so absorbed by the context. They never thought they were capable of doing such things. They learned, to their sorrow, the power of context.

So where does choice come into play? Are we slaves to our context, helplessly being defined by it without any chance to be anything different? The answer to this question is no, we are not slaves. Victor Frankl learned from his own experience that there is choice in context. In his book *Man's Search for Meaning*, he explained that you could take away every freedom from someone and humiliate them in every way, as what happened to him in a Nazi concentration camp, yet people still had the ability to choose their attitude.[11]

However, simply asserting the fact that we have choice and that we are, therefore, immune to the power of context when we choose to be is as incorrect as the idea that we are total slaves to context.

We underestimate the power of context at our own peril. We need to build an awareness of the contextual and systemic forces of where we are. We need to see how they seek to define us and what they seek to bring out in our actions and attitudes. We need to understand that as human beings we are not infinitely strong, and we need to develop an understanding that there are choices we can make that effectively eliminate our options. Our plans should not be made for just when we our strong; our plans should be made to protect us when we are weak, as we all sometimes are as human beings. We can't trust our willpower to save us when we make choices that place us in a context where strength of will is not enough.

We can use our power of choice to help us not be defined by context when context would push us toward things that are harmful to ourselves or others. The most powerful choice you can make to avoid being defined by a context is to not participate in the negative context when possible and to choose to exit a context when it becomes corrosive. It helps to go into new contexts with open eyes and with willingness to question and think critically about all of the contextual factors and pressures that exist there. Never ever assume that you are not being affected by your context, either online or in the real world. Making that assumption is the most certain way to ensure your context will control you.

Economic Trends of the Cyber-Scape

All that being said, a thoughtful, careful approach to the cyber-cultures we encounter is not characteristic of the way most people seem to interact with the Internet. Instead, most of us seem to dive right in with a large dose of curiosity and a minimal amount of caution. In this mindset, it is easy to get swept away in the tides and totally caught up in trends before we've even thought to examine and evaluate them.

This tendency was recently demonstrated on a large scale. The country of Myanmar launched its first social networking site in 2013. BBC News summed up the results of this launch with the pithy tweet: "No abusive comments but lots of nude selfies as Myanmar tries first social-networking site."[12]

It seems that the people in Myanmar caught on to, and were caught up in, some powerful contextual forces of the cyber-scape rather quickly. The way they were rapidly assimilated into this shallow and impulsive mindset and the resulting shenanigans can be revelatory to the rest of us about what some of the most powerful tides are in this phenomenon of online social media.

In my mind, the entry of the Myanmar population into the cyber-scape seems to support my observation that approval and attention are the two dominant currencies in the cyber-scape. They are not the only motivators that exist online, but in my observations, they are the most powerful, the most plentiful, and the most coveted forms. In the economy of the cyber-scape, sex, image, risk, and imitation appear to be the most common trade goods exchanged to get the currency of approval and attention. In many areas of the cyber-scape, this kind of economic interchange has become the path of least resistance. It is a path that is easy to travel a great distance down without ever stopping to question where the road leads.

Strangers in a Strange Land

Imagine for a moment that you are considering going on a long trip to a country you know very little about. In this country, they speak a different language that you haven't learned. You can pick up bits and pieces of it, but you have to extrapolate and guess at a lot of the meanings. You don't really understand the culture of the country very well, nor are you familiar with its history. There are competing political and economic ideas and philosophies there, but you haven't learned about them. You don't know anything about the public health conditions there. You have no idea if the water supply is safe to drink, what potential diseases you may need to defend against, or even what to expect of the climate in this country. Lacking this knowledge, you have no way to adequately prepare to journey there.

You hear that some people go there and have a lot of fun. Some people who visit this country gain an excellent education and are able to put it to good use upon returning. However, other people seem to become strangely brainwashed during their time there, losing sight of their priorities and their identity. They wind up getting lost in trivialities and odd ideas. Some people's lives are complicated or even ruined by the fads they get caught up in while they are exploring this new country. More alarming than that, some of the people who go there end up abused, traumatized, or even killed. However, you don't know what makes the difference between those who benefit from their visit and those who suffer from their visit.

What do you do in this situation? Do you just throw caution to the wind and head out, trusting in your wits and reflexes? Do you simply follow wherever the situation takes you? Do you think, *When in Rome, do as the Romans do*? Do you follow whatever trends you encounter? Do you take time to observe what is going on, and then make your decisions from there? Do you take time to learn more about this country before you determine where to go and what to do when you get there, and where and what to avoid? Which of these choices have you been making about the cyber-scape?

Now, imagine for a moment that instead of you being the one going on the trip, it is your child who wants to go. Your child is highly enthusiastic about the idea, and they point to the fact that so many other kids are going there and without any parental supervision. You have no idea how to guide or counsel your child in their visit there, because you simply don't have enough information. All you know is that many other parents seem to take no thought of sending their children there, alone.

What do you do in this situation? Do you decide not to let them go at all? Do you take comfort in seeing so many other parents send their children there and send your child off into the unknown, hoping for the best? Do you take some time to learn about this country, with its potential benefits and pitfalls, and then talk with your child about how they can safely and beneficially navigate their time there? Do you set up a system to check in with them about how things are going there? Do you choose to go there with them for a time? Which of these choices have you been making about the cyber-scape?

Plotting Our Course

It has been my observation that most of us tend to travel through the cyber-scape with little thought and insight, and that we also tend to send our children unguided into unfamiliar territory on the cyber-scape with little to no guidance. The naiveté we have about what our children are encountering on the cyber-scape is profound.

Consider this: right now, the words *sex* and *porn* are among the most commonly searched terms by children as young as seven years old.[13] We teach our children not to accept rides from strangers or walk into traffic because we know they lack the judgment and experience to navigate those kinds of experiences. However, when we send them off unin- structed and unmonitored into the cyber-scape, we place them in a posi- tion where they can easily get themselves into equal or greater danger. Why do we collectively seem to just assume that our kids will "figure it out" on their own in the digital realm when we can be so aware of how much they need guidance and models and external controls while they mature and develop internal controls in their interactions in the physical world? This is a baffling and unjustified contradiction in our thinking.

Liz Gumbinner advocates for parents to start having the *tech talk* as an ongoing conversation with their children from the moment they are old enough to first play around with electronics. She says, "Keep an eye on your kids' computer time and Internet usage, know who they're communicating with and be honest about it. It's not spying if you talk about it openly."[13]

I believe there is great wisdom in this counsel. On the cyber-scape, we can find things that enrich our lives and benefit us in a multitude of ways. At the same time, we can find things that at best can bog our lives down with meaningless drivel and at worst can become a major disruption to our lives, if not the source of our downfall. The poten- tial benefits and risks of the cyber-scape are woven right into the very nature of its existence. Unfortunately, it's easy to accidentally stumble upon the destructive trends. Indeed, experience indicates that is the path of least resistance, but it is not the inevitable outcome. I believe that what we experience in the cyber-scape—either to our benefit or our detriment—has a great deal to do with how we choose to navigate within it.

Endnotes

1. Hawking, S. W, and Mlodinow, L. (2008). *A briefer history of time.* London: Bantam.
2. Indiana University (2012). We live our lives within our media, rather than simply with it, expert says. *Science Daily.* Retrieved October 25, 2013, from http://www.sciencedaily.com/releases/2012/10/121029131825.htm.
3. Chamorro-Premuzic, T. (2013). Sharing the (self) love: The rise of the selfie and digital narcissism. *The Guardian.* Retrieved April 4, 2014, from http://www.theguardian.com/media-network/media-network-blog /2014/mar/13/selfie-social-media-love-digital-narcassism.
4. Keating, F. (2014). Selfies linked to narcissism, addiction and mental illness, say scientists. *International Business Times.* Retrieved April 4, 2014, from http://www.ibtimes.co.uk/selfies-linked-narcissism-addiction -mental-illness-say-scientists-1441480.
5. Bohannn, J. (2013). Who's afraid of peer review? *Science, 342*(6154), 60-65.
6. DNEWS. Social networks and online games rule our lives (2013). Retrieved April 4, 2014, from http://news.discovery.com/tech/social-media-online-gaming-rule-lives.htm.
7. Cornell University (2012). Facebook and Twitter are rewriting the world we've always lived in. *Science Daily.* Retrieved November 1, 2013, from http://www.sciencedaily.com/releases/2012/10/121005134629.htm.
8. Britney, F. (2013). Lady Gaga to little monsters: Stand down in Perez Hilton, Deadmau5 feuds. *The Hollywood Gossip.* Retrieved April 10, 2014, from http://www.thehollywoodgossip.com/2013/08/lady-gaga-to-little-monsters-stand-down-in-perez-hilton-deadmau5/.
9. Public Library of Science (2013). For Wikipedia users, being 'Wikipedian' may be more important than political loyalties. *Science Daily.* Retrieved November 1, 2013, from http://www.sciencedaily.com/releases/2013/04/130403200204.htm.
10. Zimbardo, P. G. (2007). *The Lucifer effect: Understanding how good people turn evil.* New York: Random House.
11. Frankl, V. E. (1963). *Man's Search for Meaning.* New York: Washington Square Press.
12. BBC News (2013). No abusive comments but lots of nude selfies as Myanmar tries first social-networking site. Retrieved April 10, 2013, from https://twitter.com/BBCWorld/status/385964126872535040.
13. Wallace, K. (2014). Replace the "sex talk" with the "tech talk?" CNN. Retrieved December 23, 2014, from http://www.cnn.com/2014/12/23/living/feat-replace-sex-talk-tech-talk-parents/.

CHAPTER 3

MAPPING OUT THE CYBER-SCAPE: SOCIAL MEDIA

Social Media Benefits and Pitfalls

An exhaustive examination of all the potential benefits and potential pitfalls of social media would be immense and too ponderous for the purposes of this discussion. In this chapter I would like to examine certain aspects of both the positive and the negative potential of social media before we focus on areas of special concern regarding social media.

Benefit: A Broader Reach for Philanthropic Efforts

For people seeking to raise funds, rally supporters, and develop resources for a broad range of humanitarian and philanthropic causes, social media is fantastic. It provides humanitarian-oriented organizations with easy access to a large potential audience, creating an effective means for connecting with people. It is great at reaching people who are already actively trying to find ways to give and is an effective tool in persuading people who otherwise might remain uninvolved. It is also much more far reaching than the door-to-door method of contribution collections of yesteryear.

The usefulness of social media in humanitarian efforts was illustrated by a recent campaign on Facebook designed to get people to sign up to be organ donors. The results were impressive and dwarfed all previous organ donor initiatives. Thousands of people signed up.[1] This was also a very cost effective option, since social media sites often allow organ donor registries and other similar charitable organizations to advertise at no cost. Using social media to rally support, nonprofit organizations can get a much better bang for their buck. More of their resources are used in helping the people they seek to assist, rather than spending time and money on expensive and ineffective ways to garner support for their causes.

Benefit: Earlier Detection of Adverse Medication Reactions

Social media can be used to monitor trends in disease and its treatment in a rapid fashion. For example, one research project currently underway is designed to harness people's blog posts and tweets about health related issues to improve the early detection of adverse medication effects:

"The National Science Foundation has awarded a $130,000 grant to a team co-led by University of Virginia professor Ahmed Abbasi to fund research that will analyze social media, including tweets and online discussion forums, to identify adverse drug reactions—a process that promises to be much faster and perhaps also more accurate than the existing methods of identifying such reactions."[2]

The ability to collect and identify this kind of information more quickly and more efficiently has the potential to save lives. We have the potential to catch side effects and dangerous reactions sooner, evaluate the effectiveness of existing medications, and speed up the research and development process for new medications. This also potentially allows the FDA to have access to information they would not otherwise have, since their current methods are to wait for people to directly contact them with medication concerns. Utilizing complex algorithms to track health chatter in online forums has the potential to provide the FDA with a much more representative view of a medication's effect on the general population. This has the potential to provide more accurate medication recommendations, and dare I venture to say, better and more cost effective outcomes for healthcare consumers.

Pitfall: Misinformation about Health and Spreading of Erroneous Healthcare Trends

Just as the Internet provides easy access to positive, accurate, and helpful healthcare information, there is a virtual deluge of misinformation, pseudoscience, and attempts at extorting other people's health concerns for profit. Given the earlier discussion of the general problem people have with evaluating the validity and reliability of the information they find online, this yin and yang of accurate and questionable health data online can create a considerable conundrum for those who go online seeking information to guide their health care decisions.

Among the perils and pitfalls of seeking answers for medical questions is hypochondriasis, the condition of being highly anxious and suggestible. We have a tendency to conclude we have a disease when we hear about it simply because certain features match what we are experiencing.

Medical students and psychology students often experience some degree of hypochondriasis as they go through their training. When they learn about a certain disease or disorder, they are more likely to erroneously attribute symptoms or signs they have to a specific disease or disorder that they are currently learning about.

This can and does happen fairly frequently to people in the general population as they search the Internet for answers to symptoms they are experiencing. Interestingly enough, this can move beyond hypochondriasis and progress to an actual conversion disorder (with things like blindness, paralysis, or other negative neurological symptoms based on psychological—rather than biological—causes) or psychogenetic movement disorder (with twitches, seizures, or other positive neurological symptoms for psychological causes instead of physical causes).

In these cases, there is a real (not imagined or faked) increase of the identified symptom, and even the psychological creation of the other symptoms you have read about as a part of the disease or disorder you now think is the cause of your symptoms—all with no biological basis for the symptoms! In other words, the person with this kind of disorder is not sick, at least, not in the way you think they are, but because they are *convinced* that they are sick, their body creates all of the signs and symptoms of the illness. It's things like this that remind us that psychology is not for wimps!

Apparently, hypochondriasis, conversion disorders, and psychogenetic movement disorders can become virtually "contagious" through social media. For example, a recent case in upstate New York involved approximately twenty teenagers who were having seizure-like symptoms. This "disease" started when several girls developed facial and body twitches similar to those in Tourette's syndrome. These teenagers went to social media such as YouTube and Facebook to describe and demonstrate their symptoms, hoping that someone could provide an answer for them as to the nature of and cure for their symptoms. Interestingly enough, their disease appeared to spread as they shared it online, and other teens developed the same symptoms in response to seeing them posted online.

A reporter for *Discovery News* wrote about the phenomenon: "Experts have diagnosed the problem as a form of mass hysteria in which an individual, usually a young woman, becomes ill during a period of stress, and others in the same community, school or workplace begin to show the same physical symptoms."[3] Again, these were not people faking their symptoms, but literally creating a shared experience of a psychogenetic movement disorder.

Part of what this indicates to me is that not only do we need to take what we read on the Internet with a grain of salt, but we need to take ourselves with a grain of salt as well. It is very easy for us to figuratively put blinders on and become over-focused on our anxieties and our search for answers. Then we charge off in the wrong direction like Don Quixote jousting with windmills as if they were giants. To me, this is an important thing for us to keep in mind when we go online looking for information about the most effective diet, the causes of cancer, how to prevent hair loss, how to build muscle mass, the safety of an illegal drug, or anything else that may have bearing on our health and well-being.

While cyber-hypochondriasis may be a more dramatic example of odd things that can happen to health because of online activity, the much more common risk is the potential for receiving, believing, and embracing erroneous health information, thus leading to negative health outcomes. It is hard for the average consumer to know who to believe amid the loud, confident, and insistent voices on the cyber-scape. This is especially the case when there is any degree of controversy involved in a healthcare matter, such as the causes of autism, the causes of cancer and its treatment, the potential health benefits and dangers of cannabis, the benefits of a gluten-free diet, the potential benefits (or lack thereof) of eating only organic foods, and so on.

Entire controversies are manufactured where the results of reliable data and its implications are clear, but many people have fallen for the trap of emotional reasoning. They are cherry picking results to support preferences or preconceived ideas. Worse, sometimes they are committing the all-too-frequent error of spurious correlation, believing that since two things happened in close succession to each other, the one must have caused the other. In other words, our online discourse creates confusion and controversy where the science is actually clear and unmistakable. The average consumer is poorly equipped to reliably measure for themselves the difference between this kind of pseudo-controversy and a legitimate controversy. To be confused in a perplexing situation is understandable, but to be confused when the facts are actually relatively clear is a tragedy.

Benefit: Health and Well-Being of Elderly People

Social media provides a wide range of resources that can have significant benefits for the health and well-being of elderly people, especially in cases of illness, disability, and isolation. Websites and forums can provide accurate and useful health information on a wide variety of topics. Elderly people are able to network with each other and with online resources, as well as have easier access to distant family members. They can find social interaction online to alleviate the frequent later-life stressor of loneliness and isolation. In addition, having online availability to social contacts, doing their own shopping, volunteer opportunities, and so forth can enhance elderly people's feelings of autonomy, usefulness, and self-efficacy in a time of life when there is a risk of feeling deficient in those areas.[4]

Pitfall: Health, Well-Being, and Exploitation of Elderly People

Did you ever receive an email that went something like this? "Hello, good Mr. Sir or Madam. A most prestigious friend of I me give your name. I am prince in Nigeria, and must transfer much fortune in gold to America. Much dollars, very value. If you me help, I much money share with you. Only your bank information I need to transfer much money, then I let you keep one million American dollars."

The classic "Nigerian prince" email con tactic has become so infamous, it would seem that everybody would know about it by now. And yet this email and variations on its theme still get sent out, which indicates to me that some people must still actually fall victim to it; otherwise it wouldn't still be used as bait. I always wondered who fell for these things. Then again, not all Internet scam tactics or phishing emails are quite so obvious. For cyber-scape newcomers and those without enough background and experience to recognize the various con tactics online, the potential to be seriously exploited on the cyber-scape is significant. The highways of the world wide web are infested with cyber-robbers just waiting for unsuspecting prey to come along.

Someone my age may think that it is common knowledge to never click on a link in an unsolicited email, or to check to make sure the URL for the site they are visiting is correct, or that those "Your computer has been infected! Click here to fix it!" scareware tactics are all bogus. Those things may indeed be obvious to many of us; however, elderly people for whom the cyber-scape is a foreign culture are at risk of falling victim to a number of seemingly obvious exploitation tactics. They often suffer as the targets of fraud or identity theft. When elderly people fall victim to online cons, they may hesitate to seek help because they either do not realize they have been scammed or they feel ashamed for having been taken in.

Beyond that, as elderly people encounter the online profiles of other people—which often portray only a highlight reel of everything happy, fun, and exciting in their lives—it can lead to a sense of depression about their own lives. This is a common result of making unfavorable social comparisons due to the overly positive or self-aggrandizing online presentations they see others parading in front of them.[5]

Thus, for elderly people unfamiliar with the cyber-scape, venturing out into the realm of the Internet has the risk of being counterproductive or even abusive and exploitive.

Benefit: Facilitation of Crisis Communication and Response

The speed and immediacy of social media makes it a highly efficient way to spread news. Indeed, information on world events tends to break sooner, faster, and in more rapid succession on social media than news coming through traditional and established news sources (imagine how that complicates making a living as a journalist these days). The interactive nature of social media in crisis events makes it a powerful tool for not only reporting on the events, but actually intervening upon the events directly in real time. Thus, social media can be a powerful tool for alleviating catastrophe and preserving lives.

An example of this was the London riots of 2011. This particular series of riots—stirred by public anger at the police—was memorable due to the intensity, danger, and destruction that they brought, resulting in five deaths and more than two hundred injuries, along with a large amount of property damage. While the rioters were using social media to organize themselves and stir up greater anger and discontent, the police also took to social media to try to help calm the situation down. The police successfully utilized a Twitter account to coordinate relief efforts, correct rumors, answer questions, and ultimately help defuse the entire situation. The rapid-fire nature of Twitter provided both danger of high-speed escalation of the situation and the opportunity for rapid intervention and resolution. Ultimately the tone and consistency of the message from the police were found to be important factors in making this real-time crisis communication and intervention effective.[6]

The potential benefits of social media for crisis situations were also illustrated in the Boston Marathon bombing in 2013. Those affected by the bombing were deeply and intensely humanized through the social media coverage, which was colossal on social media entities such as Facebook, Reddit, YouTube, and Twitter. These media, and the highly personal touch they added to the events, offered avenues for sharing information and led to a massive outpouring of compassion and support, and opportunities to both give and receive needed aid.[7]

Pitfall: Crisis, Sensitive Information, and Vigilantes

The Boston Marathon bombings also clearly illustrated some of the perils of social media. Social media users in the path of the police pursuit were texting, posting, and tweeting up-to-date, detailed information about the manhunt for the bombers on public forums such as Twitter. One of the major problems this presented is that it also provided the two bombers with the very same information, leaking to them important tactical information about where and how the search for them was being carried out. This allowed them to make very informed decisions about how to evade their pursuers.

This should have been a fairly obvious issue, given the highly public nature of Twitter, Reddit, and the other forums being used to share this information, but social media users had become used to snapping pictures and sending tweets in real time, with little critical thought about what they were doing and with little consideration about possible consequences. In this manner, social media users had become unintentional accomplices to the bombers evading law enforcement. Finally, the elite hacktivist group Anonymous intervened. They posted a statement advising social media users to stop tweeting and posting this information, pointing out that law enforcement was being thwarted by having their plans and maneuvers revealed.[8]

Another tragic use of social media happened during the Boston Marathon bombings. Reddit users created a subreddit called *findbostonbombers*. Together, they engaged in a CSI style crowd-sourced investigation, searching through photos of the bombing scene to try to identify the bombers. The passion and confidence of this group ran very high, and they proceeded with all the righteous zeal of an inquisitor during the Salem Witch Trials. Ultimately, they ended up erroneously indicating a number of innocent people as prime suspects for the bombing. The person they identified as their standout suspect for the white cap bomber was Sunil Tripathi, partially because he fit the general image and because he had not been seen for a month leading up to the bombings. Tripathi was later found floating dead in the waters off India Point Park, with all indications that he had been dead for some time.[9] Reddit apologized profusely to Tripathi's family for their dangerous speculation and the forceful and dogged public accusations they had made against him. Reddit moderator Rather_Confused stated, "We're creating villains from innocent bystanders. . . . We have to be responsible."[10] Pitchfork mobs of yesteryear are still pitchfork mobs today, even though they are carrying smartphones instead of farming implements.

There were several elements that went into creating these tragic dynamics. First was the overconfidence and overzealousness of the social media users in this case. (Remember the previous observation of how we tend to be "confident idiots?" That totally applies here.) It seems to me that they knew they were skilled and savvy in technology and their social media tools. They mistook this skill as being transferable to being accurate and effective investigators, when in reality they had less experience in this area than even the most rookie cop on the street. Sure, they had professional tools, but they also had amateur skills and understanding and they seemed to have no awareness of this limitation.

Second, they utilized social media to bypass the due process that was constitutionally set in place by the government of the United States to safeguard the innocent from false accusations, harassment, and unjust punishment. They made their own rules, and there were no checks and balances in place. They abandoned concepts that are central to the democratic system of justice. In this way, they bypassed the law, and their attempt at crowd-sourcing justice became more akin to anarchy, lynch mobs, and vigilantism.

Third, these social media users exhibited the blind self-assurance that has become the hallmark of the online political mentality.

While it is true that the technology of the cyber-scape allows us to accomplish more things faster than ever before, it gives no assurance that we are moving in the right direction. The cyber-scape allows us to climb metaphorical mountains more rapidly than any time in history, but it also allows us to dig a bigger, darker, slipperier pit for ourselves at a pace much faster than ever before if we are not mindful. The sheer speed with which things move in the cyber-scape in conjunction with the riptide effect caused by the dynamic motions of the cyber-crowd can be so rapid as to prevent us from taking part in the process of both self-awareness and situational awareness. Sometimes serious, real world consequences follow in the wake.

Pitfall: Trauma Boundaries

The real-time, unfiltered nature of social media brings with it another potential hazard: increased trauma. When a tragedy happens, such as a terrorist attack, the images of it are shot out into the world almost as soon as they happen. Indeed, something that I often feel a little sick about is coming across an accident or injury and seeing a swarm of people taking pictures with their smartphones rather than finding a way to help. May I take a moment now and say, in general, put down the phone and lend a hand.

As these images are transmitted, there appears to be little to no consideration for the impact these images will have. Terrifying scenes of raw human carnage and suffering play themselves out in front of a wide audience. As a result, many people experience secondary trauma that is almost as real and as powerful as if they were present. I have had quiet moments of reflection in which it occurred to me that the people who impulsively send out all of this raw footage are in some ways helping the terrorists in their goal of causing the largest traumatic impact of their actions possible. I know they don't mean to do this, but the functional result of their behavior plays out this way. Our impulsive, knee-jerk reaction use of social media runs the risk of actually empowering terrorists.

I will never forget the terrorist attacks on the World Trade Center on September 11, 2001. I can still feel, as a visceral memory, the shock that ran through me. What I thought, at first, was a tragic aviation accident transformed into confused suspicion as the second plane collided with the second tower. I can still sense in my gut the inexpressible horror of catching glimpses of bodies falling from the buildings, knowing those were people's fathers, mothers, husbands, and wives. I still see the crumbling of the towers vividly in my mind. When I think about it too much, powerful emotions of helplessness and shock still sometimes come to the surface. I was traumatized, as were many others, and I think in some ways those sounds and images will stay with me forever. I wasn't even there. I was in my small apartment in Provo, Utah, preparing to go to work that day, and I watched it play out in front of me on a television screen.

I have often wondered what my experience would have been like if the technology we have now would have been available then. Even though the events of September 11 were played out in real time in front of a worldwide audience, there was still some degree of discretion in what images were publicly aired. As traumatizing as that day was for so many of us, what would it have been like if we had been exposed to the same degree of raw, live coverage of the events of that day as we are to tragedies today?

I think a quote from Michael Crichton's *Jurassic Park* is applicable: "Your scientists were so preoccupied with whether or not they could, they didn't stop to think if they should."[11]

Perhaps we have become so enamored with what our social media technology *can* do that we have not taken the time to adequately consider what is *prudent and wise* to do with it, especially as it applies to crisis and tragedy.

Benefit: Increased Political Participation

Many societies that hold elections and rely upon the political participation of the general populace struggle with getting people politically involved. It is also difficult to get pertinent political information to the voting public. I was in Brazil during a presidential election, and I thought it was interesting that a popular way of soliciting votes was to hire cars with sound systems to drive around and play a catchy jingle advertising a candidate's name and voting number.

I still remember those jingles to this day, though I couldn't tell you a single thing about the platform of any of the candidates. The thing is, I'm not alone in that. I believe a fairly large portion of their population probably knew very little about their candidates or the political issues at stake, and they probably voted based off of whichever jingle resonated with them the most. This didn't strike me as an ideal way to inform one's political decisions. Then again, who's to say that the voting public of the United States is any better informed? How many of us make political decisions based on sound bites and things we have heard on one-sided political talk shows? I kind of want to know the answer to that question, but I kind of don't want to know, either. I get the feeling it would depress me.

The cyber-scape has been shown to be an effective means of spreading political information (as well as misinformation, slander, and propaganda). It also serves as a ready forum for people to express their political views and recruit other people to them. The more informed people are politically, the more likely they are to vote, volunteer, and so forth, all of which are things the democratic process depends upon in order to function well. Young adults who post about their political beliefs online have been found to be more likely to actually participate in public affairs, and getting people politically active online appears to result in more real-world political involvement.[12]

Potential Pitfall: Political Polarization and Gridlock

Of course, the million-dollar question in this case is this: what is the nature of this increased political involvement? Does it mirror the increased polarization and extremism demonstrated in online political discussions? If so, does it contribute to factors leading to a decline in civility and the inability to compromise and cooperate in politics that is having a crippling effect on the political process of the nation? Is it productive to involve more people in politics using online methods, or is it merely more polarizing and thus sabotaging? Is it the very building block from which we construct political gridlock?

More is not always better. It's just more. The trends thus far seem to indicate that this increased political activity falls into the polarized realm. Research is showing sharper divisions along political lines, a greater tendency to demonize those with differing views, a disrupted ability to negotiate and compromise, and even a decreased ability to tolerate living among people with differing political views.

All of this is driven by an increasing trend for the most polarized people on the right and the left of the political aisle to scream the loudest and be the most politically active. This is pushing the political agenda of their own parties to extremes, while mutually riling each other up to amplify the rancor and animosity toward the other political party. This dynamic is demonstrably bogging down the whole democratic process in a mire of ineffectiveness.[13]

The cyber-scape has proven to be a powerful recruiting, indoctrinating, and deploying tool in this process of self-righteous political self-destruction. This is a spectacular and disturbing display of group-think, which we will discuss in detail later. To be clear, that's not a good thing.

Benefit and Pitfall: Screening Potential Employees

Social media provides a new source of information for employers to screen potential employees. Having access to social media allows employers to see beyond applicants' resumes to parts of their lives and personalities that they do not volunteer on their own. This can help employers make a much more educated decision about who they hire.

However, this may place certain job applicants at a significant disadvantage compared to other competing applicants. For example, research has shown that young adults, men, Hispanics and those with lower Internet skills are less likely to keep potential future employment opportunities in mind when posting on social media.[14] In other words, they are less likely to think, *Is this something I would want a future boss to see? Is this something that would make people less inclined to hire me?* Rather, they tend to make the ill-conceived assumption that the only people who will see what they post are their online friends and followers. Little do they suspect the rants they have written and the questionable pictures they have posted will be laid before the eyes of those who make decisions about whether they get accepted into a college or whether they get hired for a job.

Some people have expressed significant objections to the practice of screening job applicants' social media.

Dr. Lori Foster Thompson, a professor of psychology at North Carolina State University, explained, "Companies often scan a job applicant's Facebook profile to see whether there is evidence of drug or alcohol use, believing that such behavior means the applicant is not 'conscientious,' or responsible and self-disciplined."[15]

However, Foster and her colleagues have found no significant correlation between conscientiousness and an individual's willingness to post content on Facebook about alcohol or drug use, which is funny to me, because the very definition of conscientiousness would imply that someone would think twice before posting that kind of content. The internal logic of their statement is kind of shaky.

Nonetheless, Will Stoughton, a PhD student at North Carolina State University, made the following objection: "This means companies are eliminating some conscientious job applicants based on erroneous assumptions regarding what social media behavior tells us about the applicants."[16] The researchers did find one correlation between the desirable traits of agreeableness and conscientiousness: people who manifested these traits were very unlikely to insult other people on Facebook.

While this is an interesting finding, it is one that bears some critical thinking. Logically, conscientious people should appear conscientious across contexts, whereas people who are merely trying to appear contentious to garner a positive opinion of themselves will have breaches in it in areas where they do not expect to be monitored. The authors of the most recently mentioned article did not find a correlation between conscientiousness and people posting about drugs and alcohol on social media. It would be easy then, in light of this finding, to assume that it is not reasonable to try to predict a potential employee's behavior based on what they post on social media. However, that would be overextending the application of the findings of this particular study. All it is really able to say is that they found no significant correlation between the way they measured conscientiousness in a person and their willingness to post about drugs and alcohol on social media.

The question remains, then, if posting about dangerous or illegal activities is actually a good predictor of people engaging in illegal or dangerous activities in the real world. It turns out that there is good reason to believe so. One example of this was a study that demonstrated that a teen's texting about anti-social topics and behaviors does in fact accurately predict higher levels of rule-breaking and aggression in the real world. The researchers noted, "Texting with a peer about rule-breaking activities may not only provide easy access to information about illegal and antisocial behavior, but may also reinforce the notion that these activities are accepted within the peer group."[17]

While this study does not directly look at adults and at potential job applicants, it does raise our awareness to the fact that there is a demonstrable correlation between someone's online activity and their real-world activities. As much as people like to think they can successfully compartmentalize their lives, we are holistic beings: what we do in one area of our lives tends to spill over into the other aspects of our lives. What we try to do in some hidden, dark, locked cavern inside ourselves becomes a powerful molding force of our minds and our characters. Therefore, there is good reason to believe that examining someone's social media can provide accurate predictions for what their behaviors will be. It is up to the employer to decide if they think these behaviors displayed on social media would be an asset or a liability to their business practices and culture.

Yin and Yang of the Cyber-Scape

This chapter has illustrated a number of ways in which the world of social media has both positive and negative elements. A reckless approach to the cyber-scape brings with it the opportunity of stumbling upon beneficial aspects, but also considerable risks of charging deep into dangerous territory. It is my opinion that there is no part of the cyber-scape that exists without risk. Indeed, I don't believe there is any part of life where we can exist in a risk-free environment. Just as understanding the risks in life and choosing thoughtfully which ones to engage in and which to avoid can help us grow, mature, and enjoy our lives in the physical world, applying this same approach to the cyber-scape can help us reap the rewards and avoid the traps.

Self-Examination

As you consider the information that has been presented thus far, I encourage you to carefully answer the following questions. In addition, I invite you to discuss both the questions and answers with at least one person you trust and get their perspective and their observations.

1. How much time do you think you spend online? Now think back through your day and count the minutes as precisely as possible. How much time do you actually spend online? Is there a gap between the two?
2. Where do you spend your time online?
3. What cyber-nations are you a part of (groups, websites, etc.)?
4. What are the cultures of these various groups? What are the common attitudes, actions, and patterns manifested in these groups? What attitudes and opinions are supported in these

groups? What attitudes and opinions are looked down upon or even punished in these groups?

5. In what ways have you adopted the culture of these groups? This may be very hard to discern on your own, so consider asking a trusted friend for help. Culture shapes us in ways we often can't perceive. Our lack of perception is not the same as a lack of being influenced.

6. What do your social media profiles look like? What would they look like to a college considering your application? What would they look like to a potential employer considering offering you a job?

7. In what ways is the manner you present yourself online similar to the way you present yourself in the real world? In what ways are your online and real-world image, attitudes, and behaviors different?

8. What cyber-leaders do you have (these can be individuals like Ashton Kutcher, George Takei, Lady Gaga, and Bill Nye, or groups such as FOX News and "Mormon Mommy" bloggers)? Whom do you see as authorities you trust online? Whose online opinions are influential for you? Whose online opinions are you likely to accept without challenging?

9. How does your membership in these online groups and your connection to these online personalities affect your thoughts, feelings, and actions?

10. How conscious are you of the impact of your media use on you?

11. How conscious are you of the impact of your media use on other important people and priorities in your life?

Endnotes

1. The Hastings Center (2012). 'Facebook effect': Thousands registered as organ donors via Facebook, dwarfing other donation initiatives. *Science Daily*. Retrieved November 1, 2013, from http://www.sciencedaily. com/releases/2012/09/120911125305.htm.

2. University of Virginia (2012). Sifting social media for early signs of adverse drug reactions. *Science Daily*. Retrieved November 1, 2013, from http://www.sciencedaily.com/releases/2012/09/120921111034.htm.

3. Discovery News (2013). Is social media spreading twitching hysteria? *Discovery News*. Retrieved November 15, 2013, from http://news.discovery.com/tech/twitching-disorder-social-media-120203.htm.

4. Université du Luxembourg (2013). Social media can support healthiness of older people. *Science Daily*. Retrieved November 1, 2013, from http://www.sciencedaily.com/releases/2013/04/130415204824.htm.

5. Ibid.

6. Fraunhofer-Institut fuer Angewandte Informationstechnik (FIT) (2013). Twitter for crisis communication: Study shows benefits for the police. *Science Daily*. Retrieved November 1, 2013, from http://www.sciencedaily.com/releases/2013/04/130430092328.htm.

7. Halverson, N. (2013). Social media superorganism keeps Boston story personal. *Discovery News*. Retrieved November 25, 2013, from http://news.discovery.com/tech/apps/social-media-superorganism-boston-marathon-bombing-130419.htm.

8. Ibid.

9. Bidgood, J. (2013). Body of missing student at Brown is discovered. *The New York Times*. Retrieved April 18, 2013, from http://www.nytimes.com/2013/04/26/us/sunil-tripathi-student-at-brown-is-found-dead.html.

10. Stanglin, D. (2013). Student wrongly tied to Boston bombings found dead. *USA Today*. Retrieved April 4, 2014, from http://www.usatoday.com/story/news/2013/04/25/boston-bombing-social-media-student-brown-university-reddit/2112309/.

11. Crichton, M. (1990). *Jurassic Park*. New York: Ballentine Books.

12. Taylor & Francis (2012). How does social media help young adults become politically active? *Science Daily*. Retrieved November 1, 2013, from http://www.sciencedaily.com/releases/2012/10/121026084346.htm.

13. Pew (2014). Political polarization in the American public. Retrieved June 12, 2014, from http://www.people-press.org/2014/06/12/political-polarization-in-the-american-public/.

14. Northwestern University (2013). Young job seekers, check your privacy settings. *Science Daily*. Retrieved November 14, 2013, from http://www.sciencedaily.com/releases/2013/07/130712161103.htm.

15. North Carolina State University (2013). Companies look at wrong things when using Facebook for hiring, study shows. *Science Daily.* Retrieved November 14, 2013, from http://www.sciencedaily.com/releases/2013/07/130702095938.htm.
16. Ibid.
17. Ehrenreich, S.E., Underwood, M. K., & Ackerman, R. A. (2014). Adolescents' text message communication and growth in antisocial behavior across the first year of high school. *Journal of Abnormal Child Psychology* 42(2), 251-264.

CHAPTER 4

SPECIAL SOCIAL MEDIA CONCERNS

In the previous chapter, we explored how the cyber-scape is a realm that includes a wide variety of potential benefits and pitfalls. I believe some potential pitfalls merit special attention, either because the magnitude of the risk they pose is greater, the chance of encountering them is very high, the general societal trends around them are prominent and concerning (thus leaving us less likely to think critically about them because they are so common), or any combination of these three factors.

"Multitasking," More Appropriately Known as Distraction

If there is one widely shared observation about the cyber-scape, it is that our involvement with it is often a source of considerable distraction for us. Cyber-distraction has become a juggernaut of a phenomenon, especially with the easy availability of texting and Internet access via smartphones. Given that there are approximately 1.4 billion smartphones in use in the world at the time I am writing this[1], roughly one-fifth of the world's population now has another sensory-rich, compelling, easily accessible world constantly beckoning to them from their fingertips, purses, pants pockets, or other creative place they have chosen to store their smartphones.

While the accessibility of this cyberworld has many advantages, I constantly see examples of the cyber-scape intruding upon the real world in disruptive and even destructive ways, with screens interrupting, interloping, and even interdicting important events, relationships, and opportunities. It is my observation that unless we are mindful and purposeful about our relationship with the cyber-scape, this cyber-hijacking of the real world is the most common outcome. Most people seem to be oblivious to the fact when it is happening to them. I do not believe that this disruptive clash of the digital and physical realm is inevitable, but it does seem to be the path of least resistance and thus the path most often taken.

I often hear people refer to their constant use of smartphones as "multitasking." What a comforting word that is to us. When we say it in relation to our own actions, we give ourselves the soothing impression that we are actually successfully doing multiple things at once. We often take pride in what we see as our ability to multitask, as if it were a great accomplishment. Many jobs tout multitasking as a requirement. Business articles about work-life balance recommend multitasking as a solution. The idea that we can multitask seems to promise that we can get more of what we want out of life while accomplishing more of what we have to do. Multitasking sounds like a way we can have it all, and have it all now. It has been interesting for me to see how the multitasking mindset has risen to the status of a proselytized Western value of nearly religious status, in stark contrast to the Eastern value of mindfulness, which promotes the worth of focusing fully on one thing at a time. Guess which value I hope my brain surgeon will be expressing should I ever find myself in need of neurosurgery.

The question is, are we really as good at multitasking as we think we are, and does it accomplish what we think it does? There is grim irony in the results of a study that found that the better people think they are at multitasking, the worse they actually perform in actual multitasking measures.[2] In other words, the more confident we are in our multitasking skills, the more certain we should be that we are not doing a good job at it. Mounting evidence suggests that effective multitasking is merely a myth, implying that we might justifiably expect Bigfoot, El Chupacabra, and the Loch Ness Monster to be good at multitasking. But if we think we are doing a good job at it, we are most likely mistaken.

This reality is aptly demonstrated in the alarmingly growing phenomenon of injuries and deaths sustained as a result of using smartphones while driving. It seems all too easy to believe that we can divert our attention from the steering wheel to a smartphone screen to read a text or Facebook post while staying fully in control. How easy it is to forget that while we are driving, we are essentially piloting high-velocity, 1.5 ton, steel battering rams. This is a weapon the Roman Legions would have loved to get their hands on when laying siege to a city. Yet driving these high caliber, human-piloted ballistic projectiles has become such a common experience that we often fail to do the math and comprehend what is actually happening when we take the steering wheel.

Do we realize that while we are driving at 55 miles per hour, we cover 22.5 feet per second? On average, when a person sends or reads a text, they take their eyes off the road for 5 seconds,[3] meaning that at 55 miles per hour they cover 112.5 feet. That's a lot of distance in a very short amount of time. A lot can change in that amount of time and space, and the speed of vehicles on the road leaves only fractions of a second for reaction time at best. If a 1.5-ton sedan collides with something—another car, a tree, or a child crossing the street at a crosswalk—at 55 miles per hour, it does so with 82.5 tons of force. In that collision, an unbuckled driver weighing 150 pounds would impact the interior of his or her vehicle with 8,250 pounds of force.[4] I don't know about you, but I wouldn't step into a boxing ring with an opponent who could hit that hard. If I were ever crazy enough to do so, I'd expect to leave that boxing ring either in a body bag or as a liquid. The numbers alone indicate to us that this is not a matter we should take lightly, although many of us often do so. Texting while driving is an irrational act of unjustified pride and overconfidence with huge potential for human tragedy.

Reality has ways, often tragic ones, of trying to remind us of this fact. In 2012 in the United States, 421,000 people were injured and 3,360 people were killed in motor vehicle accidents involving distracted drivers. That rate has been increasing year after year.[3]

RYAN J. ANDERSON, PhD

Even though there has been a public outcry against texting while driving and other forms of distracted motor vehicle operation, at any given daylight moment, approximately 660,000 are actively manipulating cell phones or other electronic devices as they drive. That number has continued to increase in spite of efforts to raise awareness about the problem.[5] In a recent survey, even though 98 percent of drivers admit that they believe that texting and driving is dangerous, 75 percent of drivers admitted to texting while driving, and of course, those are only the ones that admitted to it.[6] Even though we collectively know that distracting ourselves with smartphones while driving is a big issue, our behavior in this area is not improving. Indeed, it is clearly getting worse, and even your own personal commitment to not text and drive does not protect you from the risk incurred by having so many other people on the road texting their way into trouble. You could say that the zombie apocalypse has arrived in the form of zoned-out drivers. They're everywhere! Your zombie apocalypse survival kit will not save you from the growing menace of smartphone-distracted drivers on the road.

There are a number of possible reasons our choices in this area are getting increasingly destructive, in spite of all we know about the danger. It appears to be human nature to think that we will be the exception to the statistics. Many people tend to unconsciously think of themselves as surrounded by an invincible force field of sorts, somehow protected from the cause and effect nature of this universe that can wreak havoc on those around us. I have observed that people also have a tendency to think, *Well, even though I am looking at my smartphone, if something truly important was happening, I would notice.* However, that thought does not hold up under the light of scrutiny.

Ask yourself this: if I was on a commuter train and a man came onboard with a gun and searched through the crowd for a random person to shoot, would I notice? Most of us would like to think that we all would. Contrast that with reality. In San Francisco, that very situation occurred.

CNN reported:

> The security footage of the incident is chilling. The man, donning a baseball hat and smile, lifts a .45-caliber handgun in plain view, three or four times. He waves the weapon as if choosing who he wants to kill.

Some [passengers] are only two or three feet [away from the shooter while he is waving his gun around to select his target]. At one point, he even wipes his nose with the gun. But nobody seemed to notice until the blast goes off. . . . Why? [The passengers] were too into their smartphones.[7]

While this is a particularly dramatic example, this sort of incident is not at all unique or unusual. In the same news report, San Francisco District Attorney George Gascon noted, "We're seeing people that are so disconnected to their surroundings. This is not unique. People are being robbed, people are being hurt, people are being run over by cars because they're so disconnected because of these phones."[7]

It seems that we collectively have developed cyber-blindness with our smartphones and other mobile devices; we have become blind to our surroundings, and we have become self-blind, lacking insight into just how disconnected we have become. Who is more blind than the person who does not know they are blind? Confucius may not have known about social media or smartphones, but his teaching that "if you chase two rabbits, you catch none" appropriately apply to this context. The funny thing with smartphones is that you chase two rabbits, you catch none, but then you end up thinking that you've caught three rabbits and mistakenly conclude that was a far more productive way of hunting rabbits. Smartphones lead us to some pretty dumb thinking at times.

Accessible, Yet Inaccessible; Connected, Yet Disconnected

Many of us are excited about smartphones, texting, and social media because we have a sense that these are tools that help us to be more accessible and more connected to the people and things we care about. That's the whole reason I joined Facebook in the first place—to be more connected to family and friends.

Indeed, when we are using social media, I believe most of us feel somehow woven into the digital threads of a grand tapestry of information and access points that is not limited by distance or speed. I don't know about you, but sometimes I really hate the limitations of time and space, so the thought that there is something out there that can help me overcome those types of limitations is appealing.

In some ways, the Internet creates the sensation of being able to transcend some of these frustrating limitations of the human experience, and as such feels both exhilarating and liberating. The warm glow of that sensation seems to lead us to be very poor judges of just how much we can try to divide our attention before it means that we are not really paying attention to what is most immediate and to what matters most.

Our attention, when divided, tends to trickle down to the lowest common denominator, and our divided attention and intelligence feel like they are feasting when indeed we are just nibbling away at triviality. This can be a very convincing illusion. Under the hypnotic spell of this mirage, we miss a basic yet vital truth: our attempts to give attention to everything lead to the reality of us being unknowingly inattentive to everything.

There is compelling evidence that the most common result of our heavy use of smartphones, texting, and social media is not to make us more accessible and connected, but rather to make us less accessible and connected to the people we are actually with.

I found a study by Andrew Przybylski and Netta Weinstein to be particularly revelatory about this dynamic. They found that the mere presence of a smartphone in a conversation between two people in the same room had a dampening effect on the conversation relative to people having conversations without their smartphones present. This was found to be the case even though the phone did not ring or give any notifications of texts, posts, or messages. Even with the phone doing nothing at all besides sitting there looking pretty and high tech, there was a suppressive effect on the closeness, connection, and conversation quality between the two people. The more intimate and personal the topic being discussed, the more pronounced this dampening effect was. The more real and meaningful the conversation, the more the presence of the phone sapped it of substance like some kind of techno-parasite.[8]

This study did not make any conclusions as to why the phone had such a disruptive effect, but the researchers suggested some hypotheses that I think have real merit, including the idea that the smartphone could serve as a representation of a larger set of social relationships competing for the time and attention of the other person we are trying to talk to, thus edging out a sense of intimacy, immediacy, and openness in a fashion similar to trying to discuss personal issues in a crowded room.

Another hypothesis was that we have collectively become conditioned to smartphones constantly interrupting our lives, and thus merely having a phone with us sets us up psychologically to expect to only have a fraction of the other person's attention. In this way, smartphones could potentially be turning our conversations in closer relationships into the equivalent of trying to talk to someone at a business networking event who is only half-listening to you while scanning the rest of the crowd for someone more interesting or important to talk to. We end up leaving the most important people in our lives "playing second fiddle" as a result.

One may ask, *Well, what if I am connecting with my spouse/friend/ child on social media? Shouldn't that help us be more connected?* While there is reason to believe there are ways it can be used as a form of connection, social media connections have the potential to damage even very strong relationships. A study by Dr. Bernie Hogan of Oxford University found no evidence to suggest that connecting with one's spouse on social media strengthens marital relationships. In fact, the opposite is sometimes true. He stated: "Over 24,000 people in marital relationships took part in the new research, using 10 media channels. We found that those using more media tend to report no greater relationship satisfaction and some even reported decreasing satisfaction. This work suggests that media, which now includes online social media, still operates as a signal of ties of strength in relationships. However there may be a cut-off point after which the increasing complexity of maintaining so many separate communications threads starts to undermine relationship ties."[9]

In other words, while being able to text our spouse or send him or her a message via Facebook can be a mode of connection, connecting with them through too many social media routes can actually cause some distance. One possible contributor is that each added form of media for connection also adds many other connections and potential distractions. If I connect with my wife on Facebook, I now have several hundred other people I am connected with there as potential distractions. If I add to that the people I have on Tumbler, Twitter, and Words with Friends, I have created four ways to be connected with my wife, but hundreds and maybe thousands of other contacts are competing for my time and attention through those channels. While there is nothing wrong with using a social media site as a point of connection with my spouse, I may find that I get more connection with her by using fewer social media sites, even if I am connected with her on each one. In the end, I don't think anything will ever prove to be a good substitute for a one-on-one, face-to-face conversation. Call me old-fashioned if you must, but I think the research will ultimately support the idea that the best human interface is the old human face-to-face.

This concept received further support in a study from the University of North Carolina. Some of the romantic couples in this study text each other up to 500 times per day. It would not be unreasonable to hypothesize that this amount of contact would help couples stay connected, increase their relationship satisfaction, and help solidify attachment and commitment to the relationship. However, the data in this case suggest that the opposite, in fact, is true on each point. They found some interesting trends: the more couples text with each other, the less they tend to communicate with each other using other forms of communication, such as a face-to-face conversation. In other words, texting tends to replace other forms of communication rather than supplement them, and that appears to be especially true as the volume of texting increases.[10]

Texting lacks the depth and breadth available in other forms of communication: after all, texting is intended to be brief and succinct, to the point we have invented an entire simplified dialect for texting. Texting just doesn't have the same substance as other forms of communication. Reading my wife text "lol" is not the same as hearing and seeing her laugh, not by a long shot. Replacing in-person communication with texts, tweets, and posts is like substituting a steak dinner with beef jerky. Yes, these two foods are technically made out of the same thing, but there is a huge difference between the two in the substance and depth they offer. There's a reason beef jerky is not on the menu at Ruth's Chris Steakhouse. There is an entire dimension of communication that is missing in social media. Thus, in relationships where texting is a predominant mode of communication, the researchers found that relationship satisfaction is lower than in relationships where a larger portion of communication occurs through means other than texting. This was, unsurprisingly, also associated with lower levels of commitment to the relationship. If your relationship is becoming as two-dimensional as Flat Stanley, it's hard to build up the type of commitment to it that will weather the inevitable storms and challenges all relationships face.

To me, a second set of findings from this study are even more elucidating. The researchers examined the attachment styles of the romantic couples who participated in the study.

Regarding attachment styles, Dr. Joseph Nowinski explained that people are placed in one of three styles:

> **Secure attachment style**. These people have a healthy self-image. They are neither overly insecure nor narcissistic. They feel that they are lovable. They are able to enter into committed relationships and do not require excessive reassurance that they are loved.
>
> **Insecure attachment style**. These people seek frequent reassurance that they are loved; are highly conflict avoidant; are prone to feel inferior; and often experience anxiety when separated from a partner.
>
> **Avoidant attachment style**. These people value independence, prefer to maintain some emotional distance, and usually seek to be in control in a relationship.[11]

The researchers in the North Carolina study found that the men and women who were high volume texters exhibited the insecure and avoidant attachment styles—styles that tend to have difficulty building and maintaining healthy and satisfying relationships in families, with peers, and in the workplace.[10]

The most obvious conclusion to draw is that people with problematic attachment styles are more drawn to replace deeper forms of communication with texting in relationships, and I feel confident that is true. However, I think there is more to it than that. To fully explore the possible implications of this information, we must keep in mind that humans are not written in stone from a biological or psychological standpoint. We are moldable, due in part to the fact that our brains show a high degree of neuroplasticity and are constantly altered by our experiences and choices.

The degree to which we are moldable on a biological level may come as a surprise. One recent study, published in *The Proceedings of the National Academy of Sciences,* even discovered that being exposed to things such as poverty, family conflict, and stress can actually alter children's genomes.[12]

Environmental factors, including our own behavior and our relationship patterns and the ripples these create in our environment, have the potential to readjust our biological hardwiring to some degree.

What that means is if I act like someone who is insecurely attached in my relationships, I run the risk of actually becoming insecurely attached—both emotionally and even biologically—whether or not that was my predominant attachment style beforehand. Thus, heavy levels of texting in relationships likely not only reflect an insecure or avoidant attachment style but may actually help to promote and create insecure and avoidant attachment styles.

Time and further research will likely shed more light on this, and judging from the data that exist thus far, I feel confident that my analysis of the circular causation in this dynamic will be supported.

The constant use of smartphones has potential not only to disrupt the quality of our romantic relationships, but our effectiveness as parents as well. Dr. Susan Engle wrote a thought-provoking article in which she observed:

> [Smartphones] are going to cause long term damage if parents aren't careful. Again and again I see parents and their children in situations where, up until a few years ago, they had invaluable opportunities for the kind of idle chat that turns out to be essential to optimal intellectual development in general, and specifically to a child's future ability to read. But now, instead of the exchanges researchers know to be important, I see little to no exchange—while children are looking around, or playing, their parents are glued to some kind of communication device. . . . The point I am trying to make is this: parents who are concerned about their children's school success and happiness should fuss less about the amount of sugar in the cereal, or whether the school provides enough challenge for their very bright child, and instead make sure that while they are hanging around conducting everyday life, their cell phone is turned off and put away and they are available for the casual conversations that are the best school readiness program there is.[13]

When it comes to the slow accumulation of parent/child connection moments that establish firm bonds, encourage development, and provide a foundation for successfully navigating the challenges of parenting when our children reach their teens, there just isn't an app for that. In fact, it would seem that the way people tend to use apps can help us accomplish the opposite, interfering with constant, small, but important parenting moments. That's not a parenting goal I think any parent would purposefully set, nor is it a process I think we would tolerate if we were aware of the degree to which it is happening.

I find another trend in our disconnectedness from the physical world increasingly concerning. I have observed, as have many others, that as smartphones become more common, people tend to default to recording situations where human intervention would be helpful. Instead of helping to prevent suffering and save lives, with an almost trance-like reflex, they take pictures and videos and send texts and tweets rather than actually respond to someone in trouble.

Jessica Shiffer wrote the following in a thoughtful article:

> Over the last few years, our tech-induced predilection for documenting everything that we do and see seems to have taken a turn for the very dark. This was highlighted most recently by the video recording of a woman being sexually assaulted in Egypt's Tahrir Square during the inauguration of president Abdel Fattahel-Sisi. Displaying the victim not only during the attack but bloody and stumbling as police eventually pull her out of the crowd, the terrifying recording raises important questions about what seems to be a growing trend of bystanders opting to observe and document crimes and their victims, rather than interfere with or interrupt the situation.[14]

Many of us seem to be falling into the trap of thinking more about what we will present to our virtual audience than actually doing anything about what is right in front of us. In so doing, we become the equivalent of voyeurs of not only other people, but of our own lives, rather than agents of action.

Opportunity Cost

By filling our time with what comes easiest (and the stimulation of smartphones seems to be one of the easiest things to fill our time with), we run the risk of stuffing our time so fully with trivia and frivolity that we settle for pursuits that really don't mean that much to us and don't spend time nurturing the things in our lives that have greater meaning and value to us.

In fact, this habit of filling our time with the all-too-easy activation of a smartphone can be so hypnotizing as to keep us from realizing how empty our lives are becoming because we are not taking the time to talk to the people around us, notice and appreciate our surroundings, or simply have our attention free enough to see and take advantage of the countless unanticipated opportunities that come in the flow of the average day.

We run the risk of trading our most effective parenting moments for beating one more level on Candy Crush Saga or exchanging an emotionally meaningful moment with a friend to check a text that just says, "k." When put in that manner, do these trade-offs feel worth it? To me, they do not, and yet it is so easy for us to fall right into that trap.

Everything we do, including our use of smartphones and social media, has a cost. There are two major kinds of cost to consider. First, there is *direct cost*. For example, the direct cost of a Ferrari GTB Fiorano at the time I am writing this is $280,000. No matter how you twist it, if you want to park that new Ferrari in your garage, you are going to have to pay the Ferrari dealer $280,000. Otherwise, there will be no Ferrari for you. With our smartphones, there is the financial cost of the phone and the service provider, and there is also the direct cost of the time we spend using them.

The second kind of cost is what is known as *opportunity cost*, which encompasses everything else you could have spent your resources on besides the thing you decided to purchase or invest in. In any business, the greatest cost is always opportunity cost.

Going back to our previous example, the Ferrari costs you $280,000 as well as whatever else you could have bought with that $280,000. So, when you paid that money for a Ferrari, you also paid the cost of a nice house in Utah, a mini-mansion in West Virginia (or a cardboard box on the corner of Manhattan, the last time I checked on home prices there), or 280,000 orders of French fries off the dollar menu at your local fast food restaurant. Thus, the opportunity cost of buying the Ferrari was that nice house in Utah, that mini-mansion in West Virgina, and all that fried potato goodness. Your cardiologist and dietitian both thank you for that last one.

Another example of opportunity cost is that I can choose to date Sarah or I can choose to date Amy, but I can't choose to date them both at the same time. The price of marrying Sarah is that I don't get to marry Amy. If you feel tempted to think otherwise, just ask Sarah; she'll be more than willing to tell you all about it and set the record straight. Just be aware that conversation might be a little painful, but only if you consider compound fractures and the scorn of a woman spurned uncomfortable.

Although we may not like to think about it, our use of smartphones, texting, and social media has both a direct cost and an opportunity cost. The time, energy, and investment we make in using our smartphones is time, energy, and investment we no longer have to spend on other things. Chances are, the more time we spend using our smartphones and social media, the more things that are truly important to us will fall into the category of our opportunity cost for using our technological toys.

What is most concerning is how blissfully unaware we become about this opportunity cost. All too often, life is that thing that goes on in the background while we are distracted by our smartphones. Exactly how much time do we spend living this way? The average American spends twenty-three hours per week online, emailing, using social media, or texting (this isn't counting offline games, gaming consoles, portable gaming systems, games on smartphones, and so on). That means in the average year, the average American spends about 50 full days online. Or, if we just limit that to 16 waking hours per day, that's nearly 75 days' worth of waking hours. That's about 14 percent of your lifetime.[15] I am not saying that all of that is wasted time, but to me this information indicates there is likely a very high direct and opportunity cost in the way we tend to use the cyber-scape. Yet, due to the distracting nature of the cyber-scape, one of the things we are most likely to be distracted from is an awareness of the cost. We rarely find what we are not looking for, especially when we are preoccupied with something else. Thus, what we are usually most blind to is the source of our blindness.

I found the following two video links to be thought-provoking when considering the direct and opportunity costs of what have become the social norms for smartphone and social media use. If you are reading this on an e-reader, just click the links. If you are going old-school and reading a paper copy of this book, I highly recommend you take a moment to watch the following two video clips.

"Look Up"[16]
    https://www.youtube.com/watch?v=Z7dLU6fk9QY
"I Forgot My Phone"[17]
    http://www.filmsforaction.org/watch/i_forgot_my_phone/

Does this mean that technology is bad for relationships? My observation has been that if we merely follow the path of least resistance with our smartphones (which appears to have become the social norm), the answer is that it can be, and often is. However, the answer is also no, not inevitably so. It is the habits, trends, and dynamics we have built around our relationship with technology versus the people and the world right in front of us that are in fact damaging to relationships, and thus damaging to us.

My observations suggest that these destructive trends are becoming the majority. However, I believe a more mindful approach to both our technology and our relationships can help us avoid having our relationships negatively affected by our smartphones. Right now, we serve our devices. If we are thoughtful, we can find ways to make them serve us.

Shallow Thought

I am also worried about what we are becoming by communicating the way we do through smartphones. There are some legitimate questions to be asked about how our methods of texting, tweeting, and posting affects not only the way we communicate but also the way we think and what we value.

A study by Dr. Lisa Sinclair and Dr. Paul Trapnell from the University of Winnipeg utilized a sample of 2,300 college students and found 30 percent texted more than 200 times per day and 12 percent texted more than 300 times per day. Young adults who text more than 100 times per day are 30 percent more likely to be focused on wealth, superficiality, and general vanity and less likely to be interested in ethics or morals when compared to young adults who texted 50 or less times per day. Those young adults who texted more frequently also reported significantly less reflective thought than those who texted less frequently. In addition, the heavier texters showed more features of racist and stereotypical beliefs and attitudes, which is a form of polarized thought. Furthermore, Sinclair and Trapnell observed that there have been significant annual declines in their measures of reflective thought in young adults since they began this study in 2006.[18]

In other words, the trend is for people who are high utilizers of the cyber-scape to be less and less thoughtful, more and more superficial, and more impulsive and immature in their thought processes.

This study was designed to test (and ultimately provides strong support for) what is known as the "Shallowing Hypothesis," put forth by Nicolas Carr in his book *The Shallows: What the Internet is Doing to our Brains.*[19]

Carr's hypothesis states that ultra-brief social media interactions—such as short texts, short Vine videos, microblog entries, Tweets, communicating through memes, and relying on brief "sound bites"—encourage rapid, relatively shallow thought. In other words, by constantly communicating in a sort of ultra-simplified shorthand with no room for nuance or details, we train our brains to think in a shallower, more two-dimensional fashion. The tools we use, including the tools we use for reading and information gathering, actually shape us on a neurological level. Carr states that as a result of the nature and mechanics of social media technology, we are training ourselves to become adept at skimming and scanning, but by over-focusing on these skills, we are diminishing our abilities to reflect, concentrate, and contemplate. Thus, if this hypothesis holds true, very frequent use of such media should not only be associated with but should in fact be a direct causal contributor to cognitive and moral shallowness not just mentally but biologically.[20]

Following the logic of this hypothesis, it is not only the fact that the content of much of what is shown on social media is shallow (self-aggrandizement, pornography, polarized viewpoints, commercialism, consumerism, materialism, mindless imitation, and so on) that leads to it promoting and invoking more shallow thought, it is the actual mechanics of how this information is shared and consumed. One of the ways the human brain learns is through sequence learning (which we will discuss in detail later). As we repeat a series of behaviors, our brain places that series in a large "chunk" so that we don't have to think about every little piece of the behavior. Once we have practiced routines enough, we don't have to consciously think about them at all. It becomes second nature and as such is something we do without reflective thought or active awareness of choice. When applied to the mechanics of social media and texting, sequence learning means that the repetitive cycle of "scan, click, read a snippet, and move on" teaches our brains not only shallow content but a shallow thought process. And, like any other behavior, that which we consistently repeat becomes a practiced, unconscious, automatic reflex. So, if we constantly use quick, easy, shallow means to take information in, we develop an automatic reflex of taking in and evaluating information in quick, easy, and ultimately superficial ways. It becomes our way of thinking. How we use our brains actually molds and recreates our brains.

One way to think of this is to compare it to the Microsoft Windows Start button, particularly from older versions of Microsoft Windows. Let's say I want to play a game. I click on the Start button, go to the Games folder, and browse through the games until I find *Mine Sweeper*. I click on *Mine Sweeper*, load it up, play it, and have a good time. I mean, come on! It has explosions and a yellow smiley face that wears sunglasses and flashes a big smile to give me positive reinforcement. How could I not have a good time?

Microsoft Windows's programming teaches it to be efficient. If Microsoft Windows notices that I go through this sequence several times (Start button, Games, *Mine Sweeper*), it will then place a shortcut on the Start Menu. That way, when I press the Start button, the option for *Mine Sweeper* pops up at the bottom of a list of commonly used programs. I can then access it without having to browse to the Games folder and sort through that folder to find *Mine Sweeper*. How considerate of it!

If Microsoft Windows notices that I select *Mine Sweeper* from the Start Menu several more times, it will start moving it higher and higher on the list of commonly used programs until it gets to the top of the list.

Now, if Microsoft Windows functioned more like the brain, the more I choose *Mine Sweeper* from off the top of the list, Microsoft Windows would start leaving off other programs from the list of commonly used programs. As *Mine Sweeper* is repeatedly chosen, the list would keep getting smaller and smaller. It would appear like my options for doing something other than playing *Mine Sweeper* are shrinking, when in fact they are not. They are just being moved to other parts of the user interface that I have to work harder to access. Pretty soon, the only option that would pop up on the list of commonly used programs is *Mine Sweeper.*

Again, if Microsoft Windows functioned more like our brains, it would take another step: it would start to generalize. It would start to add *Mine Sweeper* into all the other folders. Do I want to write a paper? Well, it would place *Mine Sweeper* in the Microsoft Word folder. As time went by, it would hide the other icons in that folder. Pretty soon, everywhere I looked I would see shortcuts for *Mine Sweeper.* It would seem as if *Mine Sweeper* was the only program I had on my computer. That smiling yellow face would have changed from my mine-avoiding friend to a yellow-tainted Orwellian Big Brother, watching my every move with his sinister intentions hidden behind his pixelated sun shades. (Perhaps that part was a little melodramatic, but I think you get the point.)

This same process occurs with us when we are repeatedly thinking with a shallow process, thinking about shallow things, or doing both simultaneously, as social media is adept at inviting us to do. This process literally shapes both the structure and functioning of our brains, and this style of thought and value begins to generalize into the way we think about other things, not just what we post or read in texts or on social media. Therefore, by repeatedly training ourselves with shallow thinking in this one area of life, we set ourselves up for shallow thinking in all areas of our lives, and this appears to be even more true the more frequently we engage in such thinking, which falls in line with what we know from neuroscience about how the human brain learns. We're shaping our brains, people. That organ might come in useful for something at some point in time in our lives, so molding it is not something I think we should do carelessly.

Narcissistic Playground

Besides shaping our minds, our social media use can shape our very personalities—often in some concerning ways. Dr. Brittnay Gentile observed, "Despite the name 'social networks,' much user activity on networking sites is self-focused."[20] Indeed, social media profiles have widely become a sort of persistent online marketing program for people, their image, and their ideas, many of which are heavily padded by facades and exaggerations of all kinds. Dr. Elliot Panek and his associates observed that social media profiles can also be used as a mirror.[21] We can go through a process of putting out an image, seeing how other people respond to it, and then identifying more strongly with that unrealistic image as our identity. "[Posting and tweeting are] about curating your own image, how you are seen, and also checking on how others respond to this image." They also described how people have a tendency to use social media as a megaphone. We shout out our ideas to the world, and they are often responded to with a flurry of comments, likes, and retweets (although oftentimes it seems to me like the equivalent of yelling nonsense words into an echo chamber). Other people praise us for our wit, humor, and style. We are reinforced for doing something as trivial as taking a picture of what we are eating for breakfast and finding that enough people consider this important enough to click "like" and post the obligatory but all-too-predictable comments of "yum" and "I'm jealous!" Whereas celebrities often flee from the invasiveness of the paparazzi, on social media many of us become aggressive paparazzi to ourselves and bask in the warm glow of attention, affirmation, and adulation we receive as a reward.

As a result, Panek concluded, "People may over-evaluate the importance of their own opinions." Both ways of using social media—as a mirror and a microphone—were found to be reinforcing of narcissistic personality traits. This harmonizes with the findings of Gentile and her colleagues that narcissistic personality traits were associated with having a higher number of "friends" on social networking sites. They also found that social media sites that have less interaction but are focused more on maintaining a profile (for example, Myspace and Live Journal) were more highly associated with narcissistic personality traits. It would seem that while the Internet can be a source of knowledge, it can just as easily be a source of powerful reinforcement for the mistaken notion that you know it all. We can create the illusion that the universe really does revolve around us. Narcissism has become the prime "virtue" of social media.

Narcissism, Fragility, and the Mask Prison

I have always found narcissism to be a curious personality trait. It is often defined as "excessive self-love," but I have come to see it differently. While it is true that a narcissistic perspective tends to lead a person to be self-absorbed, rather than loving themselves too much, it seems that they struggle to love themselves if they are anything less than extraordinary, perfect, and a cut above the rest of the mere mortals who surround them. If they are not feeling overly catered to—practically worshipped—they do not experience a sense of validation. As a result, narcissistic personality traits tend to make us very fragile. When we experience a narcissistic mindset, we cannot tolerate any awareness of our own imperfections, need for growth, or even our equality with those around us. Coming face-to-face with evidence of such things feels like an attack to a person looking out on the world from a narcissistic lens. The narcissistic style of thought compels us to cling tenaciously to our errors and self-defeating behaviors, because to recognize them as such would shatter our self-image. Thus, a narcissistic paradigm ultimately results in the inability to handle reality and a constant, dogged quest to reinforce the personal myth of exceptionalism and immunity from the rules, ideas, and cause-and-effect nature of the universe that govern other people. The costs of this quest are felt first and most powerfully by the people the narcissistic person interacts with. He or she blinds him or herself to the damage he or she does, blaming the emotional and relational carnage on the failings of others. It is a sad, slow, and painful death spiral for someone to go through, and I have observed it to be a cause of significant human suffering. Yet, in spite of its costs, narcissism seems to be the end goal of many of our misunderstandings, follies, and misguided efforts in the search for self-esteem.

Social media, with its focus on image and self-promotion, encourages and rewards narcissistic thoughts and behaviors. The struggle of choosing between promoting a personal image and developing real personal substance has long been a battle in human relationships and mental health. The dynamics of social media have taken that battle and intensified it to such a degree that whereas before it could have been appropriately compared to medieval knights dueling for honor on the field, now it is more aptly compared to nuclear warfare between world superpowers.

There is a story that I believe is a good parable for the challenge that the focus on image—intensified in the realm of social media—provides for us. This tale introduces us to a young man who lived in a quiet village. He was an ordinary young man like many others, longing for what he imagined were the freedoms of adulthood but still trudging through the trials of adolescence. His life was filled with the work of his apprenticeship, and he had settled into a routine that he found mundane and predictable. He was not disliked by his peers, but there was nothing about him that made him stand out. He often felt like he merely blended in with his drab, unsophisticated surroundings, and this led to him feeling unsettled, hungering for something more.

The one thing the young man looked forward to was the merchants who travelled from village to village, bringing stories from other places and goods that he could never find in his provincial little town. One merchant in particular had caught the attention of the young man. While this merchant had many interesting trinkets in his cart, he always kept one item displayed off to the side. It was a remarkable mask, unlike any the young man had ever seen before. He did not know why, but the mask seemed to draw him in. He asked the old merchant about it, and rather than give an explanation, the merchant simply took the mask from its stand and placed it over his own face. Immediately, the merchant seemed to be transformed by the mask. Behind its cover he seemed strong, wise, and charismatic, even without saying a single word. This apparent transformation transfixed the young man, and he begged the merchant to let him try it on himself. "No, young one, you cannot try on this mask unless you are willing to buy it."

"But I am willing to buy it! I will give you whatever you want for it!" the young man replied.

"There are many things I want that you cannot give me, young man. Indeed, at my age, much of what I want, no one can give me. So, do not make promises you cannot keep," the merchant replied. "No, this mask is not for sale to you today. You must be committed to buy this mask, and it will cost you a great deal."

As the young man left the merchant's cart that day, he felt determined to do whatever it took to acquire that mask. He worked harder than he ever had. He saved everything he earned. He sold off his other scant possessions, all in the hopes that the next time, he could convince the merchant to sell him the mask.

When the merchant returned, the young man sought him out eagerly and laid all he had earned out in front of the old merchant. He told the old man all he had done, all he had sacrificed. "You said I needed to be committed to buying the mask. Don't my sacrifices show my commitment? Surely, you can't deny me the right to buy the mask now!"

The old merchant considered the young man for a moment and then said, "Yes, I will accept this sum, although I doubt you know right now just how much this is costing you. The day may come when you understand the price. I wonder if you will think it was worth it on that day." He then took the mask off its stand and handed it to the young man. The young man exulted as he felt it in his hands for the first time. He could not wait; he immediately slipped it on over his face. He was overjoyed to see that the mask not only changed how he looked but how he felt. When he wore it, he felt smarter, more powerful, more in command of himself and all around him. "I can tell you right now, old man, this was worth the price. This was worth everything I could have paid and more!" he cried.

"You are too quick to judge, young one. Time will tell," the merchant said softly as the young man departed.

The young man raced home, eager to show the mask to his friends and neighbors. As he tried it on in front of them, he treasured the way they looked at him. Whereas before when others did not seem to pay him much heed, he now saw respect from old men and young men alike, and admiration and attraction from the women. He no longer blended in. This promised to be the beginning of a whole new life for him. As he prepared to sleep that night, he held the mask tenderly for a few moments and wondered, "How did I ever live without this?"

As the days went by, the young man basked in the light of the many advantages of the mask. He was given greater leverage in business, more prestige in social gatherings, more credence in his opinions, and more power in decisions. He began wearing the mask more and more each day. He couldn't see a reason not to, with all the obvious advantages it brought to him. And so, the weeks and months passed in this fashion. The young man could not imagine it was possible for anyone to feel more satisfied with their life than he felt about his.

One day, the young man attended a social gathering. He had come to greatly enjoy entering a room and seeing all eyes turned upon him. This time, however, as he watched the admiration in the eyes of all who were present, he noticed another emotion, one he did not immediately recognize because it was so unexpected. He was confused by it, and so he attempted to push it aside for the remainder of the evening. However, as he returned home that evening, the surprising feeling returned and haunted him as he tried to sleep. He felt resentment. "Why would I feel this way? This mask gives me everything I want. I have friends! I have power! I have respect! I have opportunity! Why would I resent my friends for looking upon me with such admiration?" He had a long and sleepless night as he wrestled with this question.

It was only as the gray, predawn light illuminated his weary mind that the young man began to understand. He did not resent his friends for looking at him so fondly with the mask on. Rather, he resented the growing, nagging feeling that they would not look on him the same way without the mask. He resented that it was not him that they respected but the image the mask portrayed. He resented the surge in his awareness that he no longer knew who he was without the mask. He resented that he would not know where to go, what to do, or even what to think without it.

He tried to shove these thoughts and feelings aside as he went about his business of the day, exhausted from the sleepless night. But with the early morning revelation fresh in his memory, he could not help but notice the feeling of resentment resurging again and again each time someone agreed with his opinion, affirmed his position, or treated him with respect. "It is like everything they supposedly give, they give to someone else instead of me. It is all given to the mask and I am left with nothing! I thought the mask was making me rich in every way, but it has left me poor! When the old merchant told me I needed to be committed to the mask, I did not know he meant I would be committed to it the same way a man is committed to a prison!" It was true; he had become the mask's prisoner. It owned him, and he owned nothing.

That evening, the young man sat on his bed, holding his masked face in his hands and feeling very, very old. He found himself at a moment of choice. "Do I remove the mask? What would my life be without it? But how can I continue to live with it?" As much as he wanted to rip the mask from his face, his fear prevented him. He could not bear the thought of how others would look at him with his regular, unremarkable face, his average intelligence, and his very normal life. He was trapped. The mask had won, and he hadn't even known that it was trying to beat him. And so he lived out his life, an empty man in a compelling mask.

That's not a very satisfying end to this tale, is it? All too often, though, that is the end to this tale in real life, with the mask as the victorious foe. Imagine, for a moment, how this story would be different if, instead of there being just one such mask, the young man lived in a world where there were many masks. Imagine that the young man spent his life watching others receive apparent benefits for wearing their masks. In those circumstances, how much more appealing would the idea of having his own mask be? How much more difficult would he find the idea of removing his own mask? We live in such a world. We are encouraged in many ways to wear masks of unrealistic strength, wealth, power, perfection, self-determinism, confidence, stereotypical versions of beauty, fearlessness, independence, victimhood, political enlightenment, religious or atheistic zeal, righteous indignation, intellectual superiority, disdain for social norms, rigid masculinity and femininity, unfettered sexuality, or emotional invulnerability, among others. I suspect that nowhere is our world more persistent in its promotion of these masks than on social media. Thus, the risk of becoming prisoners to our own masks is compounded on the cyber-scape, in good part due to the fact that we encounter so many other people there using their masks so prolifically and being heartily rewarded for it, or so it seems. When we fall victim to our masks, we often do not notice we have lost. In fact, we may have never noticed there was a battle going on in the first place.

Groupthink

While the cyber-scape brings with it the risk of being narcissistically self-absorbed, it also carries the very real peril of being absorbed by a hive mind, herd mindset, or mob mentality. This hive mind phenomenon is often known as *groupthink* and has been observed to be the cause of such events as the space shuttle *Challenger* disaster (in which multiple highly educated professionals knew the parts were faulty and a launch would end in tragedy, but they bowed to the pressure of the prevailing thoughts of their group), the Salem Witch Trials, lynch mobs throughout history, the Rodney King riots in Los Angeles, runs on the bank during times of economic crisis, subprime lending practices leading to a housing boom and eventual bust in 2008 in the United States, and many other situations in which normal, rational people seem to lose intelligence and insight as they team up with a larger group and goad each other on in an increasingly extreme mindset, often with disastrous results.

Lubor Ptacek described groupthink as "a well-documented psychological phenomenon where a group of people, usually insulated from any counterbalancing point of view, ends up making gravely irrational decisions."[22] Groupthink has long been observed as a destructive phenomenon in the physical world, but the cyber-scape's ability to connect larger groups from around the entire world has facilitated the ability for groupthink to form larger, more quickly, and more completely, and has also extended its reach to absorb individuals into the collective mind to a global scale. In other words, groupthink on the cyber-scape is groupthink on steroids.

Beyond expanding the reach of groupthink—and thus adding to the strength of the insularity of thought that groupthink thrives upon—the very mechanics of social media lend themselves well to reinforcing groupthink. For example, if Facebook literally showed you all of the status updates and pictures of all of your friends, the average user would be inundated with such a colossal stream of updates that you could never keep up with it and your experience with Facebook would ultimately be frustrating. That is not good for Facebook, because it would result in users abandoning Facebook and hurting their business. Therefore, Facebook uses algorithms to trim down the sheer volume of data and only displays for us the posts that it believes we will most want to see, thus leading us to have an emotionally satisfying experience with Facebook and helping improve Facebook's bottom line. Facebook is a business, after all. Thus, Facebook algorithms turn it into a sort of sycophantic "yes man" for your expressed preferences and opinions.

Ptacek observed,

> If you like a post about kittens the algorithm will reason that you like kittens and chances are you will be seeing more posts about kittens. Over time, you end up "liking" various comments, pictures, and pages. Based on your liking, Facebook starts presenting you more of the stuff you like from the people [whose posts you have indicated you like, by interacting with them or "liking" the posts]. That happens at the cost of all other news in your newsfeed. As a result, you get exposed only to views from friends who you "like" more and more and you won't get exposed to anything else. This is a fertile breeding ground for a group-think with all its shortcomings.[23]

Randall Ridd made a similar observation: "The Internet also records your desires, expressed in the form of searches and clicks. There are legions waiting to fill those desires. As you surf the Internet, you leave tracks—what you communicate, where you have been, how long you have been there, and the kinds of things that interest you. In this way, the Internet creates a cyber profile for you—in a sense, your 'cyber book of life.' As in life, the Internet will give you more and more of what you seek."[24]

Due to the commercial interests and economic purposes that help drive the Internet, in many ways the algorithms of various social media and even some search engines function to show you more of what you want to find, not necessarily more of what is actually out there. Because of that, our search for knowledge on the Internet can often be subject to a sort of stealthy circular reasoning, with us being introduced to sites and online communities that tend to reinforce our preconceptions and prejudices. The Internet is not designed to do critical thinking for us, nor to illuminate for us how our opinion is an artifact of the limited scope of our search (not to mention the whole mess with evaluating the validity and reliability of data that was discussed earlier in this book). The cyber-scape will never respond to our search results with the text, "Hey, I can see that you have been searching a lot about topic X, but you haven't really considered the unintended consequences. I can see you also haven't run any searches at all for topic Y, which would probably lead you to interpret what you are finding about topic X in a different light. Besides that, the methodology of what you are reading about topic X is weak, and the authors are often grossly overextending their conclusions." Even when we do find contradictory information in our searches, I believe that most of us are not very good at seriously considering opposing points of view. Usually, the human method for handling contradictory opinions is to listen to them long enough to construct a shallow caricature of the point the other side is trying to make, just detailed enough to feel satisfied, superior, and informed when we shoot down our shallow representation of their thoughts, feelings, and position. We then turn back to our like-minded crowd, who congratulate us for our prowess in dismantling the feeble claims of the poor fools who dare to think differently than we do. What a satisfyingly smug feeling that is!

I have seen many people balk at the idea that groupthink actually changes people's opinions, and they feel that they are certainly immune to the phenomenon. The idea that we could be so gullible and so moldable is disturbing to us. And yet, there are many ways in which this phenomenon plays out right in front of us on the cyber-scape, and not just to other people, but to ourselves.

Sohn reported on a study from the Massachusetts Institute of Technology that demonstrated groupthink at play on a large scale.[25] Sinan Aral and his colleagues conducted a study on a social media website where users post articles, reviews, and comments and can vote either positively or negatively on each other's posts. The researchers chose comments at random to receive either positive or negative votes. Over the course of five months, they randomly rated more than 101,000 comments, which resulted in more than 10 million views, and then were voted on by other users 300,000 times. This allowed the researchers to analyze the votes that followed their own to see if there were any discernible patterns that emerged.

They found that when they randomly assigned a post a single positive vote, regardless of the content of the post, it received a 25 percent spike in subsequent positive votes compared to the control group of comments that were assigned no rating at all. Interestingly enough, when the researchers randomly assigned a single negative vote, they observed a similar spike in subsequent negative votes, but then a backlash of positive votes that seemed to overwhelm the possibility of a negative spiral in the voting. As the researchers delved in greater detail into the history of the users who voted on items, they found evidence to support the idea that seeing other people's ratings actually changed their opinions about posted news items. It was not merely a matter of certain groups responding in greater numbers to one news item or another based on its content.

It appears that as a whole, we have come to empower "the collective" of the Internet as a trustworthy authority figure. Perhaps this indicates some sort of faith in the idea that the truth lies in the mean, and that the mean will be accurately reflected in the massive numbers of the population of the Internet. Perhaps this is an extension of the mentality that "50 million Elvis fans can't be wrong." Whatever the cause, people frequently turn to online ratings when making decisions about hotels, movies, vacations, fashion, news reports, parenting, home repairs, television shows, educational trends, and political candidates, among countless other things. These online ratings exert a powerful influence on our decisions. A survey by Dimensional Research found that 90 percent of their respondents reported that reading positive online reviews influenced their decisions about purchases, and 86 percent stated that their buying decisions were influenced by negative online reviews.[26] Another survey found that more people trusted the opinions of strangers online than those who report they trust the opinion of their friends.[27] It makes me want to take a step back and say, "Wait, just who are we trusting again, and why?"

Examples of groupthink on the Internet abound, from websites for and against various drugs (which can lead to ridiculous claims on both sides), discussions about politics, debates about educational practices, discussions about social trends, examinations of various religions and philosophies, and so forth. This is concerning to me because, as Irving Janis observed, "[People under the influence of groupthink] quickly reach consensus decisions with amazing disregard for obvious warning signs that they are on the wrong track. Extremely cohesive groups, oriented around a strong leader, will ignore or punish dissenting opinions."[28] If there was a way to accurately measure just how many of our thoughts, opinions, and beliefs are determined or influenced by groupthink, I believe we would find the results rather chilling. On the cyber-scape, groupthink is a risk for all of us, and most of us who fall into its mental clutches do so entirely unawares. The most dangerous prisons are those of the mind, and the most frightening of those are the ones we don't even know we are in.

Mindless Imitation

While getting sucked into a hive mind is a concerning risk on the cyber-scape, there is also the potential to have our minds willingly pummeled and numbed by a long line of trivial, ridiculous, and in some cases dangerous "stupid human tricks." It is as if there is a section of the cyber-scape that is set aside for human beings to attempt to prove Darwin's theory of evolution wrong by doing things so inane or idiotic that it makes the idea that we are actually evolving to a higher level of intelligence hard to believe. It's interesting how infectious this phenomenon is, since we tend to respond to these trends through spreading them, imitating them (in a process I have come to call "me too-ism"), or seeking to "one up" them. It is like there is someone on the Internet who shouts out the commands to a bizarre square dance written by the Mad Hatter:

> Plank yourself everywhere you go.
> Allamande left, but don't tip toe.
> Make a cat-themed video!
>
> Side step forward, make a dash!
> Wear an ironic mustache!
>
> Dance that Gangnam Style again!
> Chasse right to the count of ten.
>
> Circle to the right like a flag unfurled.
> Quote "The Most Interesting Man in the World!"
> (He doesn't always dance, but when he does, it's a square dance!)
>
> Greet your over-attached girlfriend!
> Dance like the world is going to end!

Punch a text into your phone!
Don't end up forever alone!

Throw down an archaic rap!
Make the Nyan cat take a nap!
Admiral Ackbar: "It's a trap!" Take a selfie while you drive.
Boy, I hope that you survive.

Everybody facepalm, do-si-do now!
Yeehaw!

On and on the caller drones, and people seem to flock to follow the commands in vast herds. After all, it looks like fun.

I am not trying to say that nonsense is a bad thing. I believe we can all benefit from some humor and silliness. That is why you will just as easily find me quoting Pinky and the Brain and Strong Bad as well as Shakespeare and Socrates. Indeed, many of these memes start out quite clever and funny, although both the cleverness and the humor tend to get diluted the more times each theme is riffed upon. Mental fluff itself is not necessarily a problem unless we are indulging in so much of it that it begins to take up the time and energy we would place into things that have mental substance. Filling our time and our minds with endless hours of Internet memes, remakes of videos, and other pointless trivia can contribute to the shallowing effect mentioned earlier and can also exact a high opportunity cost.

Consider the huge amount of time and energy put into viral videos. Perhaps one of the most well-known examples of the viral phenomenon is the Harlam Shake. For those lucky souls who don't know what this is, the Harlam Shake is a viral video that starts with a single person doing some kind of dance (usually while wearing a helmet or some kind of headgear) in a setting where no one else seems to notice them. Then, when the bass drops in the music, the scene transforms to everyone dancing, often in various costumes and also often in various stages of being less than fully clothed. The original Harlam Shake went viral in February of 2013. By February 10, the rate of its spread had reached 4,000 new versions being uploaded to YouTube per day. By February 14, there were reportedly 40,000 different versions uploaded.

That is not reposts or shares; those are different versions. This same pattern has occurred before with the viral videos of the songs "Call Me Maybe" and "Gangnam Style," or more recently with various remakes of "Let it Go" from the Disney movie *Frozen*. Each new wave is bigger and grows more quickly than its predecessor.

Some of these viral fads and memes can actually be dangerous. The cinnamon challenge is an example. This challenge, as the name implies, requires the contestant to consume one tablespoon of cinnamon in sixty seconds without drinking any water. This is a painful experience that leaves the contestants with a horrible burning sensation and causes forceful coughing. According to cinnamonchallenge.com, more than 40,000 people have participated in the cinnamon challenge and posted the results on YouTube. Those who took the challenge have received a lot of attention, affirmation, and support. A good time was had by all, no doubt (and yes, that was a sarcastic comment). However, the cinnamon challenge is more than just uncomfortable. It is so dangerous that the professional journal *Pediatrics* published an article on it. This report demonstrated that the Cinnamon Challenge is actually damaging to the lungs,[29] can trigger asthma attacks, and has even resulted in poisoning and hospitalizations. And yet, this is something we encourage and reward? Yes, it is. Every view and every like is a vote for more people to participate in this activity, and it has real world consequences.

Somehow, we seem to compartmentalize between the cyber-scape and the physical world. Either we don't think at all about the crossover between the two, or we minimize it. However, our herd-like online behavior can have very real consequences in the physical world. A humorous example of this is found in the form of an innocent-looking online celebrity known as Meet Eater, a plant that gets watered when people become its Facebook fans or post things on its Facebook wall. The problem is, Meet Eater's fan base has proven to be fatal. Meet Eater and its successor have actually died twice from being overwatered by people flocking to like it and write on its Facebook wall.[30] Moderation does not seem to come naturally on the cyber-scape.

While the death of two plants may seem relatively harmless (gardeners and environmentalists, please don't send me hate mail for saying that), let's put some thought into how this plays out for human beings.

For a long time, we have been able to watch the destructive downward spiral of many celebrities' lives—especially child celebrities—that seems to stem from them feeding off of the constant attention they get for their edgy or outrageous behavior. Indeed, it has become almost a tradition of sorts to watch some bright young Disney star or starlet transform themselves into the polar opposite of their previous public persona as they grow up. The more outrageous they become, the more notoriety they receive, and this appears to be a very intoxicating elixir. Even when they get negative attention, they still seem to feed off of having the public limelight. They thrive off of those who applaud their boldness and audacity, like those who vigorously and publicly approved of the controversial VMA awards show "twerking" performance by the apparently aspiring parseltongue Miley Cyrus and her dance partner Robin Thicke. They think their critics are merely secretly jealous or at worst giving them free publicity, since even bad press is still press, ergo the quote often attributed to P.T. Barnum, "I don't care what they say about me, just make sure they spell my name right!"

The whole phenomenon appears to act like an addiction. Those who get a taste for attention and notoriety build up a tolerance to it and need a higher "dose" to get the same fix as time passes. For example, Dennis Rodman apparently used to be able to get a buzz by wearing a woman's gown in public. Eventually, that grew to be old hat and no longer got any attention. Rather than stopping and asking himself the pointed and sage question of "What the heck am I doing?" he worked his way up to palling around with North Korean dictator Kim Jong Un. Once that grows old, it's going to be tough to top. Perhaps he could become an advocate for something even more universally despised, like paper cuts or telemarketer calls in the middle of dinner time—or telemarketers giving paper cuts at dinnertime. That might do the trick.

With the advent of social media, this elixir of attention and its resulting downward spiral is no longer limited to celebrities. The average Joe or Jane can receive the same intoxicating attention by posting a picture of him or herself "planking" in a dangerous location. They can be encouraged in their bullying of another by their peers liking and reposting their attacking remarks and memes. They can push themselves to extremes to imitate or "one up" something someone else has done online that garnered attention. They can injure themselves by attempting some stunt such as amateur Parkour. When it goes awry, they may even abase themselves by posting their embarrassing resulting injury, since humiliating Parkour "fails" get as much attention as amazing Parkour escapades. If we can't be famous for being good at something, we've become comfortable with being famous for acting like an idiot, although the shelf life of such fame is extremely short.

A recent example of the real life damage this dynamic can cause is the viral drinking game "Neknominate." This so-called game involves a player filming him or herself drinking a beverage—usually alcoholic and usually in large quantities—and posting it to social media. Then they nominate someone by name to try to outdo their record. The nominations have evolved (*devolved* may be the more accurate word) with each round to be more extreme, more outlandish (including ingredients such as a dead mouse or motor oil), and significantly more dangerous. This viral trend has predictably led to a number of fatalities.[31] Did we not see that coming? These deaths were both foreseeable, preventable, and completely unnecessary. I find myself wondering if the people who participate, watch, or give "likes" to these videos give any thought to their contribution to these tragic outcomes. While news of fatalities as a result of this dynamic may rouse some interest, I have also observed that it is easy for us to ignore problems that are just as real but not as dramatic, such as bullying, insecurity, over-reliance on image, fostering impulsiveness, and so forth.

With imitative memes and viral videos, the cyber-scape has a large cultural impetus toward quick, impulsive, dangerous behavior and one-upsmanship without consideration or critical thought about one's own intended actions. *Think, then act* is not exactly a mantra that is compatible with this mindset of the cyber-scape. It is as if the cyber-scape has a whole choir of voices that shout out in unison, "Do it! I dare you! I triple dog dare you!" whenever we have an inclination to do something foolish. Indeed, sometimes I see the antics that go on in the hallowed halls of the Internet and feel inclined to say with Shakespearean flair, "Oh, frontal cortex, where art thou?" or "The more we get together, the stupider we shall be." (The second one is admittedly not Shakespearean, but it is a traditional British folksong.) For me, this pervasive cyber-culture that rewards impulsive actions is a particularly concerning dynamic when it intersects with child and adolescent brains that are still developing and as such already struggle with things such as self-regulation, long-term thinking, insight, and delayed gratification.

Oversharing and Triangulation

The cyber-scape excels at overcoming boundaries. In some ways, this is wonderful. We can stay in contact with other people much faster and easier than ever before. We can collaborate in our work efforts with people all over the world in real time. Information and resources that used to be incredibly difficult to hunt down are only a Google search away. Genealogy research, for instance, used to consist of spending endless hours in library archives, poring through microfiche, writing to people around the globe, gleaning information at extended family reunions, and so forth. Putting together just a few generations of a family tree could take weeks, months, or even years. Today that same process can be done in just minutes using sites such as family-search.org, ancestry.com, or billiongraves.com. Information in other languages can instantly be translated into ones we understand. People who would never be able to have their ideas published can now have a worldwide audience. In this way, the boundary-breaking abilities of the cyber-scape have been immensely liberating, more so than perhaps anything else in the history of the world. To me, this is unarguably a good thing.

We tend to think of boundaries as oppressive, constraining, and undesirable. While that may be true of some boundaries, thinking of all boundaries that way is yet another example of polarized thinking and is merely a two-dimensional model of a three-dimensional dynamic. In reality, some boundaries are helpful, empowering, and desirable. For example, the field of family therapy has long noted the importance of boundaries within families. Family therapy pioneer Salvador Minuchin noted that emotional and relationship problems occur when there were boundary violations, such as when "parents intrude in sibling conflicts, or adolescents disqualify parents or intrude into the spouse's area, or grandparents join with grandchildren against their parents, or spouses bring their parents into coalition against their spouse," and explored how creating and sustaining appropriate boundaries in families leads to increased functioning, well-being, and happiness of all involved.[32] Boundaries are often an important part of solutions, and boundary violations are often key causal factors of problems.

One specific type of boundary violation has been found to be particularly harmful: triangulation. Although triangulation has several different "flavors," in general it is a conflict between two people. Let's call these fictional folks Person A and Person B (any resemblance to real persons, living or dead, is purely coincidental, although chances are as I explain this, you will think this applies to you or someone you know). Rather than addressing that conflict directly between Person A and Person B, one or both of them draws in a third party, whom we will predictably call Person C. So, this could look like a pair of newlyweds having an argument, resulting in the young bride turning to her mother to complain about how immature her man-child of a husband is. Her mother then chimes in to talk about how she never really liked the guy anyway, and they go on to commiserate about men and pontificate about how to fix them. Those darn Y chromosomes can be so troublesome!

This kind of triangulation is known as an *alliance*, as daughter and mother team up and express empathy for each other in their plight with the clear villain being the new husband (which, by the way, often results in the fallout of resentful feelings toward the mother's husband as a form of collateral damage). However, it does nothing to fix the tension between the newlyweds. Curiously, due to the energy and emotion she invests in turning to her mother, the young wife is likely to feel like she has put in all kinds of efforts in to fixing the marriage, all of which are yielding no fruit. She will typically be blind to the fact that she hasn't actually put energy into fixing the marriage with the other person in the marriage. When you leave a major partner of the problem and the solution out of the process, you don't end up with a solution. I use women in this example of triangulation, but men can and do equally fall into this same trap. Triangulation plays no favorites when it comes to making fools out of people and creating misery. It's progressive like that.

Triangulation can also look like a father and mother who have been neglecting nurturing their marriage and focus their time and energy on the antics of their troubled teen. The young and wayfaring lad or lass may indeed have problems to be fixed, but their difficulties now provide a distraction so the mother and father can now ignore the sense that they are strangers to each other by focusing on fixing the teenager's rebellion. Thus, they feel united in purpose with a sort of pseudo-intimacy, even though they are emotionally no closer than they were before their child went rogue.

Triangulation can become a complicated, interlaced mess of overlapping alliances as Person A and Person B each seek out multiple allies. Triangulation can and does happen rather prolifically in marriages, families, businesses, societies, and governments. Triangulation tends to result in an odd kind of stability. It releases just enough pressure to keep things from completely disintegrating, but it also doesn't do anything to resolve the cause of the pressure. Triangulation helps people get stuck in misery and dysfunction, while thinking they are doing what is needed for a solution, and the problem is clearly being perpetuated by the other jerk in the conflict.

Triangulation takes a toll, not only on relationships and mental health (resulting in depression, anxiety, divorce, ineffective parenting, low self-esteem, poor personality development, and other such issues) but also on physical health as well.[33] It does this not only for Person A and Person B, but for the third party or parties they triangulate in as well.[34] Triangulation truly is that diabolical gift that just keeps giving—or, probably more accurately put, the gift that just keeps taking.

The Internet provides endless opportunities for all forms of triangulation. The scary thing is, when we enable someone in destructive triangulation, we usually feel like we are helping them with their problems, and we don't see how we are merely providing them with a pressure release valve and helping to prevent them from actually solving their relationship difficulties. When we enlist someone as our partner in triangulation, we often feel we are just getting help, and we feel we are putting so much effort into solving the relationship problem that we are frustrated when things don't get better. Somehow, we miss the fact that we are not doing anything to directly heal the problems in the relationship with the person we have the relationship with in the first place. Thus, our self-awareness that we are engaging in this destructive dynamic—online or offline—is often highly unreliable.

Furthermore, triangulation on the Internet can provide a high-speed highway for the development of online affairs. It's easy to think, *My spouse doesn't appreciate me, but this other person is so kind, loving, and supportive. I think my life would be so much better with them.* As we fall into this line of thought, we fail to recognize that it is easy to seem supportive and perfect from afar and that in most cases, we are falling for the illusion that the grass is greener on the other side of the fence.

The cyber-scape is equally adept as a tool for breaking both maladaptive and adaptive boundaries and is a ready facilitator of all kinds of emotional triangulation. We seem to experience a sudden rush of freedom from breaking of boundaries. This exhilarating, visceral sensation can blind us to when the breaking of boundaries is actually an act of self-sabotage and even self-destruction. Sometimes that shattering sound we hear when boundaries break is actually the shattering of our own bones as we hit the ground after taking a foolish leap that felt like freedom at the time.

Besides triangulation, another form of boundary violation that happens frequently in the cyber-scape is oversharing. Some forms of oversharing are relatively harmless. I probably don't need to know that Ashton Kutcher is eating yogurt for a snack. There probably is such a thing as a saturation point for how many pictures of your cat you can put on the Internet before it becomes meaningless. These things may be fluff and trivia, and they are not necessarily harmful by themselves, beyond how they may contribute to the *shallowing effect* discussed previously.

Other forms of oversharing tend to get a little more serious. These include posting pictures of every wound, scrape, or gruesome injury we sustain without thinking how it might impact those who see it. These also include posting rants and other public criticisms, spewing unfiltered mental sewage across a large area of cyber real estate. We often say things in anger that are twisted by our distorted emotional thinking and that frequently turn out to be inaccurate and unwise. As we impulsively slander the name and the image of other people in moments of anger or indignation, we ring a bell that we cannot unring. What we post online is permanent. Once we send that photo, tweet, or post, we are making decisions about someone else's online footprint without any thought to their rights to have some control in this area. We appoint ourselves their judge, jury, and public executioner. (Isn't that a good definition of tyranny, where one person is given all of those powers without any system of checks and balances? Are we sowing the seeds for a society of vigilantes, bullies, and tyrants?) Anger makes fools out of even the wisest people, yet how much of what is shared over the cyber-scape is motivated by anger? How much of what we share and overshare stems from our intellect and character at their weakest points? That would be an interesting question to be able to answer. I reckon we would be shocked to discover it.

Oversharing also includes our tendency to take pictures of other people, often in situations we consider embarrassing or shameful, and posting them in a public forum for ridicule. This can range from posting pictures we have taken of people we find odd at Walmart to publicly posting pictures of our children crying and then including witty or pithy statement about why they are crying. These pictures and posts can oftentimes become the cyber-equivalent of a lynch mob, with scores of people "liking" and commenting positively on our clever, contempt-motivated public flogging or execution of the target person's dignity. When put that way, it doesn't sound quite so harmless, both in how it affects the other person and in how it shapes our own character.

Oversharing can be taken to a deeper, more destructive level. One sad, cautionary example of this degree of oversharing is former US Congressman Anthony Weiner. His oversharing through sexting led to his very public transformation from a husband, father, and public servant to God's gift to satirical newspaper columnists. Even after his tendency to send lewd pictures of his sexual anatomy to young women on the Internet cost him his position in Congress, and even when he was trying to make a comeback to politics in the New York mayoral race, Mr. Weiner continued his habit of oversharing through sexting, violating not only his boundaries as a professional but his martial boundaries as well. This resulted in a second very public debacle of humiliation for him and his family and the ruination of his career.[35] He made himself into the epitome of the type of candidate every politician prays will run against him or her in their next bid for reelection.

It would be easy to stand back and point a mocking finger at Anthony Weiner, feeling secure in our self-righteousness and superiority. However, we would be wise to keep in mind that he just happens to be one of the people who was caught and displayed in a public manner. He is not alone, not even close. A recent study found that 54 percent of all smartphones belonging to adults in the United States contain sexy photos or texts, with 16 percent of respondents admitting that they do this with complete strangers.[36] Mr. Weiner is certainly not alone in his unwise decision making process, and that's not even beginning to address the possibility that this becomes an actual addictive process for many people—but we will address that idea later in this book. Besides sexually explicit material, a large percentage of adults also shared information like passwords, email accounts, and details of their bank accounts over their smartphones. That's roughly the cyber equivalent of shouting out your credit card number across a crowded diner and then repeating it even more loudly when someone says, "Sorry, I didn't quite catch the last two numbers. Could you say that again?" People do this apparently unaware that smartphones are unsecured platforms and that any and all information they transmit with smartphones is likely to be intercepted by sources besides their intended recipient.

The potential for exploitation in this area is significant, even if these kinds of images and information are not intercepted by a third party and even if they are shared only with someone with whom you are in a relationship. One prominent example of this potential for exploitation is the growing trend of revenge porn, in which an ex-lover decides to disseminate sexually explicit pictures of his or her ex on the Internet, often accompanied by the person's name, phone number, and address.[37] The victims of this trend tend to most often be women, and the experience of being targeted this way is often publicly humiliating and very difficult to clean up. At the time of this writing, only two states have laws protecting people against this kind of exploitation, and states that are seeking to make such laws fight an uphill battle against groups such as the American Civil Liberties Union, which sees this kind of expression as being protected by the constitutional right to free speech.[38] In fact, revenge porn was even actively promoted by a man named Hunter Moore, who created a website specifically to host revenge porn and crowned himself the King of Revenge Porn (while simultaneously earning himself the epithet of The Most Hated Man on the Internet). Moore, incidentally, was later arrested for paying someone to hack into private computers to steal nude photos.[39] A word to the wise: if someone is willing to help you exploit someone else, you can assume they will be just as willing to exploit you, especially on the Internet.

One reliable tool for life is to develop a filter between our thoughts and our actions, including our words. A well-developed and mature brain works something like this: have a thought, wait, evaluate that thought, refine that thought, then either act or speak about that thought based on how you have refined it, or let that thought pass without action or comment. This is a simple yet brilliant process that can bring about a great deal of good and prevent a lot of harm. Yet, the light speed pace of the cyber-scape makes it very easy for us to have a thought process that looks more like this: have a thought, post it as quickly as I possibly can! Faster! Faster! The world needs to know! Now, now, NOW! When it comes to the temptation to take and send sexy pictures, we need to slow down and think, *I know I am in a romantic relationship with this person right now. How certain am I that I will be in this relationship for life?* We need to ask ourselves, *Would it be a problem for me if someone else intercepted this information that I am about to text, email, or post to social media from my smartphone?* With the way the Internet functions now and with the sheer number of people monitoring it in various ways and for various motives, it may not be an overstatement to say that everything we transmit via our smartphones has a high probability of being seen by someone other than our intended recipient, and we should treat it as such.

Old Sigmund Freud might say that our impulsive, appetite-driven, immature id is the part of our psyche that has decided to hog our smartphones and social media accounts with all the vigor and sophistication of a caffeine-infused Chihuahua, leaving our more rational ego and more principle-minded super-ego out in the cold. I think one of the most clever—and funniest—examinations of this phenomenon was done by the sketch comedy group Studio C called "The Facebook Friends Song." It's worth checking out: www.youtube.com/watch?v=gl-VaMyDRpII.

Perceived Anonymity and Moral Reasoning

Let's be clear about something: human beings have always been capable of making really dumb decisions and screwing up their lives. Oversharing, boundary violations, groupthink, and these other dynamics we have discussed thus far have always been with us. They were not artifacts and inventions of the cyber-age. However, the cyber-scape seems to be a place in which we are more vulnerable to them. Why is that? Why do we seem to be more likely to act in impulsive and foolish ways in texts, tweets, posts, emails, and online chats? Why do our moral and ethical standards seem to take a dive there?

Part of the answer, at least, can be found in a story included in book two of Plato's *Republic*. The story is about a mythical item known as the Ring of Gyges. Plato spins a tale of one unnamed ancestor of treacherous king Gyges who finds a cave that housed a ring with the power to make him invisible. With the aid of this ring, the man had no fear of any accountability for his actions or any retribution for his misdeeds. With that ability in hand, this ancestor seduced the queen, killed the king, and ascended to the throne. Some authors suspect that this story became J. R. R. Tolkein's inspiration for the character of Gollum in the *Lord of the Rings* series.

In the tale of the Ring of Gyges, as also in the story of Gollum, there is something about being able to be invisible, with a sense of a buffer between one's actions and any consequences for them, that appears to have a corrosive effect upon our sense of personal morals and ethics. Before anyone gets too self-righteous and claims this sort of thing could never happen to them, let's consider another context in which this same phenomenon frequently occurs: driving. Each of us with any degree of experience on the road have experienced, either in ourselves or in other people, a Dr. Jekyll and Mr. Hyde sort of transformation that can occur when someone gets behind the wheel of a car. People who otherwise would not yell, scream, bully, intimidate, or cuss someone else out anywhere else in their lives are found doing that very thing behind the wheel of a car. This phenomenon is all too common. Walt Disney pictures even poked fun at this widespread trend in the 1950s cartoon short "Motor Mania" (www.youtube.com/watch?v=m-ZAZ_xu0DCg), in which the mild mannered Mr. Walker transforms into the maniacal and sociopathic Mr. Wheeler as he mounts his automobile. Who knew Goofy had such a dark side? But then again, part of what makes it funny is the fact that it is true.

I believe that a part of why this happens to people while we are in our cars is that there is something about the experience of being in a car ourselves and seeing other people encased in the metal frames of their cars that distances us just enough from the "flesh and blood" experience of seeing the other person as a person. They seem less real to us. It is easier to disconnect ourselves from their emotions and their experiences and merely see them as an annoyance in our plans and our convenience.

I see this with combat veterans. Post-traumatic stress disorder can be a terrible burden for any soldier returning from a war. But, as I have known and worked with veterans and as I have associated with colleagues who specialize in the treatment of combat veterans, I have observed that there is a difference in how traumatic it is to take a life as an infantry soldier on the ground who often sees the very human aspects of his kill when compared to a pilot who strikes from such altitude and distances that he or she may never really see the human carnage and death that results from their attack. The pilot may imagine it, but they don't have to see it. Something about having to actually see the other person, look in their eyes, and see their expression connects a close range, ground pounding soldier more to the reality that they are actually killing another person. Something about that seems to increase the potential for trauma. It makes the enemy less anonymous, less abstract, and more human.

In the cyber-scape, we experience both a sense of invisibility in the cloak of perceived anonymity and privacy, as well as a potentially dehumanizing digital emotional distance between us and the "flesh and blood" reality of the people with whom we interact. Furthermore, we also experience a sense of compartmentalization, as if our cyber-life was in a neat silo on one side of a chasm and our real world life was in a silo on the other side of the chasm. We seem to expect that we can keep these two worlds entirely separate. We seem to have the idea that there will be no cause and effect relationships between what goes on in our cyber lives and what goes on in our real lives. I believe that the combination of these three factors—perceived anonymity, dehumanizing psychological distance, and a sense of compartmentalization—create an unstable and potentially explosive compound that frequently plays itself out to the tune of a Greek tragedy.

Perhaps nowhere is this Gollum/Gyges syndrome more apparent on the Internet than in the phenomenon of Internet trolling. For those lucky individuals who are unfamiliar with Internet trolls and thus need an introduction to them, Farhad Manjoo describes them as "agitators who pop up, often anonymously, sometimes in mobs, in comment threads and on social networks like Facebook and Twitter, apparently intent on wreaking havoc. The term is vague precisely because trolls lurk in darkness; their aims are unclear, their intentions unknown, their affiliations mysterious."[40] Trolls are the masked drive-by shooters of the cyber-scape, cyber-terrorists of humanity in general, assassins of character and emotion who appear to enjoy inflicting pain on others and revel in the sense that they can do so with impunity due to the sense of invisibility and anonymity that the Internet provides.

In their online personas, Internet trolls are a lot like jackals and vultures, descending in packs to finish off weakened prey or to feast upon the downfall of others. They swoop in upon human tragedy and vulnerability to rub salt in the wounds and maximize humiliation and suffering. They operate like the cyber-counterparts of the Westboro Baptist Church, which celebrates the death of American soldiers and protests at their funerals with signs reading, "Thank God for dead soldiers," "You're going to hell," and "Planes crash, God laughs" (in reference to the 9/11 terrorist attacks). The actions of this church sparked intense outrage all over the world, but their acts are matched and exceeded online every day by the actions of countless legions of Internet trolls.

Trolls kick people when they are down and somehow walk away from the experience feeling like they have accomplished some kind of conquest, like a college student beating up kindergartners and then strutting around like he or she had won a championship in mixed martial arts. An example of this were the trolls who decided to capitalize upon comedian Robin Williams's tragic death by assaulting his daughter, Zelda, with accusations that she was the reason for her father's suicide and morbidly photoshopping images of his body to taunt her.[41] Internet trolls seem to take great delight in watching the reaction such ignoble actions provoke.

Trolling on the Internet has a decidedly sexist slant to it. A study out of the University of Maryland found that the average female chat room user is bombarded with one hundred threatening or sexually explicit messages per day, whereas the average male user receives only four.[42] The Internet has become a safe haven for expressing and proselytizing attitudes of hostility and sexual objectification of women. Those with the courage to speak out against the strong misogynistic threads of gaming and online culture risk the considerable wrath of the trolls. For example, Anita Sarkeesian, the creator of a thoughtful series of online videos entitled "Tropes vs. Women in Video Games," examined the entrenched sexist themes in video game culture. When she released an episode that analyzed the objectification of female characters in video games and exposed a trend of violence against sexualized female nonplayer characters (NPCs), Internet trolls attacked *en masse* with threats against her and her family that were so severe that she was forced to abandon her home and seek shelter.[43] Rather than silence her, the Internet trolls adeptly proved her point most effectively. Casey Johnston pointed out the "profound irony" that "one woman who dared to point out some of the misogyny in video games was so deluged by misogynistic threats over how there is no misogyny in video games that she was driven into hiding."[44] I somehow doubt that the trolls see it that way, though. And I very much doubt that they intend to leave her and those who listen to her alone as she continues to try to share her message.

Trolls often function like mobs on steroids and methamphetamine, sometimes using aggression and intimidation for a purpose, but often using these methods for no other reason than the fact that they can. Their cloak of perceived anonymity and invisibility on the Internet emboldens them to abandon any sense of moral constraint upon their actions, and thus they consistently demonstrate there are no limits to the depths to which Internet trolls will sink in their campaign of social vandalism and verbal violence. Trolls are not going anywhere anytime soon. In fact, they seem to be multiplying and getting stronger. Manjoo said, "The Internet may be losing the war against trolls. At the very least, it isn't winning. And unless social networks, media sites and governments come up with some innovative way of defeating online troublemakers, the digital world will never be free of the trolls' collective sway. That's the dismal judgment of the handful of scholars who study the broad category of online incivility known as trolling, a problem whose scope is not clear, but whose victims keep mounting."[45]

Because a sense of anonymity and invincibility enables this kind of cowardly villainy from trolls, removing their experience of impunity can help curb the trolls' atrocious behavior. For example, Riot Games, the producer of *League of Legends*, has experimented with a system that penalizes people who troll by reducing the number of messages they can send to other players per match. The general idea is that if you are going to use messages to be abusive, you get less of them, which can then hamper your ability to actually communicate the way you need to in order to effectively play the game and win. This seems to have yielded some encouraging preliminary results. Trolling players who received the penalty showed a 20 percent reduction in complaints against them following their punishment. This was 4 percent more effective than the standard intervention of temporarily banning players for trolling behaviors.[46] The Gollum/Gyges syndrome displays itself outside of the realm of Internet trolling in various ways. I have often thought that if Gollum and Gyges's unnamed ancestor had a favorite app in common, it would be Snapchat. Snapchat openly promised complete anonymity, claiming that all images sent through Snapchat are only visible for a number of seconds and then they somehow disappear completely and untraceably into the netherworld. Snapchat quickly became a veritable Valhalla for sexting and other shady things, such as arranging drug deals and similar illegal activities. This was, after all, the intention of its designers. That's not slander or extrapolation: emails obtained by the Los Angeles County Superior court in an investigation against Snapchat clearly document this as their intention. To quote one of the founders of Snapchat, it's "the best way to sext."[47]

Adam McLane points out that the founders of Snapchat "refer to themselves as '*certified bros*' who brag about their fraternity getting kicked off Stanford's campus. And they refer to women, their target demographic, as '*betches*.'"[48] They promised a magical world in which anyone could do anything with no fear of oversight, consequences, or accountability. This, however, is nothing but an illusion. McLane continues, "SnapChat knows who you are, where you are, and they store it all. (They are legally bound to). Even though their marketing copy says they don't. . . . their terms of service say that they do store it AND they have the right to sell that information as an asset to the company which they can sell."

The evidence suggests that they knew from the very beginning that what they were marketing and what they could actually offer were not the same. Even their own privacy policy states, "We cannot guarantee that deletion will always occur within a given timeframe." The truth is, deletion does not occur at all. That's why they can't guarantee it. In his exposition against Snapchat, McLane reveals, "All the SnapChat app actually does to make it so you see if for just a few seconds is change the name of the file so that you can't see it. *But it's still there.*"[49] Forensic researcher Richard Hickman supports this conclusion: "Metadata is stored for SnapChat images, as shown by the com. snapchat.android_preferences.xml file, and that it contains metadata about expired 'snaps' as well as unexpired 'snaps', and that images that are sent via Snapchat are indeed recoverable, and do not 'disappear forever.'"[50] Snapchat's claims of providing anonymity have fallen apart so completely that they have settled with the Federal Trade Commission to settle charges brought up against them for their false claims.[51]

Have you heard the saying, "What happens in Vegas stays in Vegas"? This marketing ploy is used to get people to lower their inhibitions and empty their wallets with the promise that the foolish things they do there won't spill over into their lives. Try telling that to a sexually transmitted disease or a drained bank account. "I'm sorry, HPV, but since I contracted you in Las Vegas, you have to magically disappear and leave me with no consequences once I cross the city limits. I'm sorry, missing money in my bank account, but since I spent you in Las Vegas, you have to magically reappear in my bank account as soon as I leave." It doesn't work in Las Vegas, and by and large it doesn't work online, no matter how certain you are that what you are doing is anonymous and private.

In general, perceived anonymity is a dangerous thing. First, it is dangerous because it is merely a perception. The number of conditions in which we are truly anonymous—even online—is very small and growing increasingly smaller if my observations are correct. Thus, when we operate under an assumption of anonymity, we are often operating with a misunderstanding of the very reality of our situation. When we perceive and act upon something that isn't real, our thinking is really no better than the thinking of someone who is in an active psychotic episode. Our insistence that the delusion should be real doesn't make it so. Second, the disinhibiting effects of perceived anonymity tend to jam our moral and ethical compasses. This carries a great risk for eroding our integrity, character, discretion, and trustworthiness. Families and societies fall apart in a manner directly proportionate to the degree that we allow these principles to degrade within ourselves.

The "Privacy" Issue

The issue of so-called Internet privacy is definitely worth a more detailed examination. As mentioned previously, people in general seem to have an expectation of online privacy and anonymity that does not match up with reality. High school students in Connecticut demonstrated this during an assembly that was designed to raise students' awareness of just how public their social media and other online information are. As the *pièce de résistance* of the presentation, the students were shown a slide show that featured pictures that had been culled from their own social media sites, which they had assumed were protected and private. The presentation backfired entirely. Rather than having an eye-opening experience and walking away gratefully, the students were outraged. They directed their wrath at the police and at their social media providers, calling it an outrage and a violation.

Some students went so far as to decry Twitter as "corrupt." Rachel Ehrenberg's take on their reaction was, "People who have grown up online seem to have developed sophisticated standards of privacy in the very public sphere of social media that their parents don't really appreciate."[52] While I agree with that observation, I feel compelled to point out that the teens' reaction was a fine example of shooting the messenger. Yes, those who have grown up in a world of online interactions have an expectation of privacy about what they shout out to the world (just read that sentence again and listen to how unrealistic of an expectation that really is), but that expectation does not match up with reality, nor can reality be reasonably changed to meet that expectation.

It is, plain and simple, a delusion—a popular and prolific one, but a delusion nonetheless. It is not evidence of Twitter's corruption that we tend to share that delusion. Rather, it is evidence of our naiveté.

Responding to the truth that online privacy is largely a figment of our collective imaginations with indignation doesn't change anything. Public is not private, even online, and the idea of online privacy treads close to the line of being justifiably called a contradiction in terms. Merely calling something private does not make it so. It's like siblings sharing a room, with the older brother drawing an imaginary line across the middle of the room and declaring, "This is my side of the room. You can't cross this line!" Do you want to guess just how long the younger sibling will wait before showing that line can't stop him? (Hint: it is likely to be so fast, you may wonder if the younger child managed to break the laws of physics.) In the case of this high school assembly, the people who crossed the imaginary line of privacy to create the slide show had no intentions of exploiting these teens. The students failed to see that everyone with exploitive intentions could just as easily do the same, and throwing a tantrum or having imaginary "rules of honor" is no protection against that fact. It just makes them an easier target because they walk along in pseudo-blissful ignorance of the truth in this matter.

Here's the ironic part: the fact that social media information is not private or anonymous is not a secret. It is all spelled out for us in the user agreements of these very programs and apps we use. Of course, nobody ever reads those. I guess that is why GameStation now owns the souls of 7,500 of its customers. I'm totally serious. As an April Fool's Day joke, they included the following in their end user license agreement (EULA):

> By placing an order via this Website on the first day of the fourth month of the year 2010 Anno Domini, you agree to grant us a non-transferable option to claim, for now and forever more, your immortal soul. Should we wish to exercise this option, you agree to surrender your immortal soul, and any claim you may have on it, within 5 (five) working days of receiving written notification from gamesation.co.uk or one of its duly authorized minions. We reserve the right to serve such notice in 6 (six) foot high letters of fire, however we can accept no liability for any loss or damage caused by such an act. If you a) do not believe you have an

immortal soul, b) have already given it to another party, or c) do not wish to grant Us such a license, please click the link below to nullify this sub-clause and proceed with your transaction.[53]

They had 7,500 customers that day that agreed to this deal, although I am guessing most of them never even read it. I wonder if Jack Sparrow and Faustus were among the users whose souls they purchased. Regarding this soul-snatching transaction, John Brownlee remarked, "It's all in good fun, but it does demonstrate how dastardly EULAs can be."[53] What we are agreeing to with our social media is all spelled out for us, but how many of us have taken the time to understand the deal we are making? Probably very few, I would wager.

Talal Al-Khatib put it this way: "If a stranger approached you asking for your name, age, phone number, names of family and friends, and interests, with the intent of sharing that information to more strangers, you'd probably be hesitant to readily give up that information. Yet that's essentially what users do when they create their Facebook profiles. All of that information about you isn't owned by you. All of those personalized data points belong to Facebook, and there are ways all that sharing can come back to bite you."[54]

So what is the deal you make with social media? According to the EULA for Facebook, the deal is that they can use your name, profile picture, information, connections, and all content—yes, all content, with no exclusions whatsoever—"in connection with commercial, sponsored, or related content (such as a brand you like) served or enhanced" by the social networking site.[55] This is essentially the deal with all social media. So what does that mean in plain English? You are the product they sell. All of that information online does not belong to you. It belongs to them, and they told you so when you agreed to it in the first place, whether you were listening or not.

Social media services are not free. I know you don't send them a monthly bill so it's easy to think the service is free, but you pay them nonetheless. You pay them by giving them an audience, first of all, and then you pay them again by giving them permission to sell your information to whoever wants to purchase it. Al-Khatib said, "Facebook's business isn't just connecting users across the world; it's selling the information on those users to advertisers so that they can find out who you are, build a profile and determine what they think you'd want to purchase."[55] It bears repetition: you are the product they sell. You are social media merchandise.

Not only that, you have agreed to let them do some things you may not realize. Facebook employs a team of data scientists who are constantly exploring new ways of studying humans through social media. This was forcefully illustrated in 2014 when Facebook revealed that it had altered the posts of 689,003 of its users by removing all of the positive posts or all of the negative posts to explore how this affected what these users posted, and by extension how it affected what they thought and felt.

Hill said, "The experiment ran for a week—January 11–18, 2012—during which the hundreds of thousands of Facebook users unknowingly participating may have felt either happier or more depressed than usual, as they saw either more of their friends posting '15 Photos That Restore Our Faith In Humanity' articles or despondent status updates about losing jobs, getting screwed over by X airline, and already failing to live up to New Year's resolutions. '*Probably* nobody was driven to suicide,' tweeted one professor linking to the study, adding a '#joking-notjoking' hashtag."[56]

Facebook committed some serious errors in judgment here, as well as possible serious violations of research ethics. For starters, it only added "research" to its terms of service policy four months after it began doing this particular study.[57] In essence, Facebook had you sign an agreement for your Terms of Use and then altered it after you signed it without informing you. I believe most people would cry foul on this sort of *ex post facto* alteration of an agreement. Furthermore, this action violates the principle of informed consent, which is at the very heart of scientific ethics. That being said, though, Facebook was very clear upfront that everything you post there belongs to them.

It has been interesting for me to observe the attitude that Facebook has had to the public outcry about this event. Kashimir Hill observed, "In its initial response to the controversy around the study. . . . Facebook doesn't seem to really get what people are upset about, focusing on privacy and data use rather than the ethics of emotional manipulation and whether Facebook's [Terms of Service] lives up to [what is] usually required for academic studies like this."[58] What I find fascinating is that the attitude of Facebook seems to be a perfect model of some of the problems with perceived privacy and how it plays into the Gollum/ Gyges syndrome. The attitude expressed by Facebook seems to reflect an opinion that as long as the data are kept "private," then the ethics of what is going on within that privacy is seen as largely a moot point. So as long as we keep things a secret, what we do doesn't matter? That feels like very shaky moral and ethical reasoning to me. Hill further commented on this point:

> When universities conduct studies on people, they have to run them by an ethics board first to get approval—ethics boards that were created because scientists were getting too creepy in their experiments, getting subjects to think they were shocking someone to death in order to study obedience and letting men live with syphilis for study purposes. A 2012 profile of the Facebook data team noted, "Unlike academic social scientists, Facebook's employees have a short path from an idea to an experiment on hundreds of millions of people." [Tangentially, did they just imply what it sounded like they implied—that they believe they have the advantage of being able to do research and bypass the usual ethical oversight that governs other social science research?] Cornell University released a statement . . . saying its ethics board — which is supposed to approve any research on human subjects — passed on reviewing the study because the part involving actual humans was done by Facebook not by the Cornell researcher involved in the study. Though the academic researchers did help design the study—as noted when it was published—so this seems a bit disingenuous.

I believe that there are very valid concerns to be had about an organization that can conduct research and experiments on such a large fraction of the world's population, especially when the subjects are not actively aware they are participants and actively consenting to the specific study. At best, the most informed Facebook users have a vague notion they might be participants in some undefined studies if they happened to have read the terms of services, which hardly anyone has. These concerns are compounded by the fact that this nonspecific, vaguely disclosed research takes place without having the checks and balances system of ethical review that history has demonstrated is so crucial to prevent misuse and abuse of research subjects.

Besides some concerning issues about the ethical questions about gathering data for research without consent and manipulating Facebook users' emotions, the results of their social experiment have some interesting implications. Their results indicated that human emotions and attitudes are "contagious" through social media. In the words of the researchers involved in the study, "These results indicate that emotions expressed by others on Facebook influence our own emotions, constituting experimental evidence for massive-scale contagion via social networks."[59] Facebook's own findings only go to offer further support for the points I made previously about the pervasiveness and power of groupthink in social media.

Why does this research even matter to Facebook? Are they doing it out of pure scientific initiative to better the human race? Who benefits from this research and how? The most likely explanation is that they are conducting this research to improve their bottom line. That's not surprising, since Facebook is a product and businesses conduct research on their products. However, Facebook is a product that not only crosses the line with social science but with people's lives, beliefs, emotions, and relationships. Therefore, in the case of Facebook and other social media sites, there can be a very fine line between marketing research and large scale social manipulation. Parmy Olson adroitly analyzed the situation as follows:

> Right now Facebook's power to influence has just one objective: keeping us all on Facebook. . . . Few outside of Facebook truly understand the secret sauce that filters our news feeds. You may have 1,000 friends on the site, but only see a few of the posts they're putting up each day. What's deciding that summary? Facebook says it's showing people "the content they will find most relevant and engaging"—but those two terms are starting to mean the same thing. We now know that on Facebook, relevance doesn't just have to mean proximity in age or geography, but emotional resonance too.[60]

Facebook is not the only social media site to "experiment" on human beings. In response to the backlash against Facebook's revelation about their undisclosed manipulation in the name of research of their users, Christian Rudder, the cofounder of the dating site OkCupid also announced, "We experiment on human beings . . . It's just a fact of life online. There's no website that doesn't run experiments online . . . If you use the internet, you're the subject of hundreds of experiments at any given time, on every site."[61] While Mr. Rudder may be overstating the case somewhat—it is probably not accurate to say every website is experimenting on its users—his attitude and observations are a clear demonstration that actions that many people would consider a violation of their online privacy and informed consent have become the standing operating procedure of a large percentage of the Internet, especially social media sites. Such practices have worked their way deep into the culture of the cyber-scape and are entrenched to a degree that it is not realistic to expect them to ever change.

Even outside of the realm of social media, we are learning more and more that the cyberworld we thought was private is actually heavily monitored in a wide variety of ways by governments, private entities, and individuals, representing a wide variety of ideologies, purposes, and intentions in their monitoring of electronically transmitted information. Texts, phone conversations, private messages, and so on are heavily recorded, monitored, and mined for a wide variety of ever-evolving reasons. This was most notably demonstrated in Edward Snowden's 2013 exposure about the data-collecting policies and procedures of the NSA (which, by the way, is not the only government organization in the world monitoring cyber-information). The NSA collects Internet information from a wide variety of sources including Microsoft, Apple, Google, Skype, Facebook, YouTube, AOL, and more. Virtually everything is being monitored: email, chat, VOIP calls, videos, photos, video conferencing, texts, stored data, logins, Internet searches, and so on. Even though sophisticated methods such as Tor and virtual privacy networks (VPNs) can be used to make it harder to identify your location, your identity and information can often still be extrapolated by monitoring enough points of contact.[62]

There is a cold, hard truth that we probably need to accept about the idea of privacy online. While there may be various degrees of semi-privacy and there is not justifiable cause to go around thinking George Orwell's vision of the future has come to full fruition, the fact remains that privacy is not a realistic expectation for anything we post online or send via smartphone. In essence, complaining that someone has violated your online privacy is like complaining that someone has stolen your pet unicorn. Neither one ever really existed in the first place.

Of course, people try a number of things to alter this reality. Some of these approaches are more naïve, and some are quite a bit more sophisticated. On the naïve side, it seems to be a regular tradition now for a post that sounds something like the following to be passed around Facebook: "They've done it again! Facebook has changed its privacy policies. Quick, before they violate your privacy, you need to post this to your wall! 'In response to the new Facebook guidelines I hereby declare that my copyright is attached to all of my personal details, illustrations, comics, paintings, photos and videos, etc. (as a result of the Berner Convention) etc. *ad absurdum.*'"

I can't blame them for trying. However, this technique is just about as effective as crossing your fingers while signing a legal document or requesting a mulligan for an investment that crashed. We can all imagine how well that would turn out. You can agree to the contract to use Facebook or you can choose not to agree and not to use the service, but you don't have the ability to set the terms or alter the agreement just by posting a status update. To paraphrase an Internet meme, "One does not simply protect one's Facebook privacy with a status update."

Other people take a much more sophisticated, technologically savvy route to try to create privacy and anonymity online. Some of these approaches are actually rather ingenious. Of these, perhaps the most powerful option is Tor, which has become increasingly popular and widespread since the NSA scandal of 2013. Without going into too many details, Tor tends to work like a shifting labyrinth, transmitting encrypted data through a constantly altering network of computers. It presents anyone trying to track you with a complex and constantly shifting maze. Among other things, it helps to hide the IP address, thus making it difficult to track down the physical location of users. Thus, Tor has become a favorite approach for journalists, whistle-blowers, criminals, activists, conspiracy theorists, people trying to protect their children from online predators, people trying to evade online stalkers, and a wide variety of people who value the idea of their privacy.[63]

It can be easy to think of Tor and other similar approaches as the silver bullet that guarantees online privacy and anonymity. After all, such a sophisticated approach feels virtually invincible, and many people treat it as if it is. However, even Tor has its points of vulnerability. Security researcher John Adams pointed out that Tor can only provide data encryption during transit, and as a result, there are multiple scenarios in which information could pass through the Internet in plain text, thus exposing the data to anyone looking for it. "If a destination website you're connecting with has cookies, Javascript, or any sort of tracking information on the client, it can be de-anonymized over time. Tor will also not protect privacy if you have tracking plugins installed on your browser."[64] Tor is also vulnerable to malware attacks. Furthermore, a lot of effort has been put into busting open the Tor network. "American cryptographer, computer security, and privacy specialist Bruce Schneier penned a post showcasing how the NSA is trying to break into Tor's network: Before it can use its computer network exploitation (CNE) capabilities, the agency needs to find Tor users. After discovering one, Schneier says that the NSA would use its network of secret Internet servers to redirect the user's traffic to the government's servers, codenamed FoxAcid, thereby 'infecting' the user's computer," essentially hijacking Tor and neutralizing its anonymizing abilities.[65] In fact, because of the limitations of exactly what can and cannot be hidden, researchers from the University of Regensberg concluded that ".onion sites [using Tor] remain just as vulnerable to hacking as sites on the open Internet."[66]

Thus, when Facebook announced on October 31, 2014, that it would provide a "secret" and "secure" access point for Facebook users by utilizing Tor, many people felt that this would help ensure that their Facebook activities would be both private and anonymous. But, in some ways, adding potentially millions of users to a Tor network only creates more and more vulnerability points for the network as a whole (especially because many of those users are not at all savvy about the limitations and vulnerabilities of Tor; the Tor chain is really only as strong as its least sophisticated links, so each wannabe cybershadow denizen reduces the integrity of the Tor system as a whole), all of which can be exploited, infected, and hijacked to crack the whole network open like a ripe coconut. Therefore, I think it is very likely that Facebook's intentions on this matter are going to backfire. In fact, recent events wherein Tor has been clearly penetrated demonstrate that the efforts to compromise Tor have already been successful.

Cracking Tor is not merely theoretical. It has already been done by the NSA, the FBI, and by the hacktivist group Anonymous. As a part of its Operation Darknet campaign against child pornographers,

Anonymous targeted the child pornography site Lolita City (one of the largest such sites, clocking in at 100 GB worth of child pornography), which used Tor as a protection for the privacy and anonymity of its users. Anonymous succeeded in cracking the site wide open, posting the account information of Lolita City's users online to expose them. Their methods, for anyone interested in knowing, were as follows:

> The Anonymous operation against Lolita City began on October 14, when members discovered links to child pornography on a .onion site called The Hidden Wiki. According to the group's statement, Anonymous members removed the links, but they were reposted by a site administrator. Anonymous then moved to shut down the site with a denial of service attack. Additionally, the hackers matched the digital fingerprints of links on the site to Freedom Hosting. After sending a message demanding that the hosting service remove the content, Anonymous' hackers were able to exploit the PHP site with a SQL injection attack and extract the user database before launching a denial of service attack. "The server was using hardened PHP with escaping," Anonymous said in its statement. "We were able to bypass it with UTF-16 ASCII encoding."[67]

Another high-tech approach in trying to assure online privacy and anonymity is Geeksphones's Blackphone, a new smartphone that offers a variety of services designed to minimize the amount of information that Google and other online observers can collect.[68] The Blackphone uses a cannibalized version of the Android operating system to remove data mining features while adding privacy enhancing features. It also includes a two-year subscription to Silent Circle, which offers encrypted phone calls. With all of this, the Blackphone is essentially the Fort Knox of smartphones. If a ninja transformed into a smartphone, this is what it would turn into. Even with this highly dedicated, highly sophisticated combination of hardware and software, the Blackphone's creators do not make claims that they can make you invisible and anonymous, only that this pricey device (weighing in at $629) will "minimize" the chance and the degree of monitoring. Their careful claim seems to indicate to me that they acknowledge the fact that full privacy and anonymity online are simply not possible.

I hope I have made my point without kicking a dead horse too much: no matter what you do, you cannot assume that you have either privacy or anonymity online. While there are times when having as much secrecy online may be desirable (such spreading information in an oppressive regime, exposing corruption, helping an abused woman evade her ex-spouse after she has relocated, and so on), I also have to wonder if there are times when creating at least the illusion of online anonymity and privacy is really a good thing for most of us under normal circumstances. I have observed that all too often, this illusory ability to lead a dual life seems to compel people to put things in their online life that would be detrimental or even destructive if they spilled out into their real world life. Like matter and antimatter, when the barriers between the cyberworld and the real world break apart, the combination of what was held separately in those two realms can cancel each other out violently. We need to be very cautious about human nature and who we become under a cloak of perceived secrecy. I think it is foolish for any of us to conclude that we are immune to these effects.

A Prime Example of Cyber-Compartmentalization: Online Affairs

One of the areas in which this compartmentalization spurred by the promise of privacy and its resulting catastrophic implosion is plainly manifested is in the phenomenon of online affairs. The interactions leading up to online infidelity start out seeming so innocent and innocuous, and those who participate in them often seem blissfully unaware that they are walking a path of courtship with another when they already have a partner or spouse to whom they have made promises and commitments. After all, there is no physical contact going on between them and their cyber-"just-a-friend," so how could anyone possibly think they are having an affair? In the beginning, at least, the conversations between them tend to be nonsexual in nature, although later on they are prone to excuse sexual conversations because they are only words with no deeds attached. They protest, "How can I have an affair with someone I have never even touched?" Their perceived privacy allows them to experiment with intimacy of thought and emotion that they do not initially identify as such because they experience it in a cyber-assisted, disembodied form. Thus, it somehow seems less real than if they were going out to dinner with friends and holding their spouse's hand while playing "footsies" under the table with their friend's wife or husband. And yet, in a very real sense, that is exactly what they are doing.

People involved in online affairs become accustomed to calling their growing cyber-love affair different things: friendship, correspondence, and so on. They become defensive if questioned about it. (Tangentially, the best quote on defensiveness I have ever heard comes from the film *Star Trek: Into Darkness*: "Resorting to name calling suggests you are defensive and therefore find my objections valid." Think about that for a moment; our defensiveness is a sign that we know the other person is right but don't want to admit it.) They accuse other people of invading their privacy, of being old-fashioned and out of date, or of not understanding "the way things are on the Internet." They chide other people for simply not understanding. They protest that no one has ever understood them like their online friend, oblivious to the fact that they are experiencing an illusion of depth in the two-dimensionality of the Internet. They shift blame and refuse to engage in honest self-examination. They question everyone but themselves. After all, to do so would break the momentum, and while in the midst of an online affair, they are having a thrilling ride, one whose chills and spills they are convinced will have no cost to anyone.

In spite of the illusion of compartmentalization, online affairs have real life consequences including neglecting work, neglecting children, damage to the marriage (obviously), divorce, and bitter custody battles with children caught up helplessly in the results of decisions they had no power over. That is often the case, even when the affair remains solely within the cyber realm. However, a large number of these online affairs become actual physical affairs, as well. While there is some variation in the data thus far, one study found that as many as two-thirds of online affair partners meet in real life and have sex (often unprotected) with their online affair partners.[69]

Online affairs often carry a multitude of illusions. Dr. Kimberly Young observed, "When you see people only through their words on your computer screen, you are free to conjure up your own images of who and what they really are . . . The sound of his voice, the gaze of his eyes, the way he might touch your hand—you supply those details in your own mind. You give him automatic passing grades at all those initial checkpoints you normally would cross in person . . . And because using the Internet often makes you feel calm or even euphoric, you're naturally going to create the ideal person."[70]

While Dr. Young was referring to people you meet for the first time online, I have found that this is also true of people you may already know but whom you start wooing online, either as a renewal of an old acquaintance or as a way to attempt to enhance a friendship. Affairs have always been with us, but I think the nature of the cyber-scape makes it significantly easier for affairs to happen there. To some degree or another, we are all two-dimensional online and much easier to live with. We put out our best, most exciting, most interesting parts in our online friendships and leave out the mundane and the parts of us that are harder to coexist with. I find it interesting that we refer to our online personas as our "profiles." This is a very fitting word because that is all we really tend to portray online—an obscure, shadowy profile like a Greek relief sculpture, without all of the details and features that make us fully human and which encompass all of our complexity.

This cyber-two-dimensionality sets us each up to be a sort of Rorschach blot online, a vaguely defined shape upon which other people project their thoughts, feelings, hopes, fears, and desires. Thus, it is easy to see in someone's online persona the perfect, idealized person we have always hoped existed out there. We don't see it as the mere image it is, though. We see it as real, and we often hold this belief with zealous conviction. While the grass has always seemed greener on the other side of the fence, this has become especially true when the picture of the grass has been photoshopped to make its online profile more appealing. (And oftentimes it turns out it may not even be grass at all, as it claims to be, but rather field bindweed. But how would you know? You've only encountered its online profile!) Real life and real people can't compete with the cyber plastic surgery we give ourselves in our online profiles, so we are at risk of chasing mirages, like some poor, parched traveler stranded in a desert.

This tendency to idealize, gussy up, and fictionalize the other person (who has already been given a superficial digital extreme make-over of epic proportions) seems to be especially strong when that person shows some interest in us. We want to be wanted; we find it immensely flattering. We find it even more flattering when it appears we are wanted and appreciated by someone we are convinced is exceptional. This sense of being sought out by someone apparently superior appeals to our own narcissism and to our difficulty with loving ourselves with all our imperfections and allowing ourselves to be loved by other equally imperfect people. When we have convinced ourselves that the shiny, gilded exterior we perceive in the other person's online presentation actually indicates that they are some kind of idealized Adonis that we have always been searching for, it is just as easy, then, to want to try to transform ourselves to show what we think the other person wants to see in us. As a result, codependency finds new, exalted heights in digital form. In this process, we stand at great risk of losing ourselves. The funny thing is, we often don't perceive this as losing ourselves. Rather, we tend to think that we have set ourselves free.

This effect can be amplified when combined with groupthink. No matter the quality of the choices you are making, you will find choruses of voices on the cyber-scape willing to cheer you along and reassure you of your rectitude. As you present your point of view to your carefully selected online audience, laying out your narrow and artfully crafted story about the virtues of your online affair partner pitted against the faults of your spouse (or whatever you have selected as your justification for your decisions), you will almost certainly be able to find voices that support you regardless of the legitimacy of your argument. Granted, you will have to ignore the fact that they only know exactly what you choose to tell them and thus can have no claims to any objectivity or circumspection of any kind when it comes to giving you honest feedback and evaluation of your life and your choices. But most of us can muster up the ability to overlook such things without too much strain when it suits us. This is made easier by the fact that for every voice that asks you to reconsider or criticizes your actions, another voice will come to the rescue of your justifications. Remember how we discussed earlier that "dislikes" and critical comments tend to spur a backlash of "likes" and supportive comments? That happens in this type of situation, as well. Thus, you will find ample support to soothe your sense of cognitive or moral dissonance, and you will find a rich supply of such advice as, "A gentleman is entitled to an affair, so long as he is discreet," or "You go, girl! It's about time you found a real man! Dump the chump and step up to the stud!"

I have observed that it is usually that illusory feeling of freedom—along with the reassurances of online allies—that people use to hide from themselves the fact that their lives and families are falling down around them while they indulge in this affair. They are like Nero, fiddling while Rome burns and even tossing gasoline on the fire and then looking up from his melodies from time to time to say, "Wow, this place is a dump! I wonder who ruined it. There's nothing left for me here. I should probably move on." Thus unfolds a tragedy of Shakespearean proportions, a humorless *Comedy of Errors* that has become all too common. The phenomenon of online affairs encompasses so much of the risk of the cyber-scape discussed thus far: shallow and polarized thought, narcissism, poor data evaluation, masks, disconnectedness, self-justification, oversharing, triangulation, groupthink, lotus, and the corrosive potential of perceived anonymity and privacy. It is a poster child for the need to learn to navigate the cyberscape thoughtfully and mindfully.

Crime

When visiting any new state or country, it is worthwhile to be aware of the potential for falling victim to crime there. For example, Rio de Janeiro in Brazil is famous for its amazing beaches and vibrant culture. Sadly, it is also infamous for its shocking crime rate, especially in its *favela* shantytowns, where heavily armed drug gangs rule as a power unto themselves. The violence and level of armament there is comparable to what can be found in an actual war zone. Prior to a recent crackdown in crime, Rio had a homicide rate of 42 homicides per 100,000 people. That's not even counting other forms of violent crime such as armed robbery, assault, kidnapping, and rape.[71] Beauty, excitement, and significant danger commingle in Rio—a place where heaven and hell seem to mix seamlessly like conjoined twins—and the unsuspecting or naïve visitor is at real risk of becoming a victim or even a fatality.

The same could truthfully be said about the cyber-scape. Cybercrime is a very real and pervasive phenomenon. Estimates of the annual worldwide cost of cybercrime range from about $375 billion to approximately $575 billion.[72] This has resulted in an estimated loss of 200,000 jobs in the United States alone. Hundreds of millions of people each year have their personal information stolen, with approximately 40 million American citizens falling victim to cyber ID theft in 2013. It's not just happening to small business or those not savvy about computers: even tech titan Google, the modern avatar of technological know-how, was hacked in 2010, leading to the loss of intellectual property for thirty-four Fortune 500 companies.[73] Retail giant Target was hacked, leading to the theft of the credit card and debit card information of 40 million customer accounts.[74] A common saying among cybercrime experts is, "There are only two kinds of companies: those who have been hacked, and those who don't know yet that they have been hacked."[75]

Sometimes, cybercrime takes a more subtle route. On April 23, 2013, the Twitter account for the Associated Press was hacked. The hacker sent out a fake tweet that read, "Two explosions in the White House and Barack Obama injured." As a result, the Dow Jones Industrial Average plunged 146 points. To translate that into more concrete terms, that represents the loss of $200,000,000,000. You read that right: two hundred billion dollars annihilated by one manipulative, false tweet.[76] Now, this may seem more like the move of a cyber-vandal, someone who is just interested in mischief and mayhem but seems to not be able to profit from this action beyond satisfying their appetite for *schadenfreud* (a German word for the emotion "taking pleasure in someone else's suffering"), or possibly being a clever form of cyber-terrorism.

There is more to this kind of skullduggery than meets the eye, however, and a seemingly senseless act of cyber-manipulation can be turned to a source of underhanded profit for the enterprising schemer with the right know-how. Jesse Emspak pointed out, "A sophisticated hacker who 'shorts' Apple, that is, borrows stock and sells it in the hopes that the price will drop and then buys it back at the reduced price, would profit. Imagine that person hacking into Apple's Twitter account and tweeting something that makes other investors nervous. They sell, and the hacker profits in a matter of minutes. This is one reason that the Securities and Exchange Commission is looking into trading activity just before the tweet and after. That could be a tall order though; many funds already offer ways to short the Dow Jones

Industrial Average, and they are all used by legitimate investors. One could always claim that they just got lucky."[77]

Manipulating the stock market based on rumors is not a new tactic for trying to make a quick and not-so-honest buck, but the potential for hacking can move beyond merely starting rumors to giving the full appearance that the information is coming from a legitimate source. So much of what happens in the stock market is automated (for example, algorithms are set to automatically buy and sell in response to preprogrammed indicators), and so many investors tend to act with a "hair trigger" when apparently important indicators pop up (after all, the term "you snooze, you lose" is seen as an almost redundant truism in high pressured stock trading), that such a scam will play itself out before anyone even thinks to verify the sources of the information. After all, the sources appear totally genuine. In this way, and in many other variations of hacks, assaults, and denial of services attacks, the actions of a very few unscrupulous and technologically savvy people, or even just one such person, have the potential to inflict great financial loss on not only an entire nation, but upon the entire world.

Hacking attacks have evolved to the point where they can be used as cyber-weapons of mass destruction. These attacks are so common it has led some commentators to conclude that World War III is already upon us in the form of cyber-warfare.[78] It is a war among nations, such as the USA, China, and North Korea. It is also a war between private factions, special interest groups of various kinds (such as Anonymous), vigilantes, and sociopaths. It is a combination of large-scale total war, terrorism, and guerilla warfare, and it is deepening and evolving on a daily basis.

While big-scale cybercrime certainly seems more dramatic and more worthy of being made into a cerebral Hollywood blockbuster movie, small-scale cybercrime has equal potential to cause distress and suffering. One form of small-scale cybercrime that has caught the attention of the media is cyberbullying. Bullying itself is not new, by any means. However, smartphones and social networks make it easier to turn bullying into a multipronged assault capable of invading places that used to be a safe haven for those being bullied, including when they are shut inside the confines of their own rooms. It provides those who bully with more tools and quicker access to a larger audience in their smear campaigns and mud-slinging marathons. Public humiliation is dished out to a potentially worldwide audience at the speed of light. The cyber-scape furnishes quick and easy access to positive social reinforcement from crowds who roar their approval for the actions of bullies, like Romans in the Coliseum clamoring for the death of a wounded gladiator. All of this makes bullying easier, more efficient, and more rewarding for the bully.

Cyberbullying takes many forms. It can be found in the form of harassing and demeaning social media posts, embarrassing pictures snapped and immediately posted online, slander posted in hacked accounts, streaming video of humiliating situations, in online games, and so on. Anywhere you go online, you are likely to find cyberbullying, even in a setting as seemingly innocent and sheltered as Club Penguin. While there is variation in the data (measuring prevalence of cyberbullying can be difficult for a number of reasons), the American Academy of Pediatrics reports that approximately 17 percent of high school students are the victims of cyberbullying, with girls being two times more likely to be victims of cyberbullying than boys. The victims of these cyberbullying campaigns often suffer emotionally, socially, and physically.[79] The damage inflicted can take years to heal from, or can even last a lifetime.

Cyberbullying can also end in tragedy. There are too many stories to tell of suicides linked to online bullying, and I lack the means to do justice to all who have suffered because of it. One example is Tyler Clementi, an eighteen-year-old freshman student at Rutger's University in 2010. His roommate, Dharun Ravi, tweeted mockingly about Clementi: "Roommate asked for the room until midnight. I went into molly's room and turned on my webcam. I saw him making out with a dude. Yay." Later, when Clementi asked to have their room privately for the purpose of another date, Ravi sent out another tweet. "I dare you to chat me between the hours of 9:30 and midnight. Yes, it's happening again." Ravi turned on his web camera and sent out a live stream of Clementi's romantic encounter. Clementi reeled from his public outing and humiliation. He was overwhelmed and devastated, and clearly saw no recourse or remedy to the shame he felt at being publicly mocked and exposed. His last communication was a post to his

Facebook wall: "Jumping off the gw bridge sorry." True to his statement, he ended his own life by jumping off the George Washington Bridge.[80]

Another case that made headlines and evoked a public outcry was the death of Megan Meir. Megan was a thirteen-year-old girl who others described as "bubbly" and "goofy." She had been diagnosed with ADHD and depression, struggled with her weight, and, like many girls her age, she had difficulties with body image and self-esteem. Megan had a MySpace account and became friends with someone whose profile identified himself as an attractive sixteen-year-old young man named Josh Evans. "Josh" first befriended her, courted her, and then dumped her, stating, "I don't know if I want to be friends with you anymore because I've heard that you are not very nice to your friends." He then began to spread messages and post bulletins about her, calling her "fat" and "a slut." His last message to her was, "Everybody in O'Fallon knows who you are. You are a bad person and everybody hates you. Have a sh****y rest of your life. The world would be a better place without you." Her heartbroken response to his last post was, "You're the kind of boy a girl would kill herself over." Twenty minutes after this last exchange, Meir was found hanging from a belt in her bedroom closet. She died the next day. Later, it was discovered that "Josh Evans" was actually Lori Drew, a woman who lived four houses down the street from Megan's family and was convinced that Megan was spreading rumors about Drew's daughter. Drew had concocted "Josh Evans" as a way to torment and punish Megan to "get even" with Megan for what she thought Megan had done to her own daughter.[81] Lori Drew went on to be the country's first federally prosecuted cyberbully.[82] Drew was convicted but later acquitted, not due to lack of evidence but due to the fact that there were no laws at the time that were adequate to describe what she was being charged with.[83]

Victims of bullying tend to come to see their world as a threatening place, and many who choose to continue to live instead of ending their own lives seek ways to protect themselves. As a result, victims of bullying are forty-nine times more likely to have carried a weapon to school than nonbullied students, resulting in an estimated 200,000 bullied teens bringing guns, knives, and clubs into high schools in the United States in an effort to find some sense of security.[84] Given the right circumstances, this approach can move beyond defensively carrying a weapon to going on the offensive. Investigations into a number of school shooting incidences have revealed that lashing back against perceived bullying was a major part of the shooters' motivation.[85] Indeed, a study of fifteen school shootings found that long-term rejection and bullying was a factor in all but two of the shootings.[86]

Being bullied is not enough by itself to turn a bullied student into a vengeful gun-slinger, but when combined with other factors (such as a fascination with firearms or bombs, an interest in death or Satanism, or psychological difficulties such as impulse control issues, depression, or antisocial personality characteristics), bullying seems to serve as a trigger for those who are at risk of snapping in this tragic manner. It seems to me that if we are interested in stopping school shootings, we need to be talking about much more than gun control or arming teachers. We need to intervene sooner and more broadly. If we are only trying to figure out what to do when the would-be shooter goes in search of firearms or enters a school locked and loaded, our options are limited. Finding effective ways to combat bullying seems to me to be an important part of a more comprehensive solution.

Just as the cyber-scape offers a whole new world of tools and options for bullies, it also brings with it the ability to empower stalkers in ways that stalkers of yesteryear could only dream of. This was illustrated by the case of Alexandra Scarlett, who gave Jason Smith her phone number one night when she met him at a nightclub. A stalking nightmare of epic proportions ensued. When Scarlett refused to go out with Smith, he began sending her approximately thirty threatening messages per day via her Facebook and MySpace accounts. He ranted and raved that he would rape her mother and aunt, shoot her father, and kill her if she didn't go out with him. She tried blocking his Facebook account forty times, but he always found a way around it. Scarlett would shut down accounts and open up new ones using a variety of ways to hide her identity, but Smith always managed to find her. This daily harassment went on for two years until he was finally busted by the police.[87]

There are other ways in which the boundary between cybercrime and real-world crime tend to blend and melt into each other. As I speak with people about cybercrime, most of them seem to have the impression that it all tends to fall into the category of extortion, stealing, and other white collar, nonviolent crimes. The truth, however, is another matter all together. Violent criminals are able to take advantage of the routes provided by the cyber-scape to stalk their targets in an up close and personal way. The cyber-scape provides a sort of "fog of war" for those interested in preying upon others, with ample resources and methods of deception and misdirection available to set up their unsuspecting victims. Social media can be and frequently is used as a very effective tool for robbers, sexual predators, con men (or women, as the case may be), swindlers, flim flams, and even murderers. Teenagers and young adults are the most common targets of violent criminals on social media.[88]

One example of this is the case of fifteen-year-old Nicole Day. She had met someone online who portrayed himself as a teenage boy by the name of Brian Butterfield. She had frequent contact with "Brian" through Facebook and text messages and finally agreed to meet up with him in person because he said he would provide her with free marijuana. When she arrived at their designated meeting place, she found something very different than she had expected. In a turn of events right out of every mother's worst nightmares for her child, Nicole was ambushed by a man in a ski mask who chased her, subdued her, bound her with duct tape, and threw her in the back of a pickup truck. Her assailant was Kyle Dube, a twenty-year-old man who apparently knew Nicole and had forcefully tried to pursue her sexually, clearly indifferent to the laws regarding statutory rape. He apparently grew tired of being turned down by Nicole and devised a plan to impersonate the real Brian Butterfield online, become friends with Nicole, lure her into a real-life meeting, "pretend" to kidnap her incognito, hide her, and then "rescue" her so he could be a hero to her, apparently all for the purpose of seducing her.[89] With a plan like that, what could possibly go wrong? Plenty, it turns out. Dube claims that when he went to retrieve Nicole from the pickup truck, she was inexplicably dead, so he dumped her body in the woods. However, the medical examiner on the case has ruled Nicole's death as a homicide. If convicted, Dube faces twenty-five years to life in jail.[90]

Another case of cybercrime spilling over into real-life violent crime turned out to be a case of a dating bait and switch. Tara Bell, age twenty-four, set up a date with Josh Tyree, age twenty-eight, through Facebook. When Josh arrived with hopes for a romantic evening, he was greeted by Bell and two accomplices, Bo Gudea and Latasha Ward. They proceeded to assault, rob, and shoot Josh Tyree in the leg. The trio of assailants were arrested, charged, and made plea deals to avoid convictions on all accounts.[91] In a variation on that same theme of the blind date bait and switch, twenty-three-year-old Leah Gibbs rendezvoused with a stranger she had met on Facebook. To start off their date, Adam Minton asked her to drive him to his bookie's residence (note to everyone: when your date starts out this way, it's a good idea to just walk away or pull out the pepper spray). He then asked Gibbs to stay in the car for a few minutes while he went in to see his bookie. Imagine Leah's surprise when Minton exited the home at high speed with a knife in one hand and a bag of money in the other, yelling at her to drive them out of there as quickly as possible. That's probably the moment she realized that it wasn't her heart he was trying to steal that night. Even though she was an unwitting and unwilling accomplice, she was arrested and charged along with Gibbs later that evening.[92] I think it's safe to assume there was no second date.

There is also the case of eighteen-year-old Nona Belomesoff, an avid animal lover from Australia. She made contact through Facebook with Christopher James Dannevig, who portrayed himself as an animal welfare worker. Dannevig offered Nona her dream job: rescuing injured animals in the bush lands. He presented it as a time-limited offer; she needed to accept now or the job would be taken. Elated at the prospect, she jumped at the opportunity and set off alone with Dannevig into the wilderness. What happened next was all too predictable. When she did not return, her parents reported her as missing to the police. They recovered her body a few days later.[93]

As these cases indicate, violent criminals on social media often take advantage of situations in which people tend to make themselves vulnerable, whether it is seeking romance (which requires a degree of risk-taking and vulnerability), attending to a drug habit or addiction (where people tend to think less than critically and often feel a sense of urgency to obtain their substance of choice), procuring employment, trying to get out of an economic pinch, or pursuing their hopes and dreams. In doing so, they tend to catch victims in situations where they let their guards down, making them easy targets ripe for the taking. It is not just the elderly and those for whom the cyberworld is a foreign country with a foreign language who are at risk. As mentioned previously, the victims in these cases are frequently teens and young adults. Part of what makes teenagers and young adults particularly vulnerable to this kind of predation—aside from the fact that they are still developing cognitive abilities that they have not mastered—is that they think of themselves as technologically savvy. As a result, they are less likely to be self-aware of when they are being technologically naïve. As a result, they are at much higher risk for charging in impetuously where angels fear to tread.

No discussion of crime in the cyber-scape would be complete without acknowledging the massively widespread phenomenon of online piracy and theft. Online software, movie, and music piracy has come to be thought of as an "un-crime," partially because so many otherwise law-abiding people participate in it. It has become thought of as a victimless crime and "just the way things are now" (trademark pending). In truth, electronic theft of media is far from victimless. For example, the online piracy of music alone cost the US economy $12.5 billion in 2007, which translates into $2 billion in lost wages and 70,000 lost jobs.[94] Given the increasing trend, it is reasonable to assume that this number has continued to increase since the time of the study. That's a lot of people out of work and a lot of damage to an already sluggish national economy simply because you didn't want to pay for the latest song by Bruno Mars or Rhianna. When you think about it, pirating music from an artist you enjoy is like pick-pocketing the waiter or waitress you like the most at your favorite restaurant. It's a lousy way to "thank" them for their work and makes it harder for them to produce the very thing you so much enjoy. This is a fine example of a self-defeating behavior.

The video game industry fares no better in this piracy trend, and it is happening on a massive scale. For example, in 2009, *Call of Duty: Modern Warfare 2* PC version had 4.1 million pirated downloads in November and December alone, in contrast to having only 300,000 copies sold in November.[95] Given a retail price of $49.99, that is approximately $205 million of stolen goods from a single gaming company in just two months, and that's just the value of a single game on the market. An estimated 9.8 million PC games in total were illegally downloaded in December 2009. Video game companies are taking a beating of epic proportions due to this pandemic of piracy, making developing games for the PC very difficult economically speaking. Gamers apparently love their games so much that they are willing to steal them, all seemingly unaware that they are making the idea of producing more PC games seem like a terrible investment for game developers. Cevat Yerli, CEO of Crytek, the company that produces the popular *Crysis* series, stated, "We are suffering currently from the huge piracy that is encompassing *Crysis*. We seem to lead the charts in piracy by a large margin, a chart leading that is not desirable. I believe that's the core problem of PC Gaming, piracy, to the degree [that PC gamers who] pirate games inherently destroy the platform."[96]

There are many justifications people give for game piracy.[97] One common rationalization is the idea that games cost too much. "I shouldn't have to pay this much for a game, so that justifies me in taking it for free." However, an elementary understanding of supply and demand in a free market clearly indicates that the more people steal games, the more expensive games have to be in order for the producer not to go out of business. In other words, a significant part of the reasons games cost so much is because people pirate so much.

A second common self-justifying statement for piracy is to blame the victim. The thought is that people steal games of mediocre or poor quality, but people will be willing to pay for good games. It certainly is easy to make assertions without having to back them up with inconvenient facts. The facts tell a very different story. Just look at what is being pirated. In 2011, the top pirated games on BitTorrent were *Crysis 2*, *Call of Duty: Modern Warfare 3*, *Battlefield 3*, *FIFA 12*, and *Portal 2*—all of which are widely regarded as excellent games by critics and user reviews. So, on a societal level, the logic that people will pay for high quality games rather than pirating them turns out to be only so much hot air. But, this ersatz argument makes for a good sound bite, so software pirates quickly and easily adopt it as a slogan to soothe their moral dissonance.

Another fascinating justification is that using DRM (electronic means embedded in their program to prevent piracy as a form of copy protection) actually causes people to commit piracy, presumably because they want copies of the game with the DRM removed. This is somewhat similar to saying that having security cameras in a store causes people to shoplift. There is significant fallacy in this logic. For one thing to cause another, it has to precede it. An examination of the history of video games demonstrates that games did not start out with DRM. Rather, DRM evolved as a response to piracy. The precedent and the antecedent in this case are clearly established in space and time—this is basic cause and effect. Yet, this illogical argument that DRM is the cause of piracy persists. Indeed, the data and logic combine to suggest that the opposite of this justification is true: if gamers want to get rid of DRM, they should stop pirating.

Granted, DRM can be intrusive to the gaming experience, and as DRM gets cracked and circumvented, many game developers are resorting to more extreme forms of DRM, such as requiring the computer to be constantly connected to the Internet to verify that the copy is legitimate, like over-anxious helicopter parents hovering over their college-aged son to make sure he gets to classes on time. By the logic of software pirates, games without DRM should be pirated less. Not surprisingly in the least, that turns out not to be the case. Consider, for example, *The Witcher 2*. Critics and users agree that it is a well-crafted, reasonably priced PC game that did not include any DRM of any kind. It went against all of the common justifications for piracy, the veritable poster child for the type of game that would not be pirated if the justifications of software pirates are true. The result? More than 80 percent of people who play *The Witcher 2* are playing pirated copies.[98] I think we can safely conclude that the justifications for software piracy are—to borrow a common Internet term—an epic fail.

As the number of PC games on the market dwindles, those who are killing the industry seem to mull around in a haze, wondering what the problem is and who could possibly be responsible. (Certainly it couldn't be them!) It is not uncommon to hear the statement that PC gaming is now dead. The claim is that developers only make games for consoles such as the Xbox 360 because "that is where people are playing games now." That couldn't be further from the truth. In fact, the number of people playing PC games (both pirated and otherwise) shows that PC gaming is more alive and vibrant than ever before, but a colossal number of gamers are doing so illegally and dishonestly. Game developers are migrating to console versions of their games out of sheer survival instinct because it is harder (though far from impossible) to pirate console games. Consoles usually have to receive physical modifications or complicated custom firmware alterations in order to play pirated versions of games, so console piracy is just not as easy and convenient as PC piracy.[99] If it were, I believe we would see piracy rates on console games as high, or even much higher, as we see with PC games.

Convenience has become not just the reason people pirate games and other media, however. One of the concerning things to me about the cyber-scape is that convenience has become the moral compass of the digital realm.[100] It is a very poor compass that will point whichever direction is easiest to point, at any given time, rather than remaining constant on a trustworthy point of reference. Such a tool is useless for navigation. Indeed, such a tool can only feed our shortsightedness. We have become accustomed to things being so close, so easy, and so simple online. On the cyber-scape, it is as if everyone is walking around with their wallets and purses perpetually open and their eyes permanently averted, creating a pickpocket's paradise. It is unspeakably easy to reach out and take something from someone else. And, because the process is digital, we manage to comfortingly distract ourselves from thinking about the people whose lives and livelihood we are trading for something as petty as our convenience. This is a concerning ethical trend even if it is simply limited to our online activity. However, our character is not something we can compartmentalize. The more we get used to exploiting people online, the more we train and mold our minds to be comfortable with exploiting people in all areas of our lives. We feed that part of ourselves at our own collective peril. Piracy changes us. If we think it does not, we fool ourselves.

Thus, when you cut through all of the florid and sophisticated-sounding yet demonstrably invalid justifications for why people pirate games, I believe the real reason is this: people pirate games, movies, and music for the same reasons people steal anything else. Getting something for free is appealing. The lower the cost, effort, and risk involved in taking something for free rather than paying for it, the higher the temptation is to steal. Stealing digital media has become tremendously easy, so people steal it. Such theft has become so common and so widespread that people don't see themselves as stealing. People feel comforted by commonly repeated, canned justifications and rationalizations. They don't see themselves as personally harming the industry whose goods they are consuming or the economy they live in because they are just one of millions of people doing it. We tend not to think critically about what is commonplace. When you act in a crowd, there is a sense of diffusion of responsibility for the results. Thus, we become blind to the harm we are doing to others and the way we are shooting ourselves in our own foot. I believe it really is that simple at its core.

Aesop's ancient fable about the goose that lays the golden eggs applies: "One day a countryman going to the nest of his goose found there an egg all yellow and glittering. When he took it up it was as heavy as lead and he was going to throw it away, because he thought a trick had been played upon him. But he took it home on second thoughts, and soon found to his delight that it was an egg of pure gold. Every morning the same thing occurred, and he soon became rich by selling his eggs. As he grew rich he grew greedy; and thinking to get at once all the gold the goose could give, he killed it and opened it only to find nothing. Greed often overreacheth itself."[101] Collectively, our culture that loves media so much is currently in the act of strangling its goose that lays the golden eggs through the pandemic of digital piracy. It kind of makes me wonder how we will respond if and when the goose finally asphyxiates under our grip.

Crime on the cyber-scape also extends into an extensive black market that operates on a level often referred to as "The Dark Web," "The Deep Web," or "The Darknet." Brad Chacos describes it as "a hidden underbelly, home to both rogues and political activists, and accessed only with the help of specially designed anonymizing software. It's a secretive place, where Arab Spring dissidents can hide their digital tracks, a place where whistle-blowers can reach out safely to scoop-seeking media outlets. And, yes, it's also a dangerous place, where a lot of illicit, underground nastiness occurs. Like a demilitarized zone or a lawless land, it's not a place most people visit—nor should they."[102]

A prime example of the cyber black market that operates in the Darknet is the Silk Road. This website operates in "Onionland," protected by the Tor network, and has been nicknamed "the Amazon.com of illegal drugs." Besides drugs, users of services such as the Silk Road and its competitors can purchase weapons, fake IDs, prostitutes, hit men, hackers' tools, and all manner of dangerous and illegal wares.[103]

Business has been booming on The Silk Road, with 957,079 registered users. From February 2011 to July 2013, an estimated $1.2 billion of illegal goods were purchased there, often using the virtual currency Bitcoin, earning Silk Road's proprietor (known as "The Dread Pirate Roberts") approximately $79.8 million in commissions.[104]

For quite some time, the Silk Road appeared to be a nearly impregnable fortress and safe haven of criminal activity. However, in October of 2013, the FBI managed to infiltrate the Tor network, seizing its servers and peeling back the layers of the onion to track down information on Silk Road's vendors and customers, and ultimately shutting the site down, along with two other major black market sites.[105] The message, "This hidden site has been seized," was scrawled across Silk Road's homepage. "The Dread Pirate Roberts" was arrested, as well as a large number of the website's dealers and customers. Keith Bristow, director of Britain's National Crime Agency, commented: "These arrests send a clear message to criminals: The hidden Internet isn't hidden, and your anonymous activity isn't anonymous. We know where you are, what you are doing and we will catch you."

The Silk Road did not go down easily. Like a phoenix from the ashes, Silk Road 2.0 rose in November of 2013, fortified by new defenses and run by another administrator of the original site who has taken upon himself the title and mantle of "The Dread Pirate Roberts." His first taunting message was, "This hidden site has risen again. You can never kill the idea of Silk Road."[106]

In spite of its confidence and sophistication, the Silk Road 2.0 has also fallen. In a dramatic illustration of how a whole Tor network can collapse, we need look only to the major dark net sting operation in November of 2014 that took down Silk Road 2.0 and four hundred other Tor protected sites. This raid was conducted by a joint task force of the United States and sixteen European countries and resulted in multiple arrests, including the new leader of the Silk Road.[107] Professor Alan Woodword, who advises Europol, commented, "Tor has long been considered beyond the reach of law enforcement. This action proves that it is neither invisible nor untouchable." The saga is not over, by any means. There is no doubt new sites will pop up, and no doubt both sides will evolve. But one message is clear: the dark net is not invincible . . . not by a long shot.

Recommendations for Protection

Overall, the cyber-scape is not a peaceful Utopian paradise where nothing bad can happen to you. Remember, the cyber-scape is the intersection between the cyberworld and the physical world—these two worlds weave tightly together in many ways, and the sense of separation between the two worlds is an illusion. If you are looking for trouble online, you can easily find it in great quantities there, and you can just as easily get in way over your head before you realize it. Remember that trouble can easily follow you from online to offline. Even if you are not looking for trouble on the cyber-scape, trouble is very actively looking for you this very moment. Many people are there seeking the uninformed, the naïve, the vulnerable, the overconfident, and anyone that they could exploit for their own profit. Even the computer savvy are not immune. Even the best protection available from viruses, hacking, identity theft, and the like is far from perfect, and the threats and dangers are constantly evolving. However, you can reduce your risks. The National Cyber Security Alliance has made the following recommendations, and I have interspersed my own recommendations into theirs.[108]

1. Keep a Clean Machine.

"Keep security software current: Having the latest security software, web browser, and operating system are the best defenses against viruses, malware, and other online threats."

I would recommend having both a high-grade, anti-virus program and a dedicated anti-spyware program. While there is some overlap in what they do, one will often pick up what the other misses. Make sure your virus and malware definitions are up to date, as well. Regularly run scans with both programs. Scan all downloads and attachments with both programs before opening or installing anything you have received from the web. Automate software updates; many software programs will automatically connect and update to defend against known risks. Turn on automatic updates if that's an available option. Remember that other devices such as smartphones, gaming consoles, and any web-connected device need protection. Keep in mind that thumb drives and other external storage devices can carry viruses and malware. Always scan them with your antivirus program before using them.

2. Protect Your Personal Information.

"Secure your accounts: Ask for protection beyond passwords. Many account providers now offer additional ways for you to verify who you are before you conduct business on that site." Beware of "spoof" emails from people imitating your bank, Amazon.com account, and so on. Never use links in an email to connect to a site. Always enter the URL yourself or use a trusted search engine. Spammers and scammers will create fake emails with fake log in pages to try to steal your account information.

Have robust passwords that use both capital and lowercase letters, numbers, and symbols. Don't use the same username and password combination for multiple sites. To remember passwords, write them down in an offline form and store them someplace safe away from your computer. Don't consider privacy settings on sites such as Facebook to be airtight, but make sure to set them to the maximum degree of protection. Also, my rule of thumb is that you should expect any boundaries you make this way to be semipermeable at best.

3. Connect with Care.

"When in doubt, throw it out: Links in email, tweets, posts, and online advertising are often the way cybercriminals compromise your computer. If it looks suspicious, even if you know the source, it's best to delete or if appropriate, mark as junk.

"Get savvy about Wi-Fi hotspots: Limit the type of business you conduct and adjust the security settings on your device to limit who can access your machine." Be far more cautious and conservative about any secure business you do when linked to the Internet by Wi-Fi. Also, be sure to secure your own Wi-Fi with a password and WPA2.

When banking or shopping online, check the URL to determine if the site's security is active. Look for web addresses with "https://" or "shttp://," which means the site takes extra measures to help secure your information. A URL that begins with "http://" is not secure and easily compromised.

4. Be Web Wise.

"Stay current. Keep pace with new ways to stay safe online: Check trusted websites for the latest information, and share with friends, family, and colleagues and encourage them to be web wise." Snopes.com can be an excellent source for identifying Internet scams.

Never make quick decisions on the Internet. Slow down and do your homework before you make any decisions. Don't trust online messages that encourage you to act immediately, promise something that sounds too good to be true, or solicit personal information. Be aware of your own vulnerabilities and ways you could be tricked or enticed to let your guard down, and be aware when something coming from the Internet seems to be operating on that part of you. Slow down, think it through, talk it over with someone you trust, and do some research before you make any decisions. As people target you on the Internet, they will try to figure out what the chinks in your personal armor are.

Also, always back up all your data. Consider using an external hard drive to duplicate your pictures, files, and other important electronic documents. I would personally recommend not merely relying upon cloud-based backup options.

5. Be a Good Online Citizen.

"Safer for me more secure for all: What you do online has the potential to affect everyone at home, at work and around the world." Being safe and smart about your own digital habits helps make the Internet more secure for all users. Remember, your life online is not separate from your life in the real world. Expect the two to intermingled. Don't do things with the cyber part of your life that will cause damage to your real world life. Remember that the concept of the Golden Rule applies online, as well; post only about others as you would have them post about you.

Make life harder for cybercriminals. Report stolen finances or identities and other cybercrime to the Internet Crime Complaint Center (www.ic3.gov) and to your local law enforcement or state attorney general as appropriate. By reducing the ease of cybercrime, we are more likely to make cybercriminals think twice before seeking out more unsuspecting prey.

To these general guidelines, I would personally add a few specific recommendations.

1. Do not post personal information online. Your personal information includes your full name, address, birthday, email address, phone number, places you can be located in the physical world, and so on. Many social media sites will encourage you to include most or all of this information in your profile. I recommend against providing more information than the bare bones minimum.

2. Assume that what you post on social media can be seen by anyone, and remember that not everyone has good intentions. I have seen people announce their marriage on social media and then ask people to give them their addresses so they can send invitations. I don't know how many times I have seen people respond to this very public post by replying directly to it with their address. Now anyone who is looking has their name and address—and I probably have a picture of your face from your profile picture or from browsing your wall—all of which are very useful pieces of data for identity theft. But the opportunity for exploitation goes so much further than that. For example, now that I have your name and address, I can wait for you to post about the business trip or vacation you are going on. In fact, you may even take and post a selfie as you board the plane, which only goes to reassure me that you are not home. Now I know where you live, and that your home is vacant, and based on pictures you have taken I may even know what you have in your home that may be of interest to me. I can also assume that you will be conveniently absent from your house during the wedding mentioned in the post where you replied with your address. It's practically like handing me an invitation to break into your home.

3. Be very cautious about "friending" people that you don't know in real life. In fact, my advice for teens is not to do it at all, and for adults I recommend a great deal of caution and circumspection in this area. The first rule of online social savvy is that many people are not who they appear to be. Therefore, it makes sense to take people you do not know in real life with a sizable grain of salt. One common human fallacy to be aware of is that we tend to think we are good judges of character. In fact, I have yet to meet someone who admits, they are a pretty lousy judge of character. We trust our own judgment in these matters to a fault, but when we meet someone online, we miss so much information (virtually everything that they do not choose to display to us) that we cannot realistically have a high degree of confidence in our impressions of their character. We must realize that our perception is limited and proceed with caution, fully aware of our limitations the way we would if we were trying to drive in a thick fog or navigate an unfamiliar room in dim lighting.

4. Don't arrange to meet up with people you have only met online. When I say this, I frequently get asked about dating websites. After all, ultimately meeting someone in person is the entire point of a dating website. First, some dating websites are more trustworthy and secure than others. Some actually do background checks and take some precautions to protect their clients. Some actually filter profiles and present them to you based on scientifically based measures of compatibility. Others don't.

If you decide to use a dating website, be aware that you are making yourself both emotionally and physically vulnerable. Go into the situation with your eyes wide open, and never make hasty decisions. I know it is hard to ask people not to make emotional decisions on dating websites (after all, dating happens to involve a lot of emotions), but in this situation you need to make decisions based on more than your emotions. Have a trusted confidant who will do more than "ooh" and "aah" with you over promising looking profiles and correspondences. Have someone who can help you bring a dose of critical thinking and help you identify when you may be acting irrationally. Recognize that dating websites are notorious for people controlling their image and managing their message to you. Ask yourself, *What is the part they are not telling me?* I am not saying you should be cynical, but you should have at least a reasonable level of skepticism about everything you see on the Internet, and dating websites are no exception. If anything, a larger dose of rational skepticism is called for in this setting. When you do meet up with someone from a dating website for the first several times, do not give out your home address. Meet in public locations, and do not give your dates means of tracking you down physically until you have gotten some time to get a better read on them.

5. Remember, if you are going to a website where people do illegal things, there will be people there who are willing to do illegal things to you. If you are going to websites that feature pirated music, games, and movies, it should be more than obvious that you are going to a place where people do not feel constrained by laws and morals and where, by definition, everyone is willing to take advantage of another person. Ostensibly, everyone is there to take advantage of the same people: those who own the intellectual property rights of the electronic media being pirated. However, for at least a certain percentage of the people visiting those sites, logic dictates that if they are willing to steal from the musicians, actors, producers, and developers of the media they are pirating, they would also not feel any compunctions or restraints in taking advantage of you if they can profit from it. Expect to get pickpocketed in a den of thieves.

6. Practice a healthy dose of skepticism. The other day, I got a call from a man with a thick accent and absolutely no personality saying, "Congratulations! You have been selected as the winner of a package with a whopping $3.5 million. I just need to confirm your name, address, and a few other details so we can arrange to deliver the package to you." I almost laughed out loud at how pathetic this wanna-be con man's delivery was. As I told him that didn't sound legitimate to me and I would pass, I almost wanted to give him a few pointers because he was just so bad at it. I couldn't help but wonder, though, if someone would fall for his little trap. I also couldn't help but think that he would probably be much more successful if he took his con online, where his dismal vocal performance and lack of ability to think on his feet wouldn't be such a liability.

The phrase "if it seems too good to be true, it probably is" has long been a faithful guide in helping people avoid getting scammed. This advice is even more true online. For example, in 2013 and 2014 a link was rapidly spread around Facebook that people could legally watch the blockbuster Disney movie *Frozen* online for free while it was still in theaters, heavily implying that this was completely legal. I watched as many of my friends and family members—law-abiding people who would never even consider stealing—posted the link and said, "Wow, I'm amazed that this really works. I am sitting on my bed right now watching *Frozen* for free."

Let's think this one through. Companies that make movies make their money from selling their movies. Does it make any sense from a business point of view for Disney to release one of their most popular movies of all time for free while it is still in its first run in theaters—thus decreasing their bottom line—when people are clearly willing to pay for it, thus increasing Disney's bottom line? I heard all sorts of explanations that Disney was doing it to promote their movie, but the fact is that is simply not true. Just because a reason sounds like it could make sense does not make it true. Disney didn't need to give *Frozen* away to promote it. It received incredible word of mouth marketing from people who watched it, so Disney got a huge dose of free marketing from satisfied customers. That is the holy grail of marketing, and when a business achieves it, they do not surrender it. Stated plain and simply, Disney did not need to resort to an expensive gimmick of giving the film away for free to get people to come watch *Frozen* in the theaters, so they would not do it because doing so would hurt their bottom line. Remember rule number one of running a successful business: don't do stuff that makes you lose money.

Business logic aside, the fact remains that you could indeed watch *Frozen* online while it was still in the theaters. The explanation is simple: this was a pirated version, and various people had made it accessible for viewing online. What were these people's motives? There are multiple possibilities. Perhaps some of these people are die-hard adherents to the open-source philosophy that all information should belong to everyone, and they believe that movies fall under that definition of "information." This strikes me as the least likely of the possibilities. It may happen from time to time, but I think usually there are other driving motives. Perhaps some of the people who pirated *Frozen* and released it online enjoy the power they feel when they hack and bypass boundaries others have set up for them, and they likely also get a rush out of "sticking it to the Man" (or the Mouse, in this case). Perhaps they think of themselves as a sort of digital Robin Hood, stealing from the big rich corporations and giving to the poor, although that is making a fully unsupported argument that people who pirate or steal cannot afford to buy what they are stealing. For example, many people who shoplift actually have the money to buy what they are stealing on them at the moment they commit the crime.[109] Think about it: how many people who pirate music really do not have the $0.69, $0.99, or

$1.29 required to buy it online? Even the tightest budget could afford a little digital music per month.

There is another possibility, one that frequently turns out to be true in this situation: the people who pirate movies and make them available online often have ulterior motives. These movies can be Trojan horses of sorts, with their links containing viruses, worms, adware, and other forms of malware designed to do everything from stealing people's personal information to hijacking their computers for any number of reasons, such as using them as a proxies for storing and sharing child pornography through peer-to-peer networks. While encountering the promise of free movies, games, and music may seem like we have stumbled upon a hippy's paradise where everything is free, too often it turns out to be the equivalent of the glowing bioluminescent light that demonic-looking anglerfish use to lure in their unsuspecting prey.

As the old saying goes, "There's a sucker born every minute." While that may be true, the good news is that you don't have to be one of them. Real-world logic for scams still applies online. Don't take offers online at face value. Question them. Think them through skeptically. Research them (snopes.com is a useful resource for this sort of thing). Don't ever click on pop-ups, especially ones for pornography and ones that claim your system has been infected with a virus and you need to "click here" to remove it. In fact, if you are on a site with a lot of pop-ups, get off of it, run a full virus scan and adware scan, and don't return to the site. And above all, if you encounter anything online that seems too good to be true, assume that it is and walk away. The Internet is not a magical place where the laws of reality do not apply.

Endnotes

1. Leonard, H. (2013). There will soon be one smartphone for every five people in the world. *Business Insider*. Retrieved April 24, 2014, from http://www.businessinsider.com/15-billion-smartphones-in-the-world-22013-2.

2. Sanbonmatsu, D.M., Strayer, D.L., Medeiros-Ward, N., & Watson, J.M. (2013). Who multi-tasks and why? Multi-tasking ability, perceived multi-tasking ability, impulsivity, and sensation seeking. *PLoS ONE* 8(1): e54402.

3. Distracted Driving (2012). What is distracted driving? *Distraction.gov*. Retrieved April 25, 2014, from http://www.distraction.gov/content/get-the-facts/facts-and-statistics.html.

4. Bower, D. (2011). The deadly equation. *Georgia Traffic Prevention Institute*. Retrieved April 25, 2014, from http://spock.fcs.uga.edu/ext/pubs/chfd/CHFD-E-51.pdf.

5. Pickerell, T. M., & Ye, T. J. (2013). Driver electronic device use in 2011. (Report No. DOT HS 811 719). Washington, D.C.: National Highway Traffic Safety Administration. Retrieved April 25, 2014, from http://www-nrd.nhtsa.dot.gov/Pubs/811719.pdf.

6. Worland, J. (2014). Why people text and drive even when they know it's dangerous. *Time*. Retrieved November 7, 2014, from http://time.com/3561413/texting-driving-dangerous/.

7. Lah, K., & Mungin, L. (2013). Train riders too consumed with phones to see gun before shooting. *CNN*. Retrieved April 25, 2014, from http://www.cnn.com/2013/10/10/tech/san-francisco-shooter-phone/index.html.

8. Przybylski, A. K. & Weinstein, N. (2013). Can you connect with me now? How the presence of mobile communication technology influences face-to-face conversation quality. *Journal of Social and Personal Relationships 30*(3), 237-246. Retrieved May 8, 2014, from http://spr.sagepub.com/content/30/3/237.full.

9. British Psychological Society (BPS) (2013, April 9). Social media: The perils and pleasures. *Science Daily*. Retrieved December 12, 2013, from http://www.sciencedaily.com/releases/2013/04/130409211859.htm.

10. Luo, S. (2014). Effects of texting on satisfaction in romantic relationships: The role of attachment. *Computers in Human Behavior, 33*, 145-152.

11. Nowinski, J. (2014). Reading between the lines of your partner's texting. *Psychology Today*. Retrieved July 17, 2014, from http://www.psychologytoday.com/blog/the-almost-effect/201404/reading-between-the-lines-your-partners-texting.

12. Madhudsoodanan, J. (2014). Stress alters children's genomes. *Nature*. Retrieved July 17, 2014, from http://www.nature.com/news/stress-alters-children-s-genomes-1.14997.

13. Engle, S. (2013). Put away your iPhone! *Psychology Today*. Retrieved May 8, 2014, from http://www.psychologytoday.com/blog/young-minds/201303/put-away-your-iphone.

14. Shiffer, J. (2014). Don't just hit the "record" button when horror strikes—do something! *Time.* Retrieved June 12, 2014, from http://time.com/2857684/dont-just-hit-the-record-button-when-horror-strikes-do-something/.

15. Mielach, D. (2013). Americans spend 23 per hours a week online, texting. *Business News Daily.* Retrieved May 22, 2014, from http://www.businessnewsdaily.com/4718-weekly-online-social-media-time.html.

16. "Look Up," YouTube video, 4:58, posted by "Gary Turk," April 25, 2014, https://www.youtube.com/watch?v=Z7dLU6fk9QY.

17. "I Forgot My Phone," YouTube video, 2:10, posted by "charstarleneTV," August 22, 2013, https://www.youtube.com/watch?v=OINa-46HeWg8.

18. University of Winnipeg (2013). Study supports theory on teen texting and shallow thought. Retrieved May 9, 2014, from http://news-centre.uwinnipeg.ca/all-posts/study-supports-theory-on-teen-texting-and-shallow-thought/.

19. Carr, N. (2011). *The shallows: What the internet is doing to our brains.* New York: W. W. Norton and Company.

20. Gentile, D. A. (2011). The multiple dimensions of video game effects. *Child Development Perspectives, 5*(2), 75-81.

21. Panek, E. T., Nardis, Y., & Konrath, S. (2013). Mirror or megaphone? How relationships between narcissism and social networking site use differ on Facebook and Twitter. *Computers in Human Behavior 29*(5), 2004-2012.

22. Ptacek, L. (2013). The social groupthink. *Lubor on Tech.* Retrieved May 16, 2014, from http://www.luborp.com/2013/05/the-social-groupthink.html.

23. Ibid.

24. Ridd, R. (2014). The choice generation. *The Ensign.*

25. Sohn, E. (2013). Online "likes" can create sheep mentality. *Discovery News.* Retrieved May 16, 2014, from http://news.discovery.com/human/psychology/online-likes-can-create-sheep-mentality-130808.htm.

26. Gesenhues, A (2013). Survey: 90% of customers say buying decisions are influenced by online reviews. *Marketing Land.* Retrieved May 16, 2014, from http://marketingland.com/survey-customers-more-frustrated-by-how-long-it-takes-to-resolve-a-customer-service-issue-than-the-resolution-38756.

27. Palmer, A. (2009). Web shoppers trust customer reviews most. *Adweek.* Retrieved May 16, 2014, from http://www.adweek.com/news/advertising-branding/web-shoppers-trust-customer-reviews-most-106391.

28. Sachs, J. (2012). Winning the story wars: why those who tell—and live—the best stories will rule the future. Boston: Harvard Business Press.

29. Grant-Alfieri, A., Schaechter, J., & Lipschultz, S.E. (2013). Ingesting and aspirating dry cinnamon by children and adolescents: the "cinnamon challenge." *Pediatrics*, 2012-3418. Retrieved May 22, 2014, from

http://pediatrics.aappublications.org/content/early/2013/04/16/peds.
2012-3418.full.pdf+html?sid=07d5c0d9-afdb-46b6-9198-
fce752764100.

30. AFP (2012). Facebook-fed plant killed by kindness. *Discovery News.*
Retrieved May 23, 2014, from http://news.discovery.com/tech/bio-
technology/facebook-plant-meet-eater.htm.

31. Wilkinson, P., & Soares, I. (2014). Neknominate: "Lethal" drinking game sweeps social media. *CNN.* Retrieved May 23, 2014 from
http://www.cnn.com/2014/02/18/world/europe/neknominate-drink-
ing-game/.

32. Minuchin, S., & Fishman, H. C. (1981). *Family therapy techniques.*
Massachusetts: Harvard University Press.

33. Kerr, M. E., & Bowen, M. (1988). *Family evaluation: An approach based
on Bowen theory.* New York: Norton.

34. Benson, M. J., Larson, J. H., Wilson, S. M., & Demo, D. H. (1993).
Family of origin influences on late adolescent romantic relationships.
Journal of Marriage and the Family, 55, 663-672. Protinsky, H., &
Gilkey, J. K. (1996). An empirical investigation of the construct of
personality authority in late adolescent women and their level of col-
lege adjustment. *Adolescence, 31,* 291-296. Larson, J. H., Benson, M.
J., Wilson, M. J., & Medora, N. (1998). Family of origin influences on
marital attitudes and readiness for marriage in late adolescents. *Journal
of Family Issues, 19,* 750-768. Smith, J. B., Ray, R. E., Wetchler, J. L.,
& Hilhail, T. (1998). Levels of fusion, triangulation, and adjustment
in families of college students with physical and cognitive disabilities.
American Journal of Family Therapy, 26, 29-38. Lopez, F. G. (1991).
Patterns of family conflict and their relation to college student adjustment. *Journal of Counseling and Development, 69,* 257-260. West, J. D.,
Zarski, J .J., & Harvill, R. (1986). The influence of the family triangle
on intimacy. *American Mental Health Counselors Association Journal, 8,*
166-174. Bell, L. G., Bell, D. C., & Nakata, Y. (2001). Triangulation
and adolescent development in the U.S. and Japan. *Family Process, 40,*
173-186. Wood, B., Watkins, J. B., Boyle, J. T., Nogueira, J., Zimand,
E., & Carroll, L. (1989). The "psychometric family" model: An empirical and theoretical analysis. *Family Process, 28,* 399-417.

35. Horowitz, J. (2013). In New York, all eyes on Antony Weiner scandal.
The Washington Post. Retrieved June 5, 2014, from http://www.wash-
ingtonpost.com/politics/in-new-york-all-eyes-on-anthony-weiner-
scandal/2013/07/24/1069862c-f4a5-11e2-9434-60440856fadf_story.
html.

36. McAfee (2014). Study reveals majority of adults share intimate details
via unsecured digital services. Retrieved June 5, 2014, from http://
www.mcafee.com/us/about/news/2014/q1/20140204-01.aspx?cul-
ture=en-us&affid=0&cid=140622 and http://www.scientificamerican.
com/article/sext-much-if-so-youre-not-alone/.

37. Brill, S. (2014). The growing trend of "revenge porn" and the criminal laws that may follow. *The Huffington Post*. Retrieved June 5, 2014, from http://www.huffingtonpost.com/steven-brill/the-growing-trend-of-revenge-porn_b_4849990.html.

38. Fuchs, E. (2013). Here's what the constitution says about posting naked pictures of your ex to the internet. *Business Insider*. Retrieved June 5, 2014, from http://www.businessinsider.com/is-revenge-porn-protected-by-the-first-amendment-2013-9.

39. Roy, J. (2014). Revenge porn king Hunter Moore was arrested, but not for hosting revenge porn. Hosting user-submitted revenge porn isn't an actual crime. *Time*. Retrieved June 5, 2014, from http://newsfeed.time.com/2014/01/27/revenge-porn-king-hunter-moore-was-arrested-but-not-for-hosting-revenge-porn/.

40. Manjoo, F. (2014). Web trolls winning as incivility increases. *The New York Times*. Retrieved August 28, 2014, from http://www.nytimes.com/2014/08/15/technology/web-trolls-winning-as-incivility-increases.html?_r=0.

41. Dewey, C. (2014). Robin Williams' daughter Zelda driven off Twitter by vicious trolls. *The Washington Post*. Retrieved August 28, 2014, from http://www.washingtonpost.com/news/the-intersect/wp/2014/08/13/robin-williamss-daughter-zelda-driven-off-twitter-by-vicious-trolls/.

42. Hess, A. (2014). Why women aren't welcome on the internet. Pacific Standard. Retrieved August 28, 2014, from http://www.psmag.com/navigation/health-and-behavior/women-arent-welcome-internet-72170/.

43. Savage, P. (2014). Tropes vs. women in video games creator driven from her home by online threats and abuse. *PC Gamer*. Retrieved August 28, 2014, from http://www.pcgamer.com/uk/2014/08/28/tropes-vs-women-in-video-games-creator-driven-from-her-home-by-online-threats-and-abuse/.

44. Johnston, C. (2014). The death of the "gamers" and the women who "killed" them. *Arstechnica*. Retrieved November 19, 2014, from http://arstechnica.com/gaming/2014/08/the-death-of-the-gamers-and-the-women-who-killed-them/.

45. Manjoo, ibid.

46. Backchannel (2015). Inside the largest virtual psychology lab in the world. Retrieved January 30, 2015, from https://medium.com/backchannel/inside-the-largest-virtual-psychology-lab-in-the-world-7c0d2c43cda5.

47. McLane, A. (2014). Why you should delete SnapChat. Retrieved June 12, 2014, from http://adammclane.com/2013/08/22/why-you-should-delete-snapchat.

48. Ibid.

49. Ibid.

50. Infosecurity (2013). Snapchat's expired snaps are not deleted, just hidden. Retrieved June 12, 2014, from https://www.infosecurity-magazine.com/news/snapchats-expired-snaps-are-not-deleted-just/.

51. Wortham, J. (2014). Off the record in a chat app? Don't be sure. *The New York Times*. Retrieved June 12, 2014, from http://www.nytimes.com/2014/05/09/technology/snapchat-reaches-settlement-with-federal-trade-commission.html.

52. Ehrenberg, R. (2013). What parents just don't understand about online privacy. *Science News*. Retrieved June 12, 2014, from https://www.sciencenews.org/article/what-parents-just-dont-understand-about-online-privacy.

53. Brownlee, J. (2010). GameStation EULA collects 7,500 souls from unsuspecting customers. *Geek.com*. Retrieved June 12, 2014, from http://www.geek.com/games/gamestation-eula-collects-7500-souls-from-unsuspecting-customers-1194091/.

54. Khatib, F., DiMaio, F., Fold.it Contenders Group, Fold.it Void Crushers Group, Cooper, S., Kazmierczyk, M., Gilski, M., Krzywda, S., Zabranska, H., Pichova, I., Thompson, J., Popovic, Z., Jaskolski, M., & Baker, D. (2011). Crystal structure of monomeric retroviral protease solved by protein folding game players. *Nature Structural and Molecular Biology, 18*, 1175-1177.

55. Ibid.

56. Hill, K. (2014). Facebook manipulated 689,003 users' emotions for science. *Forbes*. Retrieved July 3, 2014, from http://www.forbes.com/sites/kashmirhill/2014/06/28/facebook-manipulated-689003-users-emotions-for-science/.

57. Olson, P. (2014). Facebook's emotion study was all about keeping us addicted to Facebook. *Forbes*. Retrieved July 3, 2014, from https://www.forbes.com/sites/parmyolson/2014/07/01/facebooks-study-of-emotion-is-about-keeping-us-addicted-to-facebook/#10e04a2a77a9.

58. Hill, ibid.

59. Kramer, A. D. I., Guillory, J. E., & Hancock, J. T., (2014). Experimental evidence of massive-scale emotional contagion through social networks. *Proceedings of the National Academy of Sciences of the United States of America, 111*(24), 8788-8790. Retrieved July 3, 2014, from http://www.pnas.org/content/111/24/8788.full#ref-list-1.

60. Olson, ibid.

61. Rudder, C. (2014). We experiment on human beings. *Oktrends*. Retrieved July 30, 2014, from http://blog.okcupid.com/index.php/we-experiment-on-human-beings/.

62. Arthur, C. (2013). NSA scandal: What data is being monitored and how does it work? *The Guardian*. Retrieved June 12, 2014, from http://www.theguardian.com/world/2013/jun/07/nsa-prism-records-surveillance-questions.

63. Yeung, K (2013). What is Tor and why does it matter? *The Next Web*. Retrieved June 13, 2014, from http://thenextweb.com/insider/2013/10/08/what-is-tor-and-why-does-it-matter/.

64. Ibid.

65. Ibid.

66. Borland, J. (2010). Flaws in Tor anonymity network spotlighted. *Arstechnica*. Retrieved June 13, 2014, from http://arstechnica.com/tech-policy/2010/12/flaws-in-tor-anonymity-network-spotlighted/.

67. Gallagher, S. (2013). Anonymous takes down darknet child porn site on Tor network. *Arstechnica*. Retrieved June 13, 2014, from http://arstechnica.com/business/2011/10/anonymous-takes-down-darknet-child-porn-site-on-tor-network/.

68. Williams, R. (2014). Geeksphone's Blackphone promises you an unparalleled level of privacy. *Hot Hardware*. Retrieved July 10, 2014, from http://hothardware.com/News/Geeksphones-Blackphone-Promises-You-an-Unparalleled-Level-of-Privacy#!bcxF6i.

69. Hertlein, K. M., & Piercy, F. P. (2008). Therapists' assessment and treatment of internet infidelity cases. *Journal of Marital and Family Therapy, 34*(4), 481-497.

70. Young, K. S. (1998). Caught in the net: How to recognize the signs of internet addiction—and a winning strategy for recovery. New York: John Wiley & Sons, Inc.

71. OSAC (2014). Brazil 2013 crime and safety reports: Rio de Janeiro. *United States Department of State Bureau of Diplomatic Security*. Retrieved June 24, 2014, from https://www.osac.gov/pages/ContentReportDetails.aspx?cid=13966.

72. McAfee (2014). Net losses: estimating the global cost of cybercrime. Retrieved June 5, 2014, from https://www.mcafee.com/us/resources/reports/rp-economic-impact-cybercrime2.pdf.

73. Nicks, D. (2014). Cybercrime costs the world economy hundreds of billions. *Time*. Retrieved June 24, 2014, from http://time.com/2849814/cybercrime-costs-the-world-economy-hundreds-of-billions/.

74. Wallace, G. (2013). Target credit card hack: What you need to know. *CNN*. Retrieved June 24, 2014, from http://money.cnn.com/2013/12/22/news/companies/target-credit-card-hack/.

75. Perloth, N. (2013). The year in hacking, by the numbers. *New York Times*. Retrieved July 10, 2014, from http://bits.blogs.nytimes.com/2013/04/22/the-year-in-hacking-by-the-numbers/?_php=true&_type=blogs&_r=0.

76. Emspak, J. (2013). 7 shocking things you can buy with Bitcoins. *Discovery News*. Retrieved July 17, 2014, from http://news.discovery.com/tech/gear-and-gadgets/7-shocking-things-buy-bitcoin-131009.htm#mkcpgn=rssnws1.

77. Emspak, J. (2013). Hack a Twitter account, rake in stock profits. *Discovery News*. Retrieved June 24, 2014, from http://news.discovery.com/tech/gear-and-gadgets/twitter-hack-stock-market-130424.htm.

78. Tchong, M. (2013). World War III is already here— and we're losing. *Readwrite*. Retrieved January 3, 2015, from http://readwrite.com/2013/02/05/world-war-iii-is-already-here-and-were-losing.

79. American Academy of Pediatrics (2013). Cyberbullying rampant among high school students: Nearly one-third of youths also report playing video/computer games for more than 3 hours a day. *Science Daily*. Retrieved December 12, 2013, from http://www.sciencedaily.com/releases/2013/05/130505073738.htm.

80. New York Times (2012). Tyler Clementi. *New York Times*. Retrieved June 25, 2014, from http://topics.nytimes.com/top/reference/timestopics/people/c/tyler_clementi/index.html.

81. Megan Meir Foundation (2014). Megan's story. Retrieved June 26, 2014, from http://www.meganmeierfoundation.org/megans-story.html

82. Zetter, K. (2009). Lori Drew to be sentenced today. *Wired*. Retrieved June 26, 2014, from http://www.wired.com/2009/05/lori-drew-to-be-sentenced-today/.

83. Zetter, K. (2009). Judge acquits Lori Drew in cyberbullying case, overrules jury. *Wired*. Retrieved June 26, 2014, from http://www.wired.com/2009/07/drew_court/.

84. Briggs, B, (2014). Bullied students sneak thousands of guns into schools. *NBC News*. Retrieved June 25, 2014, from http://www.nbcnews.com/health/kids-health/bullied-students-sneak-thousands-guns-schools-n95781.

85. Associated Press (2013). California school shooter target bullies, sheriff says. *Fox News*. Retrieved June 25, 2014, from http://www.foxnews.com/us/2013/01/11/sheriff-teen-planned-shooting-claims-to-have-been-bullied/. Mason, M., & Zucchino, D. (2013). Bullying may have motivated Nevada school shooter. *Los Angeles Times*. Retrieved June 25, 2014, from http://articles.latimes.com/2013/oct/22/nation/la-na-middle-school-shooting-20131023.

86. Leary, M. R., Kowalski, R. M., Smith, L., & Phillips, S. (2003). Teasing, rejection, and violence: Case studies of the school shootings. *Aggressive Behavior* 29, 202-214. Retrieved June 25, 2014, from http://www.sozialpsychologie.uni-frankfurt.de/wp-content/uploads/2010/09/Leary-et-al.-2003.pdf.

87. Daily Mail (2009). "Chilling" cyber stalker terrorized girl with Facebook death threats for two years after she refused to go out with him. Retrieved July 11, 2014, from http://www.dailymail.co.uk/news/article-1226349/Chilling-cyber-stalker-terrorised-girl-Facebook-death-threats-years-refused-him.html.

88. Al-Khatib, T. (2013). Facebook felons: Violent crimes using social media. *Discovery News*. Retrieved July 11, 2014, from http://news.discovery.com/tech/facebook-felons-violent-crimes-using-social-media-20130607.htm.

89. Sharp, D. (2013). Nicole Cable affidavit reveals text messages with murder suspect Kyle Dube, before Maine abduction. *The Huffington Post*. Retrieved July 11, 2014, from http://www.huffingtonpost.com/2013/06/07/nichole-cable-murder-suspect-groping_n_3401670.html.

90. Harrison, J. (2013). Death of 15-year-old Nicole Cable was kidnapping gone wrong, affidavit says. *Bangor Daily News*. Retrieved July 11, 2014, from http://bangordailynews.com/2013/05/29/news/bangor/death-of-15-year-old-nichole-cable-was-kidnapping-gone-wrong-affidavit-says/?ref=inline.

91. Blake, B. (2011). Woman uses Facebook to lure man to town for robbery. *The Norwalk Reflector*. Retrieved July 11, 2014, from http://www.norwalkreflector.com/article/270241.

92. Al-Khatib, ibid.

93. BBC News (2010). Shock at Sydney teenager's "Facebook Murder." Retrieved July 11, 2014, from http://news.bbc.co.uk/2/hi/asia-pacific/8686417.stm.

94. Siwick, S. E. (2007). The true cost of sound recording piracy to the U.S. economy. *The Institute for Policy Innovation*. Retrieved July 14, 2014, from http://www.ipi.org/ipi_issues/detail/the-true-cost-of-sound-recording-piracy-to-the-us-economy.

95. Oxford, T. (2010). The truth about PC game piracy: The figures, the excuses and justifications examined. *Tech Radar*. Retrieved July 16, 2014, from http://www.techradar.com/news/gaming/the-truth-about-pc-game-piracy-688864/1#articleContent.

96. Groenendejik, F. (2008). Crytek and Epic lost millions because of piracy and are now switching game development away from PC. *Video Games Blogger*. Retrieved July 17, 2014, from http://www.videogames-blogger.com/2008/05/09/crytek-and-epic-lost-millions-because-of-piracy-and-are-now-switching-game-development-away-from-pc.htm.

97. DemonicSkies (2013). "Piracy is killing the PC"- Game devs predict a grim future for PC gaming. *GameSkinny*. Retrieved July 17, 2014, from http://www.gameskinny.com/yc2ux/piracy-is-killing-the-pc-game-devs-predict-a-grim-future-for-pc-gaming.

98. Ibid.

99. Ghazi, K. (2012). PC game piracy examined. *Tweakguides*. Retrieved July 17, 2014, from http://www.tweakguides.com/Piracy_1.html.

100. Sutter, J. D. (2014). I just can't quite you, Uber. *CNN*. Retrieved December 12, 2014, from http://www.cnn.com/2014/12/10/opinion/sutter-uber-delete/index.html?hpt=hp_t3.

101. Jacobs, J. (2001). *Aesop fables, retold by Joseph Jacobs*. New York: The Harvard Classics.

102. Chacos, B. (2013). Meet Darknet, the hidden, anonymous underbelly of the searchable Web. *PC World*. Retrieved July 17, 2014, from http://www.pcworld.com/article/2046227/meet-darknet-the-hidden-anonymous-underbelly-of-the-searchable-web.html.

103. Emspak, J. (2013). 7 shocking things you can buy with Bitcoins. *Discovery News*. Retrieved July 17, 2014, from http://news.discovery.com/tech/gear-and-gadgets/7-shocking-things-buy-bitcoin-131009.htm#mkcpgn=rssnws1.

104. Jeffries, A. (2013). FBI seizes underground drug market Silk Road, owner indicted in New York. *The Verge*. Retrieved July 17, 2014, from http://www.theverge.com/2013/10/2/4794780/fbi-seizes-underground-drug-market-silk-road-owner-indicted-in-new.

105. Greenfield, D. N. (1999). Psychological characteristics of compulsive Internet use: A preliminary analysis. *CyberPsychology & Behavior, 2*, 403-412. Leger, D. L. (2014). How FBI brought down cyber-under-world site Silk Road. *USA Today*. Retrieved July 17, 2014, from http://www.usatoday.com/story/news/nation/2013/10/21/fbi-cracks-silk-road/2984921/.

106. Greenberg, A. (2014). "Silk Road 2.0" launches, promising a resurrected black market for the dark web. *Forbes*. Retrieved July 17, 2014, from http://www.forbes.com/sites/andygreenberg/2013/11/06/silk-road-2-0-launches-promising-a-resurrected-black-market-for-the-dark-web/.

107. Wakefield, J. (2014). Huge raid to shut down 400-plus dark net sites. *BBC News*. Retrieved November 7, 2014, from http://www.bbc.com/news/technology-29950946?ocid=socialflow_twitter.

108. National Cyber Security Alliance (2014). *Stay safe online: Tips*. Retrieved July 18, 2014, from http://www.staysafeonline.org/stop-think-connect/tips-and-advice/.

109. Berlin, P (2006). Why do shoplifters steal? *National Learning and Resource Center*. Retrieved July 24, 2014, from http://www.shoplifting-prevention.org/whatnaspoffers/nrc.htm.

CHAPTER 5

POTENTIAL FOR ADDICTION

The previous chapter focused on a number of special concerns regarding the cyber-scape. One is significant enough to merit its own chapter: the potential for us to become addicted on the cyber-scape. Some scoff at the idea that people could actually be addicted to something like the Internet, smartphones, or video games. I've heard this kind of statement countless times: "These days, they make up psychological disorders for everything. This kind of psychobabble BS is a lucrative business! They make something up, diagnose you for it, and then charge you money to 'treat' you for it. It's a scam!" While I enjoy a good conspiracy theory as much as the next person (indeed, sometimes I make them up just for fun), I would challenge us to go beyond the knee-jerk reaction of rejecting this idea before examining the evidence in support of it.

Perhaps it will be helpful by starting with a comparison to a type of addiction that is widely accepted as valid, namely drug addiction. From working with recovering drug addicts, I have discovered that they tend to be deeply self-deceived, especially in the beginning of the process of recovery. Many of them tend to say, "Look, I can stop anytime I want. If I had a problem, I would stop." This invariably brings to mind the old joke: "I can quit smoking any time I want. I've done it a hundred times already!" That being said, most of the people I work with agree that if they became addicted, they should consider their drug use a problem. Usually, though, they wouldn't consider it being a problem before then. They start off drawing the line of "it's a problem" far in front of where they think there current level of usage is, at a point they think they will never reach. Of course, when they reach that point, they tend to reset the "it's a problem" line farther in front of them, like referees on a football field moving the first down marker. And so the process of revisionist thought continues each time they reach the point they believed would be a problem. Rather than acknowledge their situation and change their behavior, their natural tendency is to merely redefine the problem.

I find myself asking people who are addicted to drugs, "Are you saying that the only way drugs can be a problem is if you are addicted to them? Let's think about that. Take alcohol, for example. It's legal, but there are a lot of problems associated with it. In fact, the World Health Organization has found alcohol to be the number one cause of human death in the world.[1] I would argue that a lot of the problems associated with alcohol exist even for people who aren't what you would call addicted. For example, are you trying to tell me that every drunk driving accident and fatality is caused by someone who is a full-blown alcoholic?"

They can't really argue with that. That doesn't mean they don't try to argue with it, but ultimately their attempts to do so fall apart. The truth of the matter is pretty clear; merely asserting that you are not addicted to something (even if it is true, although often that assertion turns out to be highly questionable) is no defense against the fact that a behavior on your part is causing problems. Addiction is a primary problem that brings along with it myriad secondary difficulties, like a single chip in a windshield spreading into a massive spiderweb of cracks. However, problems do not only begin once we have passed the threshold into addiction.

Another conversation I frequently find myself having with people recovering from drug abuse and addiction is about functional equivalence. In brief, if you are living the life of an addict, it doesn't make any real difference if you are addicted or not. If your life revolves so much around a substance or activity that you put yourself at risk, stress relationships, blow off school or work, steal, lie, and mistreat other people, how is your life any better off than someone you would actually consider a full-blown biological addict? So even if you are not addicted *per se* in the hardcore medical sense of the word, you are living a life that is the functional equivalent of being addicted. When it gets down to brass tacks, there is no real practical difference, and the distinction between "addiction" and "functional equivalence of addiction" is nearly irrelevant when it comes to real-world application.

Our relationship with social media can be unhealthy in a number of ways. It can be excessive, obsessive and codependent, and in many ways the functional equivalent of an addiction. That alone is cause enough for significant concern. However, our relationship with social media and smartphones has the real potential to be an actual addiction as well.

Even though the word *addiction* tends to get thrown around so much that it tends to lose some of its meaning colloquially, we seem to have mutually recognized that many people's relationship to social media looks like—and may very well be—an addiction. The degree of sophistication and accuracy with which we make these observations varies. Nonetheless, the overall phenomenon of Internet addiction that we are describing is observably quite widespread.

What Is Addiction, Anyway?

What we know about addiction is evolving, and the more we learn, the more we realize we have yet to learn. One thing we know for sure is that addiction resides in the brain. While this is an incredibly basic and seemingly obvious statement, it has vast implications. I've often thought addiction would be easier to deal with if it made its home in the human elbow or perhaps the clavicle or kneecap. Alas, addiction exists in the most complex and complicated human organ of all—the one responsible for our perception, processing, reasoning, placement of relative value, dreams, ambitions, feelings, subconscious functions, and all aspects of our consciousness of ourselves and the world around us. Addiction, we are learning, has the ability to hijack every part of the brain and bend it to serve the addiction. It can take over what you see, feel, think, and value, and at the same time muffles your ability to perceive that it is hacking each of those parts of you. Addiction is the ultimate double-blind con, pulled off with all the savvy of a double cross in a Cold War spy movie. Addiction is the ultimate ninja, able to sneak in right under your nose and take everything you care about without you ever realizing it was even there.

Bethany Brookshire provided an excellent summary of some of the major brain-based contributors to addiction and the feature that binds all of these factors together: neuroplasticity.

> Every day sees a new research article on addiction, be it cocaine, heroin, food or porn. Each one takes a specific angle on how addiction works in the brain. Perhaps it's a disorder of reward, with drugs hijacking a natural system that is meant to respond to food, sex and friendship. Possibly addiction is a disorder of learning, where our brains learn bad habits and responses. Maybe we should think of addiction as a combination of an environmental stimulus and vulnerable genes. Or perhaps it's an inappropriate response to stress, where bad days trigger a relapse to the cigarette, syringe or bottle.
>
> None of these views are wrong. But none of them are complete, either. Addiction is a disorder of reward, a disorder of learning. It has genetic, epigenetic and environmental influences. It is all of that and more. Addiction is a display of the brain's astounding ability to change — a feature called plasticity.[2]

Let's examine how this works. In early research on addiction, scientists discovered that the production of several key neurotransmitters seemed to play a large role in developing addiction. The first of these neurochemical kingpins is dopamine, which is both a neurotransmitter and a hormone. Dopamine has long been referred to as the "feel good" neurotransmitter, but it does much more than regulate pleasure. It also shapes our sense of relative value and it regulates heart rate, blood pressure, voluntary movement, motivation, processing of rewards and punishments, regulation of sleep, regulation of mood, regulation of attention, working memory, and learning. It activates five different types of brain receptors and their variants, making it a very influential neurotransmitter.

The second big name in neurotransmitters and addiction is serotonin. It regulates mood, appetite, muscle contraction, and some cognitive functions such as memory and learning.

The third heavy hitter neurotransmitter is norepinephrine. It is both a stress hormone and a neurotransmitter. It helps regulate attention and responses to stimuli. It plays a major role in the fight-or-flight response. I think of it as "brain adrenaline." It helps us detect and overcome threats and also directs our energies toward activities that could be beneficial.

Processes that evoke high levels of these influential neurotransmitters are processed by the brain as highly pleasurable, stimulating, and/or desirable, regardless of any of the other consequences associated with them. Our bodies are hardwired to be motivated to seek experiences that evoke these neurotransmitters. As a part of our survival mechanisms, the brain's job is to help us seek out rewarding stimuli and avoid unpleasant stimuli, because as a general rule of thumb, the body is put together so that things that help you live and procreate (such as eating, mating, or getting out of the freezing cold) feel good, and things that could kill you off and end your genetic line (such as being dehydrated or getting burned) feel bad. Overall, that's a pretty good system for keeping us alive long enough to pass on our genes to the next generation. There are, of course, important exceptions to this rule—stimuli that feel good up front but ultimately can be detrimental, harmful, or even deadly.

Learning plays a huge role in the development of an addiction. Dr. Mark Butler identified several key learning processes that contribute to addiction.[3] The first of these processes is known in psychology as classical conditioning in which the brain notices when two or more things are paired together repeatedly and forms an automatic link between them. A classic example of this process was Ivan Pavlov and his dogs. As Pavlov was studying digestion in dogs, he noticed that his dogs would begin to salivate—which is a part of the digestive process—when he was placing their bowls out to feed them, without any food being present yet. Wild dogs and dogs that aren't fed out of bowls don't salivate at the sight of bowls. Salivation occurs as a preparation to digest food and is naturally triggered by the sight, smell, and feel of food. Thus, dogs should not naturally salivate at the sight of a bowl. To try to understand what he was observing, Pavlov decided to ring a bell when he served food to his dogs. After doing these two actions together for a time, Pavlov found that he could get his dogs to salivate merely by ringing the bell. Upon further investigation, Pavlov concluded that the dogs had formed a mental association between the bell and the food, and now the bell could serve as a trigger to salivate as effectively as the sight of food could.

In other words, when the brain sees that A and B go together frequently, it assumes that they should go together constantly and forms an expectation for B when there is A, and vice versa. Through a simple experiment, you can see how this has happened to you. For example, when I say "steak" (sorry, vegetarians and vegans!), what other food comes to mind for you? Is it eggs? Potatoes? Lobster? Rice Krispies? (Probably not, I would wager.) Why? What does a steak have to do with any of those things? The reason you thought what you did in response to the cue of "steak" has to do with what you have been accustomed to seeing paired together with steak. That's why I think "potatoes" in response to "steak," since I have constantly had those two foods served together. That's also why you probably didn't think of Rice Krispies, because chances are these two things have not been paired together in your experience. (By the way, if they have, I would really love to hear about how that came to be). So, if you are used to a good old Americana dish of steak and potatoes like I am, chances are if I just serve you a steak, you'll have a craving for a potato to go along with it. Likewise, if I give you a potato just like the kind you are used to having with steak, chances are you will feel a longing for steak to kick in. Because of the classical conditioning you have gone through, these two things feel like they should go together as if it were some sort of universal, self-evident truth. You don't have to actively think about this; it just triggers as a result of the classically conditioned learning process.

If I wanted to be diabolical, I—or anyone with a solid grasp of this process—could make your desires, cravings, and fears dance like a puppet on a string just by manipulating this dynamic. Fortunately, I have no such nefarious ambitions. However, this principle underlies a lot of the marketing that goes on in the commercial world. The old saying "sex sells" is true. That's why we see attractive people in provocative situations promoting all sorts of goods that have nothing to do with sex. Advertisers have figured out that by merely activating people's sexual response, even on a minor level, a vendor can help jumpstart a sense of desire for their product when they pair it with sexual cues that are inherently stimulating and motivating. We are more like Pavlov's dogs than we would like to think.

The second major learning process is known as operant conditioning. Its discovery is frequently credited to psychology pioneer B.F. Skinner. To state it scientifically, it is chronologically oriented correlation with inference of causation. To state it in plain English, since we aren't all walking dictionaries, it takes learning one step beyond "A and B go together" to "A leads to B, which means A might even cause B." In other words, this helps us learn cause and effect, although there is room for error here. Just because A consistently comes before B doesn't necessarily mean that it causes B. Operant conditioning can be used to mold thought and behavior fairly easily.

Operant conditioning has three subsets. The first is known as positive reinforcement. The general idea is, *I do X, and something happens that I like, leading me to feel more inherently motivated to do X.* For example, it could look like, *I tell a joke, and someone laughs (which does actually occur sometimes, contrary to popular belief). I like it when the other person laughs. It makes me feel like they enjoy being around me, and I value being loved. Therefore, I feel motivated to tell more jokes in social situations.* In a chemical addiction, this could look like, *I took ecstasy and had an exciting sensation throughout my whole body. I am therefore more motivated to take ecstasy.*

The second subset is known as negative reinforcement, although it's not what people assume it is when they hear the name. Negative reinforcement works like this: *I do X, and something I don't like stops happening, leading me to be more motivated to do X when something that feels bad to me is occurring.* In practice, it could look like, *I started studying, and I stopped failing all my classes. I enjoyed not failing all my classes and have my parents stop yelling at me. Therefore, I am more motivated to study, because it stops bad things from happening.* In a chemical addiction, this could look like, *I was feeling socially awkward at the party. I drank alcohol, and that feeling of awkwardness subsided. Therefore, I am now more motivated to drink alcohol at parties to stop myself from feeling socially awkward.*

The third subset of operant conditioning is punishment. In punishment, the equation is, *I did X, and something happened that I did not like. Therefore, I feel motivated not to repeat X.* For example, *I asked Rachel out on a date. She laughed in my face and posted mocking comments about me on Facebook. I am now much less motivated to ask Rachel out on a date again. I am also possibly much less motivated to ask anyone else out on a date again.* In a chemical addiction, this could look like, *I tried to go a day without smoking cigarettes, but I felt jittery, edgy, and just miserable. I am thus motivated to not go a day without smoking cigarettes.*

Reinforcement schedules play a powerful role in the magnitude and influence of the various types of operant conditioning. The simplest schedule is a basic one-to-one: *every time you do A, B happens.* This is the easiest and quickest schedule to learn. However, when the connection between A and B is broken, it is also the quickest conditioned behavior to stop. Imagine, for a moment, that we have a monkey in a cage. The monkey explores the cage and finds that when he pushes the red button on the wall, a banana pops out of a chute like a potassium-rich gift from heaven. Upon pressing the button again, the monkey sees another banana magically appear. One press of the button always produces one banana. The monkey will rapidly learn to press that button whenever he wants a banana. However, let's suppose we decide to deactivate the button. The monkey will press it and no doubt be puzzled and frustrated to find it doesn't work. He will try it several times, but after a relatively small number of experiences with the button not working, the monkey will abandon his attempts to get bananas by pressing the button. Thus, the one-to-one reinforcement schedule is relatively easily learned and relatively easily broken.

The second type of reinforcement schedule is a set ratio. For example, our monkey's button may have to be pushed three times to produce a banana. However, three pushes always produce a banana. Thus, it will take a little bit longer for our monkey to learn to use the button to get a banana, but once he gets the hang of it, he will consistently push the button three times when he wants a banana. When we deactivate the button, he will push the button more times before he gives up, because he is used to it taking three pushes, instead of just one. So, it takes a little longer to learn and a little longer to break. The larger the ratio between pushes and bananas, the longer it takes to learn and the longer it takes to break.

The third type of reinforcement schedule is intermittent. In this configuration, we insert a random ratio between button pushes and banana release. On the first time, it make take one push, on the second time, three pushes, on the third time, five pushes, on the fourth time, two pushes, on the fifth time, nine pushes, and only one push again on the sixth time. There is no predictable pattern, though; it is always changing. This can take more time for the monkey to learn, but it takes a tremendously long time for the association to break. After all, the monkey has learned that the reward may be just one push away. When we unhook the connection between the button and the banana release, our poor little simian friend will go on pushing that button for a ridiculously long amount of time. This is especially true if we increase the reward so that a successful button push releases a whole bunch of bananas.

Slot machines are based upon this same principle of intermittent reinforcement. There is a random relationship between lever pulls and winning, but the rewards look, feel, and sound rather big when they come. Slot machines are even more effective at producing a desired behavior from humans (that is, giving up all our money) when you place them in long rows or large rooms with many other slot machines. That way, humans hear other slot machines going off around them, and even though their own machine has not reinforced them for emptying their wallets and purses into it, the fact that other machines are paying out raises the sense that the big win is just a few lever pulls away. Casino operators have capitalized upon this even further by filling casinos with attractive people who pay a lot of attention to people playing and winning. Add to that an environment filled with various mind-altering chemicals such as alcohol, nicotine, and other drugs that make their way on the premises, and you have a perfect equation for keeping human beings from noticing or caring that they are spending all their money. Thus, classical and operant conditioning work together to make humans pull levers with as little chance of acquiring the dangled reward as our monkey friends pushing banana releasing buttons that don't work anymore.

Consequences are a big part of what makes operant conditioning work. However, some types of consequences carry greater weight than others. When we are infants, our brain is hardwired to look for immediate consequences to our actions. A newborn will begin to learn that if it cries, it will get fed, get its diaper changed, or get cuddled. Its brain focuses on what happens immediately after a specific behavior. Each time the newborn is hungry, tired, lonely, or wet, its brain will remember what worked to immediately fix the problem last time (crying), and that becomes the baby's reflexive reaction. A newborn or a one-year-old is not capable of thinking, *Hey, if I start investing two hundred dollars a month in the stock market over the next fifteen years, by the time I am thirty I will have a million dollars!* The brain is not yet wired to think of long-term consequences. It only thinks about immediate consequences.

As we grow and our ability to take care of ourselves increases, our brain increasingly gains the ability to consider long-term consequences. However, since the way we first learned was by examining immediate consequences, those remain the strongest, most visceral kinds of consequence that we learn from. Learning from longer-term consequences takes purposeful, rational thought and practice and is a skill that must be developed (and indeed, it is a skill not every adult is competent in). Engaging in addictive processes tends to hamper the development of that skill and dampen our ability to use it to the degree we have already developed it. Furthermore, when it comes to drugs or other addictive items, they feel good immediately when we engage in them. The pain from the negative effects of their use only comes later. Since our brain is more strongly hardwired to look at immediate consequences than at long-term consequences, our brain is going to be more drawn to using and ignoring the long-term harmful effects.

The third major form of learning is sequence learning. Our brain takes a long series of behaviors and places it in a large "chunk" so that we don't have to think about every little piece of the behavior. In fact, once we have practiced routines enough, we don't have to consciously think about them at all. For example, think about riding a bike. It involves a lot of complex muscle movements, balancing, hand-eye coordination, and so on. If we practice it enough, it becomes something that we do automatically, without having to consciously think about it. We call this overlearning, or learning something so well that we no longer have to give conscious thought to it. By practicing and over-learning, we can even do things that were originally very difficult for us to do. In the case of riding a bike, our brain makes this complex process into a compact, subconscious, and efficient sequence so we can focus on other things.

This is part of what makes recovery from addictions so challenging. When we use drugs or engage in addictive behaviors, we do not start using in the moment we pick up and use. There is a long sequence of behaviors that we have to go through before we can use. We have to get the substance. We have to ensure privacy. We have to use a computer or phone to go to a specific website. We have to close doors, or call friends, or go places, and so on and so forth. Using starts long before we actually do the using, and our brain begins to commit the sequence of behaviors leading up to the using in one big chunk to the point we can do it on autopilot and lose track of the choices we are making that make it possible for us to use.

Each autopilot sequence we have formed that leads to using is a major risk for kicking our addiction. These sequences can start with all kinds of stimuli: feelings, settings, events, relationships, sounds, smells—all of our senses and all of our perception, both internal and external, can serve as beginnings or steps in sequences. To disarm these potential landmines, we need to go through a process of bringing these sequences and all the choices that are a part of them back into our consciousness. We need to find ways to avoid the beginning of the sequence and ways to break the sequence once it has started.

These learning processes—classical conditioning, operant conditioning, and sequence learning—actually change the structure of the brain, creating physical neuronal paths, weaving different parts together in ways that are more complex and sophisticated than we currently understand. All learning changes the brain physically. That's a part of what neuroplasticity means. Addiction includes learning processes and changes in brain chemistry, both of which alter the structure and balance of the brain due to its highly moldable nature. Bethany Brookshire explains, "As someone takes a drug over and over, dopamine and other systems in the brain respond with plasticity — that is, those systems adapt to the presence of the drug. Receptors that control the response to chemicals like dopamine change concentration. Connections between brain cells and between different areas of the brain strengthen and weaken. The birth of new neurons decreases."[4]

Dr. Mark Butler shed light on this idea by comparing the structure and plasticity of our brain to the process of building a road.[5] If no one travels between point X and point Y, there will be no road there. The first person going from point X to point Y may use a machete to carve a path through the grass and bushes. If more people start traveling the path, eventually a dirt road will be built or will simply form itself as a result of constantly being tread upon. If more and more people travel the path, eventually the road will be paved. If traffic on the road keeps increasing, eventually the road gets widened and more lanes get built until it becomes a highway. The more traffic the road gets, the more on-ramps are built to let people access the road from multiple entry points. And, if people tend to ride the road all the way from point X to point Y, any off-ramps between point X and point Y will eventually fall into disrepair or be closed all together because their maintenance is not a priority. The structure of the landscape changes as people travel over it, which in turn changes the way people travel over the landscape.

Conversely, if people start getting off between point X and point Y, more off-ramps will be repaired and built. If people stop entering the road at various on-ramps, those on-ramps will eventually fall into disrepair and possibly get closed. As fewer and fewer people travel the road, the road will begin to be neglected and fall into disrepair until it eventually just becomes a broken down, crumbled dirt road again. You could still travel on it; it is just not as easy or as fast.

In addition to that, there are various other factors that determine our degree of vulnerability to addiction and either moderate or exacerbate our risk factors and addictive processes. These include genetic factors, mental health issues, emotional resources and coping skills, societal and cultural influences, and so forth. Of all the things we have yet to learn about addiction, I think we can safely say that addiction is brain molding and brain hijacking. Because of that fact, addiction is easy to fall into and difficult to get out of without outside help.

Process Addiction

When I speak with people about process addictions (addictions to things other than drugs such as gambling, porn, social media, or video games), I have noticed that people tend to struggle a bit with the concept. Overall, people seem to understand chemical addictions pretty well. After all, you can see a chemical going into the other person's body, and it is easy to think in a very simplistic, very linear fashion that the chemical you see going in is what the addiction is all about. Therefore, people can stumble over the idea of a nonchemical addiction. But really, that is a misnomer. All addictions involve chemicals—neurochemicals, as we discussed earlier. Some addictions use external chemicals to kick off the tide of neurochemicals, but some use other forms of stimulating those same neurochemical patterns. The first area that this idea gained traction in was gambling. People were able to observe a pattern in compulsive gamblers that looked exactly like what can be observed in alcoholics or heroin addicts. As time has passed, people have been able to recognize that this applies to processes other than gambling.

In my work, I have found that processes are potentially addicting when the following happens:

1. They evoke high levels of powerful neurotransmitters.
2. There is ample opportunity for classical conditioning, with a large number of common stimuli going through the process of becoming conditioned stimuli, leading to conditioned responses—in other words, you can connect and correlate a lot of pieces of your life to it.
3. They follow a strong operant conditioning pattern, particularly utilizing intermittent reinforcement of larger rewards sprinkled with regular reinforcement of smaller rewards.
4. The rewards, when they happen, are immediately gratifying.
5. The downsides of the process take longer to occur.
6. They are socially common.

Social media and the Internet, especially when accessed via smartphones, meet all of these criteria. Therefore, there is good reason to believe that our relationship with social media, if not carefully navigated, has moderate to high potential for actual process addiction.

Prevalence of Internet Process Addiction

One example of the use of the words *addict* and *addiction* to describe some people's relationship with social media and smartphones is a report released in April 2014 by Flurry Analytics.[6] The researchers in this study had access to 1.3 billion mobile devices and were able to track users' activation and use of 500,000 apps. This is a tremendous amount of data, capable of shedding light on broad societal trends. The researchers determined that the average mobile phone user launches apps 10 times per day. They decided to set the criteria for *regular users* as someone who launches apps 16 or fewer times per day, *super users* as those who launch apps 16–60 times per day, and *mobile addicts* as someone who launches apps more than six times more frequently than the average, at 60 times per day. The researchers provided no rationale behind their choices for the cutoff points. As far as I can tell, their criteria for a mobile addict is an arbitrary point they chose, probably because it seemed to fit the description of *this person launches apps a whole lot more than the average Joe or Jane.* There's more to an addiction than merely doing something a lot, but doing something a lot is an easily recognizable symptom common to addictions. Suffice it to say that Flurry Analytics's method of determining what a mobile addict is, is not the most sophisticated or valid tool for determining addiction, but I think it is probably fair to say that at that level, we would expect to see at least the functional equivalence of addiction. Even though their definition is somewhat weak, the amount of data they have is a powerful tool and can be useful in spite of the somewhat arbitrary nature of the rationale underpinning their criteria for user categories.

With those criteria as a measuring stick, the researchers found that the mobile addict segment was the fastest growing category, increasing at a rate of 123 percent from 79 million mobile addicts in 2013 to 176 million mobile addicts in 2014. During the same time period, the number of super users rose at 55 percent, and the number of regular users rose at 23 percent. One implication from this research is that unhealthy use of mobile apps is growing much more quickly than "regular" use. In other words, our relationship with social media is getting sicker, and that trend only seems to be accelerating. We are not getting better, smarter, or more balanced in our relationship with social media and smartphones; the opposite is true, and we are doing it at a brisk pace. This research did not track the movements of individual users from one category to the next, which is a pity, because that information would have been very illuminating.

Given that there were 2.4 billion Internet users in the world in 2013, 7.3 percent of all Internet users are considered Internet addicts by these criteria.[7] The combination of super users (remember that for some of these super users, only one launch per day keeps them out of the mobile addicts category) and mobile addicts make up 25 percent of the total number of Internet users in the world. Demographically, 52 percent of these mobile addicts were female and 48 percent were male. When you do the math, that means there were 15 million more female mobile addicts than male ones. The most common age groups for mobile addicts were teens (not surprisingly), college-aged students (18–24 years old), and middle-aged (ages 35–54). The college-aged population segment had the largest spike of mobile addicts. Surprisingly, middle-aged mobile addicts edged out teens for second place. That finding certainly flies in the face of the stereotype, although that's not to say that there isn't a colossal number of teens in the mobile addict category.

Among women, characteristics most likely to be found in mobile addicts included mothers, parenting and education, gamers, and sports fans. For men, the most common characteristics among mobile addicts were auto enthusiasts, parenting and education, gamers, and catalogue shoppers. Mobile addicts were clearly revealed not to be merely the stereotypical basement dwelling, pasty-skinned males who have never had a date in their lives or the endlessly selfie-taking teenage girls who talk in text language. Rather, mobile addicts are everywhere, hidden in plain sight and camouflaged in the thundering herd of other mobile addicts, undetected and unidentified like a single tree in the green landscape of a forest of seemingly identical trees. Strangely enough, I don't think this finding will be that surprising to many people. After all, we witness it constantly. It is just so much easier to recognize it in someone else than it is to see it in ourselves.

While this data is extremely helpful, we have the ability to be more scientific and sophisticated with how we determine what an actual addiction to social media, mobile phones, and the Internet is. Dr. Kimberly Young was the first researcher in the United States to identify the concept of Internet addiction. She presented her first paper on the topic at the annual conference of the American Psychological Association in 1996.[8] Dr. Young developed the criteria for an Internet addiction on a modified version of the DSM-IV criteria (which is the official diagnostic manual for mental health professionals) for gambling addiction, based on her observations that the same types of dynamics that underlie gambling addictions are present in Internet addictions. She developed the Internet Addiction Diagnostic Questionnaire, which is as follows:

1. Do you feel preoccupied with the Internet (think about previous online activity or anticipate next online session)?
2. Do you feel the need to use the Internet with increasing amounts of time in order to achieve satisfaction?
3. Have you repeatedly made unsuccessful efforts to control, cut back, or stop Internet use?
4. Do you feel restless, moody, depressed, or irritable when attempting to cut down or stop Internet use?
5. Do you stay online longer than originally intended?
6. Have you jeopardized or risked the loss of significant relationship, job, educational or career opportunity because of the Internet?
7. Have you lied to family members, therapist, or others to conceal the extent of involvement with the Internet?
8. Do you use the Internet as a way of escaping from problems or of relieving a dysphoric mood (e.g., feelings of helplessness, guilt, anxiety, depression)?[9]

Meeting five or more of these criteria met the threshold for a diagnosis of Internet addiction.

Other symptoms of Internet addiction include:

- Failed attempts to control behavior.
- Heightened sense of euphoria while involved in computer and Internet activities.
- Neglecting friends and family.
- Neglecting sleep to stay online.
- Being dishonest with others.
- Feeling guilty, ashamed, anxious, or depressed as a result of online behavior.
- Physical changes such as weight gain or loss, backaches, headaches, carpal tunnel syndrome.
- Withdrawing from other pleasurable activities.[10]

The Internet Addiction Diagnostic Questionnaire can serve as a useful screening instrument, due to its brevity and simplicity. Another scientifically based but simple set of criteria for evaluating Internet addiction was put forth by the China Youth Association for Network Development.[11] Based on their observations and studies, they determined that Internet addiction had one prerequisite and a few conditions. The prerequisite is that the pattern of usage must "severely jeopardize" a person's social functioning and interpersonal communication offline. In addition to that prerequisite, by their criteria a person should be considered to have an Internet addiction if they have any one of the three following conditions: 1) the person believes it is easier to find meaning, purpose, or "self-actualization" online than in real life; 2) the person experiences a sense of depression, anxiety, or agitation when not able to access the Internet; and 3) the person tries to hide or minimize their amount of Internet use from other people.

Dr. Maressa Hecht Orzack, who is the director of the Harvard Medical School affiliated Computer Addiction Services at McLean Hospital, describes Internet addiction as a loss of impulse control in which a person's relationship with the Internet has become unmanageable, and yet despite the problems caused by their usage, the person cannot seem to stop or change that problematic relationship. In essence, the computer and the Internet become the primary relationship in the Internet addict's life.[12] This may be difficult for the person with an Internet addiction to discern, largely because they may conceptualize what they are doing as having relationships with people on the Internet, and they thus have great difficulty in distinguishing the fact that their relationship with the Internet has overshadowed their relationship with people. The development of an Internet addiction blurs that line very effectively in the mind of the addict. The neurological training that results from the repetition of their unhealthy Internet usage changes the way the Internet addict conceptualizes relationships, pressing them through the distorting lens of the shallowing effect to the point they cannot recognize their own superficiality and distractibility in their online relationships and the way it spills over into their offline lives. The development of any addiction greatly reduces the ability to discern the addiction, largely because addiction literally alters both brain chemistry and brain structure, and the brain is needed to detect the addicted pattern. With a mind altered in this way, it is very easy to mistake a relationship with social media as a relationship with people because the content of social media is placed there by other people.

One common phenomenon that seems to illustrate this point is the way teens gather together, only to have each one of them pull out their smartphones and get on social media. The fact that they may be posting or messaging to each other as a part of their interaction on social media hides from them the uncomfortable truth that in that moment, they are giving preferential treatment to the Internet and social media over the friends they have right by their side. They are together but isolated, and they show no awareness of that fact.

Dr. Kimberly Young has also developed a more advanced diagnostic instrument for Internet addiction: the Internet Addiction Test (IAT). It has been shown to have strong reliability (the scores are consistent across time and are not affected by other factors such as mood) and validity (it accurately measures the phenomenon it is designed to measure) in English, French, and Italian, making it the first empirically validated international measure of pathological Internet usage.[13] In other words, this isn't your average Facebook quiz; it won't just tell you which Harry Potter character you are or which breakfast cereal is the same color as your aura. This test has some solid science behind it. The IAT can be taken online for free (yes, it is kind of ironic that an Internet addiction test can be taken on the Internet), where it will automatically be scored, at https://psychology-tools.com/internet-addiction-test/. Or, you can take it below and score the answers yourself.

Internet Addiction Test (IAT) by Dr. Kimberly Young

Internet Addiction Test (IAT) is a reliable and valid measure of addictive use of Internet, developed by Dr. Kimberly Young. It consists of twenty items that measures mild, moderate, and severe level of Internet addiction.

To begin, answer the following questions by using this scale:
0- Does not apply
1- Rarely
2- Occasionally
3- Frequently
4- Often
5- Always

1. How often do you find that you stay on-line longer than you intended?
2. How often do you neglect household chores to spend more time on-line?
3. How often do you prefer the excitement of the Internet to intimacy with your partner?
4. How often do you form new relationships with fellow on-line users?
5. How often do others in your life complain to you about the amount of time you spend on-line?
6. How often do your grades or schoolwork suffer because of the amount of time you spend on-line?
7. How often do you check your email before something else that you need to do?
8. How often does your job performance or productivity suffer because of the Internet?
9. How often do you become defensive or secretive when anyone asks you what you do on-line?
10. How often do you block out disturbing thoughts about your life with soothing thoughts of the Internet?
11. How often do you find yourself anticipating when you will go on-line again?
12. How often do you fear that life without the Internet would be boring, empty, and joyless?
13. How often do you snap, yell, or act annoyed if someone bothers you while you are on-line?
14. How often do you lose sleep due to late-night log-ins?
15. How often do you feel preoccupied with the Internet when off-line, or fantasize about being on-line?
16. How often do you find yourself saying "just a few more minutes" when on-line?
17. How often do you try to cut down the amount of time you spend on-line?
18. How often do you try to hide how long you've been on-line?
19. How often do you choose to spend more time on-line over going out with others?
20. How often do you feel depressed, moody or nervous when you are off-line, which goes away once you are back on-line?

Total up the scores for each item. The higher your score, the greater level of addiction is.

- **20–49 points:** You are an average online user. You may surf the Web a bit too long at times, but you have control over your usage.
- **50–79 points:** You are experiencing occasional or frequent problems because of the Internet. You should consider their full impact on your life.
- **80–100 points:** Your Internet usage is causing significant problems in your life. You should elevate the impact of the Internet on your life and address the problems directly caused by your Internet usage.[14]

Using these more scientific measures and criteria for Internet addiction, researchers from Stanford University's Medical Center found that approximately 12.5 percent of Americans exhibited one or more signs of Internet addiction,[15] and another study showed that 6 percent of Americans (approximately 19 million people) met all the criteria for Internet addiction.[16] Before you feel too comforted by the fact that this is much lower than the statistic that 25 percent of the world's Internet users fall in the category of "Internet addicts" or "super users" from the Flurry Analytics survey,[17] there is something we need to keep in mind: most research on this area relies on people self-reporting, without outside, more objective measures of their behaviors. Self-report measures are notorious for having at least some degree of skewing of the data to make respondents look healthier than they are because people tend to be rather generous in the way they rate themselves. We also have to keep in mind how much has changed in the world of tech between 1999 when that 6 percent number was produced and 2014 when the Flurry Analytics survey was performed. It would be far more illuminating to have a study that utilized scientific criteria for addiction in addition to measures of frequency of use and gathered both self-report data and outside-observer data to triangulate and increase the accuracy of symptom reporting. Based on my observations, I believe that if such a study existed (which, as far as I can tell it hasn't been done yet), we would likely find that the 25 percent of the total population statistic for "Internet addicts" and "people with the functional equivalent of an

Internet addiction" to be fairly close to the truth. My interpretation of the research is that the overall weight of the evidence suggests that this number is increasing by the year, and unless there are significant social shifts, I expect the rate of growth of actual Internet addicts and their functional equivalents to continue to accelerate.

Internet Pornography

I admit to having some trepidation about writing this section. I know it will be controversial and many people are likely to tune me out completely as I try to examine some concerns about this topic. People who speak up about this topic tend to be labeled extremists and subjected to all manner of *ad hominum* attacks and straw man lampooning without anyone honestly evaluating the validity of their points. However, I believe it would be irresponsible of me to move on from a conversation about the addictive potential of the Internet without identifying the part of the Internet that appears to have the greatest addictive potential of all: Internet pornography. Pornography has a colossal presence on the cyber-scape. Dr. Jill Manning observed: "[In 2008] there [were] well over 400 million pornographic websites on the Internet. If every pornographic web page was printed and piled up together, the stack of pornography would be over 15 miles high."[18] She notes that it has become an incredibly lucrative business. "Every second, $3,075.62 is spent on Internet pornography." Internet pornography is now a $97 billion dollar per year worldwide industry.

When a lot of money is involved, powerful people and forces are often at play to keep consumers in the business of consuming without thinking critically about the product in question. Sexuality is used to sell everything from shampoo to deodorant to woefully inadequate used cars—imagine how much easier the sale is when the product is a sexual experience itself. Saying it's like taking candy from a baby doesn't do it justice. The numbers tell the story: the rate of growth of pornography online is mind boggling. From 1998 to 2003, the number of pornographic websites grew by 1,800 percent.[19] Internet pornography has literally taken the cyber-scape by storm, to the point where it may be more appropriate to label it as a part of the cyber-atmosphere rather than merely a feature on the cyber-landscape. Internet pornography is approaching a state of cyber omnipresence and has become a persistent and powerful entity that is not only highly sought after, but actively seeks out potential users. It is the aggressive, expansionistic, idolatrous god of the Internet. It has been highly successful in its recruitment efforts. In 2008, an estimated 90 percent of young men and approximately 33 percent of young women reported using pornography. The average age of first use of Internet pornography is eleven years old. Of special concern is the fact that the average age of the onset of symptoms matching the criteria for addiction is also eleven years old.[20]

I find that Internet pornography is the most difficult cyber topic to get people to think critically about. However, some very compelling data suggest we need to take a long, thoughtful look at this trend of nearly universal Internet porn usage and how it affects us. One compelling example of the research in this field is a two-wave longitudinal study published in the scientific journal *CyberPsychology and Behavior* in which researchers in the Netherlands found that pornography has the highest addictive potential of all other Internet applications they examined, including gaming and social media.[21]

Internet pornography usage has become so widespread that it is hard to study it properly; so many people use it that it is hard to find a control group large enough to compare Internet pornography users against. That study has become more possible, however, as control groups of ex-Internet porn users have formed (driven to stop, by the way, typically by developing sexual dysfunction as a result of their pornography use). When combining this new information with previous research on pornography, what we are now learning is alarming. There is compelling evidence that Internet pornography is addictive and that it changes attitudes, behaviors, and even brain structure in those who use it in ways that have a negative impact on their emotional, relational, and sexual functioning. However, this negative impact is difficult for many people to detect in themselves, partially because people tend to start Internet pornography in their early teens or preteen years, and thus it plays a role in their development throughout the pivotal adolescent years of their sexual and intellectual growth. In this manner, the effects their pornography use has on them get lost in the smokescreen of their overall rapid development through their teenage years. Because they are going through puberty, they are changing anyway, so they lack the ability to see how they would have developed differently in the absence of Internet pornography. And because so many of their peers are involved in the same process, they often lack a group to compare and contrast their development with. Thus, pathways to easy insight on this matter are cut off to a large portion of the population. To paraphrase Internet pornography researcher Gary Wilson (stop snickering, it's not what it sounds like), if we all started smoking at age eleven, we would think smokers' lungs, chronic obstructive pulmonary disease, yellow teeth, and lung cancer were normal.

Dr. Jill Manning reviewed the most common scientifically supported negative effects of Internet pornography use.[22] These include objectification of women, buildup of tolerance and a need for more and "harder" forms of pornography, desensitization to sexual violence, internalization of misinformation about human sexuality, adopting attitudes about sex and relationships that have a negative effect on relationship quality and stability, difficulty with forming and maintaining intimate relationships, poor perception of actual sexual norms, increased risky activity (both sexual and otherwise), increases in non-sexual aggression, increases in sexual aggression, decreased desire for marriage and stable relationships, decreased desires to have and raise children, decreased trust in one's dating partner or spouse, decreased belief that long-term relationships are even realistic, sexual dissatisfaction (even leading up to actual sexual performance issues), increased risk of infidelity, increased risk of separation or divorce, distorted views of sexuality (the focus becomes a relationship with sex rather than a relationship with a person), increased risk of job loss, increased risk of belief that there are no real consequences connected to having a sexual relationship with someone you have no emotional attachment or commitment to, increased risk of developing a negative body image, and last but certainly not least, risk of addiction. That's a pretty long list of concerns that most people are either oblivious to or complacent about.

At the time I am writing this book, there have been recent public outcries about rape culture, particularly on college campuses. Rightfully so, given that rape culture has become nearly synonymous with fraternity culture, one in four women in the United States can expect to have been raped by the time they graduate from college.[23] This is completely outrageous, and many voices have been raised against this trend. Hauntingly absent from the public discourse—as far as I have been able to tell—is an examination of how Internet pornography both supports and fuels rape culture. The general conversation seems to hint around it in a tiptoeing, seemingly intimidated fashion, yet for some reason we fail to openly acknowledge a seemingly obvious connection between the aspects of pornography that help create an objectifying mindset and the result of that mindset played out in people's individual actions and our collective attitudes.

We know that Internet pornography fuels a sexualized, objectified view of women. That attitude is at the heart of rape culture. We also know that Internet pornography use tends to train us on a neurological level to disconnect how we use our sexuality from any sense of real-world consequences. Add that to the way it helps increase both nonsexual and sexual aggression, and we have a real problem on our hands. That's a perfect recipe for rape culture, and it is so widespread as to reasonably be considered functionally ubiquitous. Unless we deal with the roots of what fuels rape-friendly attitudes, we are doomed to flail away ineffectively at the branches of the problem by teaching men not to rape (can you imagine the *Not Raping People for Dummies* book that would inspire?), trying to change the college culture, teaching women to give a very enthusiastic YES so they can't be misunderstood (I wish I was merely making that one up), and so on. I'm going to go on the record as saying these efforts by themselves are doomed to miserable failure. They are too superficial, and they are missing the point. Anyone wishing to drain a swamp must start by eliminating the flow of the water into the swampy area, not just trying to bail the water out of it as quickly as possible.

I am reminded of the Cherokee legend of the two wolves in which an old Cherokee man taught his grandson about life. "A fight is going on inside me," he said to the boy. "It is a terrible fight, and it is between two wolves. One is evil—he is anger, envy, sorrow, regret, greed, arrogance, self-pity, guilt, resentment, inferiority, lies, false pride, superiority, and ego. I have felt at times a great hate for those that have taken so much, with no sorrow for what they do. But hate wears you down, and does not hurt your enemy. It is like taking poison and wishing your enemy would die. I have struggled with these feelings many times, and felt this wolf stalking within me. He is full of anger and selfishness. The littlest thing will set him into a fit of temper. He fights everyone, all the time, for no reason. He cannot think because his anger and hatred are so great. He seeks to master others and the world around him, bending them to serve his own whims. In reality, he is the slave to his own appetites and impulses. In the end, he will leave nothing in his wake but sadness and destruction."

He continued, "The other wolf is good—he is joy, peace, love, hope, serenity, humility, kindness, benevolence, empathy, generosity, truth, compassion, and faith. He lives in harmony with all around him and does not take offense. He is wise and guides his life by his wisdom, not by his impulses, his whims, or his pride. He will only fight when it is right to do so, and then only in the right way. He is master of himself above all. He can live at peace with the world around him, and it willingly lends him its strength for doing so.

"Sometimes, it is hard to live with these two wolves inside me, for both of them try to dominate my spirit. The same fight is going on inside you—and inside every other person, too."

The grandson thought about it for a minute and then asked his grandfather, "Which wolf will win?"

The old Cherokee simply replied, "The answer to that is simple, my son: the wolf that will win is the one that you feed."

Why do we feed the wolf of the objectification and commoditization of women through widespread Internet pornography use until that wolf is strong and vital and then act surprised when it goes on the prowl and makes humans its prey? I believe when we feed this particular wolf, we feed the very underpinnings of rape culture. We are smarter than this. I believe it is the seductive and addictive nature of Internet pornography that compels us to be willingly ignorant of these connections when they are blatantly obvious.

I want to be clear about something. I am not saying that Internet pornography is the sole cause of the rape culture. Nor am I saying it is where rape culture began. After all, rape culture has been with us since time immemorial. What I am saying is that the attitudes and effects of pornography are highly compatible with—and thus highly likely to contribute to—the development and spread of rape culture in individuals and in society. Americans are often obsessed with diets, yet we think little about the diet of our minds. We are affected by what we take in mentally, as evidenced by the previous conversation in this book about how susceptible we are to Internet opinions. What we feed our minds with forms neurological structures that remain with us on a deeper level than any slice of cheesecake or heaping plate of chicken bacon fettuccine Alfredo can do. If this is true of everything else we take in mentally, how could it be false of the objectifying attitudes of Internet pornography? It's time for us to become willing to really think about this.

Besides pornography's contributions to rape culture, I have been left to ponder whether there is a real and alarming connection between current stratospherically high levels of divorce and relationship dissolution and the ways that Internet pornography impairs us in our emotional regulation, relationship skills and attributes, and relationally sensitive approach to sexuality. As I examine what I know about how the human mind works and the societal trends in play, I believe there is a connection here, and I think as time goes on we will find the evidence that Internet pornography is a greater contributor to this trend than many of us would like to believe. Consider this: in 2002, the American Academy of Matrimonial (Divorce) Lawyers found that 56 percent of divorce cases that year involved one spouse having an obsessive interest in pornography. In other words, that means in 2002, Internet pornography was a major player in over half of all divorces in the United States of America.[24] Now consider this: how much has Internet pornography evolved and spread since 2002? That's sobering food for thought when it comes to the impact pornography seems to have on the stability of marriages and families.

It is not my intention to go into all the research on Internet pornography here in this book, but for those who wish to learn more, I highly suggest going to www.yourbrainonporn.com. I also suggest watching the Ted Talk "The Great Porn Experiment" by Gary Wilson, available at www.youtube.com/watch?v=wSF82AwSDiU.

What Is Realistic?

If someone has an Internet addiction, what is a realistic goal for them? Do they just need to "try harder" or "be more responsible"? Or, like someone addicted to alcohol or drugs, do they need to refrain from all Internet use? Dr. Kimberly Young, a pioneer in the field of treating Internet addictions, offers the following recommendation:

Use of the Internet is legitimate in business and home practice, such as electronic correspondence to vendors or electronic banking. Therefore, traditional abstinence models are not practical interventions when they prescribe banned Internet use in most cases. The focus of treatment should consist of moderate Internet use overall. While moderated Internet use is the primary goal, abstinence of problematic application is often necessary. For example . . . it is often discovered that a specific application such as a chat room, an interactive game, or a certain set of adult web sites will trigger Internet binges. Moderation of the trigger application may fail, however, because of its inherent allure and [people] will need to stop all activity surrounding that application. It is essential to help the [person] target and abstain from problematic application(s) while retaining controlled use of legitimate Internet usage.[25]

What that means is that when a person has discovered that their relationship with social media, smartphones, and the Internet in general has become unhealthy, several layers of change need to be undertaken in order to transform the relationship into something healthy and sustainable. The universal requirement under these circumstances will be a reduction in the amount of time devoted to social media and the Internet. From all I have seen and experienced, there is really no way to make an unhealthy relationship with the cyberspace healthy without trimming back the investment of time. In the next chapter, we will discuss specific guidelines for time limits. Beyond time limits, however, most people will find that they need to make changes in exactly which apps and sites they engage with and precisely how they interact with specific sites and apps.

As Dr. Young noted, sometimes the interface between our biological makeup and a specific app has been molded by our choices and our history with that app in such a way that it is not a realistic expectation for us to be able to engage in that specific app or site without the relationship becoming unhealthy. This is frequently the case when our relationship with a specific app or site has crossed over into full-blown addiction. This is often a very difficult truth for a person to accept. People often resist this idea and try to prove it wrong, only to fail in those attempts again and again. As hard as it may be, we need to develop an open mind to the idea that we may be able to have a healthy relationship with the cyber-scape only if we separate ourselves from our most problematic relationships online. For example, in one case I know of, a woman discovered that she needed to stop participating in political discussion sites online because she found she was not capable of using those sites without getting sucked into heated debates and groupthink.

Complete departure from specific problematic sites and apps is not always necessary. Sometimes, what needs to change are the parameters under which we use them. For example, I worked with a young man who had various Facebook accounts and operated as a moderator on a number of pages focused around Internet memes. He found that he needed to eliminate all but one Facebook account, leave his role as moderator, and focus his Facebook activities on having actual conversations with friends he actually knows in real life, rather than indulging his curiosity and boredom by riding the endless merry-go-round of memes.

Overall, if you are unwilling to make any changes, don't expect anything to get any better. In fact, the trends in this area would suggest that if your relationship with social media and smartphones is unhealthy and you are unwilling to make changes, the unhealthy aspects of the situation will only grow worse. I believe the largest challenge is to become honest with oneself. We are prone to deny our problems or to try to convince ourselves that a particular site or app that falls in the "needs to be eliminated" category really should only be in the "needs different parameters" category. It is hard to make a self-analysis in this area without entering self-deception. In fact, I have come to expect people to go through a grieving process along with this self-analysis, akin to the stages of grief identified by Elisabeth Kübler-Ross.[26] We are prone to start with denial. If our relationship with smartphones and social media is unhealthy, it is also pleasurable and immediately gratifying. The thought of having to change it is often irritating and troubling. Rather than considering that we may have a problem, we lose ourselves in a state of denial that is assisted by our cyber distraction.

In moments when our denial is pierced to some degree or other, we often respond with anger. We find the truths of our situation to be most inconvenient. Rather than face them, we may become critical of the person or people who are trying to show us the truth about our situation. We may feel that we are being imposed upon and that our rights are being violated. We may justify ourselves by noting that our behavior is not really any different than what we observe other people doing, refusing to think critically about whether the relationship is actually healthy or merely common.

When we cannot deny that the relationship has become unhealthy, we may try to bargain our way out of the implicated changes needed in our attitudes and actions. We will almost always have difficulty admitting to ourselves when a relationship with an app or a site has become so unhealthy that it needs to be discontinued. We will try to find ways to justify skirting boundaries that would clearly benefit us. We may try to reason with ourselves that by doing other good things in our lives, we have "earned" the right to maintain an unhealthy relationship with social media. Or, we may set some fictional future date in which we will make the changes we can see that we need to make. Procrastination thus becomes the ultimate form of self-deception. After all, we admit we need to change, but we placate ourselves with the myth that we will do it later. How comforting we find this lie!

When it becomes all too clear that action is needed now, we often fall into a state of depression. We focus on all the things we think we will lose through making the needed changes. We often struggle to see the benefits and the joys we will open ourselves up to through making the changes. And yet, we are finally resigned to our fate of change, and we often slowly and miserably drag our feet along the path to change, like someone condemned to death moping their way toward the gallows to be hanged.

If we persist in the process, however, we arrive at acceptance. This is not just a change of behavior but a change of heart. It is an ability to look upon our past unhealthy relationship with different eyes. It is the ability to acknowledge and embrace the benefits of the changes we have made. And, in its highest form, it brings with it a sense of gratefulness that we came to such an understanding and made the changes that we did.

This process, of course, takes time. I have found that it usually starts with our head, in our acknowledgment that we have a problem. It takes a while for the heart to catch up with the head in this process of change. In fact, it is usually only after we have started to take action that our feelings begin to change. We must often begin this journey toward greater health with the path ahead of us lit only by the meager light of the candle of our recognition of what we need to do differently. As we exercise the courage to do so, and trust in the wisdom of our fragile new vision, the path is eventually illuminated by the sunrise of our change of heart. Under that light, we find the path much easier to travel upon. In fact, under this greater light, we often come to find the journey quite liberating. But we must remember that recovery is a journey we all begin in the dark.

Endnotes

1. Medical News Today (2011). WHO study: Alcohol is international number one killer, AIDS second. Retrieved July 31, 2014, from http://www.medicalnewstoday.com/articles/216328.php.

2. Brookshire, B. (2014). Addiction showcases the brain's flexibility. *Science News*. Retrieved August 14, 2014, from https://www.sciencenews.org/blog/scicurious/addiction-showcases-brain-flexibility.

3. Butler, M. H. (2010). *Spiritual exodus: A latter-day saint guide to recovery from behavioral addiction*. Utah: BYU Academic.

4. Brookshire, ibid.

5. Butler, ibid.

6. Khalaf, S. (2014). The rise of the mobile addict. *Flurry*. Retrieved August 1, 2014, from http://www.flurry.com/blog/flurry-insights/rise-mobile-addict#.U9wDquNdWSp.

7. Meeker, M. (2013). 2013 internet trends. *Kleiner, Perkins, Caufield, Byers*. Retrieved August 1, 2014, from http://www.kpcb.com/insights/2013-internet-trends.

8. Net Addiction (2013). A growing epidemic. Retrieved August 1, 2014, from http://netaddiction.com/.

9. Young, K. (1996) Addictive use of the Internet: A case that breaks the stereotype. *Psychology Report*, 899-902.

10. Net Addiction, 2013.

11. China Youth Association for Network Development (CYAND). (2005). Report of China teenagers' Internet addiction information 2005. Beijing, China.

12. Orzack, M. H. (1999). Computer addiction: Is it real or virtual? *Harvard Mental Health Letter, 15*(7), 8.

13. Widatyanto, L. & McMurren, M. (2004). The psychometric properties of the Internet Addiction Test. *CyberPsychology & Behavior, 7*(4), 445-453. Ferraro, G., Caci, B., D'Amico, A., & Di Blasi, M. (2007). Internet addiction disorder: An Italian study. *CyberPsychology & Behavior, 10*(2), 170-175. Khazaal, Y., Billieux, J., Thorens, G., Khan, R., Louati, T., Scarlatti, E., et al. (2008). French validation of the Internet Addiction Test. *CyberPyschology & Behavior, 11*(6), 703-706. Young, K. S. (2011). Clinical assessment of internet-addicted clients. In K. S. Young & C. N. de Abreu (Eds.) *Internet addiction: A handbook and guide to evaluation and treatment*. New Jersey: John Wiley & Sons, Inc.

14. Internet Overuse. Internet addiction test (IAT) by Dr. Kimberly Young. Retrieved May 23, 2017, from http://www.globaladdiction.org/dldocs/GLOBALADDICTION-Scales-InternetAddictionTest.pdf. Used with permission from Dr. Kimberly S. Young.

15. Aboujaoude, E., Koran, L. M., Gamel, N., Large, M. D., & Serpe, R. T. (2006). Potential markers for problematic Internet use: A telephone

survey of 2,513 adults. *CNS Spectrum, The Journal of Neuropsychiatric Medicine, 11*(10), 750-755.

16. Greenfield, D. N. (1999). Psychological characteristics of compulsive Internet use: A preliminary analysis. *CyberPsychology & Behavior, 2,* 403-412.

17. Khalaf, S. (2014). The rise of the mobile addict. *Flurry.* Retrieved August 1, 2014, from http://www.flurry.com/blog/flurry-insights/rise-mobile-addict#.U9wDquNdWSp.

18. Manning, J.C. (2008). *What's the big deal about pornography?* Michigan: Sheridan Books.

19. Paul, P. (2004). The porn factor. *Time 163*(3), 99-100.

20. Carroll, J. S., Padilla-Walker, L. M., Nelson, L. J., Olson, C. D., Barry, C. M., & Madsen, S. D. (2008). Generation xxx: Pornography acceptance and use among emerging adults. *Journal of Adolescent Research, 23*(1), 6-30.

21. Meerkerk, G. J., Van Den Eijnden, R. J. J. M., & Garretsen, H. F. L. (2006). *CyberPsychology and Behavior, 9*(1), 95-103.

22. Manning, ibid.

23. Fisher, B. S., Cullen, F. T., & Turner, M. G. (2000). *The sexual victimization of college women.* Washington, DC: National Institute of Justice, US Department of Justice.

24. Manning, ibid.

25. Young, K. S. (2011). Clinical assessment of Internet-addicted clients. In K. S. Young & C. N. de Abreu (Eds.) *Internet addiction: A handbook and guide to evaluation and treatment.* New Jersey: John Wiley & Sons, Inc.

26. Kübler-Ross, E. (1969) *On death and dying.* New York: Routledge. Kübler-Ross, E. (2005) *On grief and grieving: Finding the meaning of grief through the five stages of loss.* New York: Scribner.

CHAPTER 6

VIDEO GAMES

Video games have taken a powerful and prominent position in our modern society. Whereas once they were an obscure toy for fringe enthusiasts, video games have become a mainstream phenomenon. In spite of the stereotype of the typical gamer being the socially awkward, basement-dwelling teenage boy, the average gamer in the United States is around 30 years old. What may surprise many people is that in the 25–35 year old bracket (which is the median age bracket for gamers), female gamers far outnumber male gamers, with 65 percent of women in that age group self-reporting that they play video games, as compared with only 35 percent of their male counterparts. The predominance of relatively young adult female gamers is attributed largely to the growth of social media and smartphone games such as *Candy Crush Saga* or other casual games on sites such as Yahoo!, AOL Games, PopCap games, and so forth.[1] Some hardcore, male, M-rated video game enthusiasts take great umbrage at the thought of such games qualifying someone as being a gamer. In spite of the philosophical objections of the most zealous denizens of Xbox Live, the fact remains that video games now hold a prominent role in the lives of a very large and diverse portion of our population.

When a phenomenon is common, critical thinking about it tends not to be. As with other parts of the cyber-scape, I usually observe a lot of polarized thought when I talk with people about video games. There are those who utterly abhor them as digital devil spawn and think they should be eradicated. We've all heard the statements on that side of things: video games cause ADHD, video games make kids violent, video games destroy social skills, and so forth. On the other hand, there are those who are deeply in love with video games and don't see any reason to be concerned with them whatsoever. These people often express the opinion *they're just games*, as if simply restating what they are is the end of all critical thought that may be required with this issue. With video games—and with any topic, really—I worry significantly about the quality of our thinking when we make monolithic judgment calls, judging the whole phenomenon as if there were no nuance to it whatsoever. That kind of reasoning is not all that different from deciding whether you want to buy a piece of property by examining a few square feet of it and extrapolating that what you see in those few square feet is a completely accurate representative sample of what you will find if you carefully scrutinized the whole plot of land. I have said it before, and I will say it again: polarized thinking is poor thinking, whether it be with video games or whether it be with any other subject.

I feel that I am in good company when renowned video game researcher Dr. Douglas Gentile of Iowa State University expresses the same opinion. "Polarized rhetoric is damaging and ultimately misses the point," he observes. "Video games are neither 'good' nor 'bad.'"[2] A careful and thoughtful examination of people's relationships with video games reveals the potential for both benefits and problems. Understanding why we see some people benefit and some people struggle because of their relationship with video games requires a more complete understanding of the range of what video games are and how they interact with what we are. Therefore, I would like to begin our discussion about video games by examining a number of the benefits and pitfalls we know video games present.

Gaming Benefit: Faster Visual Information Processing and Cognitive Flexibility

People who regularly play video games develop fast and accurate visual information processing abilities. While gamers develop this skill and apply it to the games they play, they benefit from these increased abilities in areas of their lives besides gaming. People who play video games regularly show advanced performance in mental visualization and rotation skills (for example, accurately thinking in 3D), visual and spatial memory, and tasks requiring divided attention. The accuracy of regular gamers on these tasks does not decrease as the speed of the tasks increases, as demonstrated both in video games and in nongaming lab tests.[3]

Another study examined the potential for the game *StarCraft* to increase people's cognitive flexibility, including the capacity to switch between tasks, think about multiple ideas simultaneously, and solve problems under time pressure.[4] The researchers recruited young adults who normally played video games for less than two hours per week (which, for this specific study, led to the research group being all female, since they were unable to find enough young adult males who played video games for less than two hours per week), and assigned them to play *StarCraft* for forty hours over a six to eight week period, averaging about five to six and one-half hours of gaming per week. The participants who played *StarCraft* for this amount of time showed substantial improvement in speed and accuracy of tasks requiring cognitive flexibility, creative problem solving, and "out of the box" thinking.

This should not be taken to mean that all video games improve cognitive flexibility. The researchers in this study also tested the game *The Sims*, a slow-paced game that requires little strategy or cognitive flexibility. They found that research participants who played *The Sims* did not show the same improvements in cognitive flexibility demonstrated by *StarCraft* players. Therefore, a game's mechanics and the way it interfaces with human cognitive processes matters when it comes to a game's ability to promote cognitive development.

Gaming Benefit: Increased Creativity

In a study of nearly 500 twelve-year-old children, researchers from Michigan State University utilized several different measures of creativity, such as drawing pictures and writing stories, to compare the creativity of children who played video games to children who did not. They found that children who played video games displayed greater creativity than children who did not play video games. They also measured several other activities such as cell phone use and texting, Internet use, and nongaming computer use and found that none of these other forms of electronic use were correlated with increased creativity; only playing video games had that connection.[5]

Gaming Benefit: Improved Overall Learning Ability

A study out of the University of Rochester found that playing action-oriented video games actually helps increase a person's overall learning ability, not just the specific mental processes that the game requires them to use. Daphne Bavelier, a research professor of brain and cognitive sciences, stated, "Prior research by our group and others has shown that action gamers excel at many tasks. In this new study, we show they excel because they are better learners. And they become better learners by playing the fast-paced action games."[6] She and her coresearchers explain that the brain utilizes templates to improve its prediction skills, and the better these templates are, the better we are at learning, analyzing, improvising, adapting, and "thinking on our feet" in general. They found that when they gave research participants a task that required them to use perceptual learning, people who played action video games outperformed those in the control group who did not, specifically displaying significantly faster adapting and learning abilities. They also found that they could improve the learning and improvising performance of non video game playing participants by having them train by playing action-oriented video games. Thus, they demonstrated that playing action-oriented video games actually created these improved abilities. These improvements held steady even a year later. It appears that playing action-oriented video games can be an effective tool for helping our brains develop the ability to create accurate templates faster, thus improving our ability to perform and adapt in unfamiliar situations that require learning.[7]

Gaming Benefit: Skills Transferable to Real Life

In spite of the research on how video games can improve various brain functions, many people express concerns that time spent playing video games is wasted time. Some critics of the concept that video games improve cognitive abilities have suggested that the skills and abilities gained from playing video games only help people play video games better and do not translate over into real-life benefits. However, recent research suggests this is not the case. Rather, video games have the potential to teach skills and abilities that can transfer over to useful and marketable real-life skills. For example, a study by the University of Texas Medical Branch at Galveston engaged teenage gamers in the same robotic surgery simulations used to teach surgery to doctors.[8] Using skills they had garnered from playing video games, these teenagers actually outperformed medical residents in the simulated surgery procedures. However, before you take this as license to play video games all day long and claim that you are preparing for your career as a neurosurgeon, you must know there was actually a "sweet spot," a balance point at which gaming yielded the maximum benefits. It was not a simple matter of "more is better." On the contrary, the best results were seen in students who played video games up to two hours daily and not those who played four hours daily. Interestingly enough (although it should not be surprising), this matches up perfectly with the American Academy of Pediatrics' recommendation that screen time unrelated to work or homework should be limited to one to two hours per day.[9] Thus, in the absence of usage becoming excessive, playing video games within the recommended amounts was actually beneficial and applicable to a wide variety of real-life situations. Maybe the next time you need surgery, you should ask your surgeon about his or her video game playing habits. It's just a thought.

Another example of ways in which gaming skills offer significant real-world benefits is the story of a game called *Fold.it*. For fifteen years, skilled medical researchers were stumped in their efforts to develop treatments for AIDS due to the difficulty of mapping out a protein known as Mason-Pfizer monkey virus retroviral protease (which, by the way, would make a great name for an indie rock band). Because conventional approaches to mapping the protein were running into seemingly impossible roadblocks, the researchers from the University of Washington decided to turn the problem into a game and release it on the Internet. The game tasked players with predicting the structure of the protein and mapping it, with better models earning more points. Astonishingly, the online players of *Fold.it* were able to solve the problem in just three weeks. Even more amazing is that only a handful of the online players of *Fold.it* had any background in molecular biology whatsoever. The players' gaming-refined spatial reasoning skills and experience allowed them to accurately resolve this incredibly complex molecular biology problem with no previous scientific understanding of the subject matter.[10] To me, that speaks volumes about the very real value of skills that can be gained from gaming.

Gaming Benefit: Emotional and Cognitive Well-Being for Seniors

Researchers out of North Carolina State University demonstrated that senior citizens can reap important benefits from playing video games. The results of the study demonstrated that senior citizens who played video games, even if they only played occasionally, reported higher overall levels of well-being. On the other hand, senior citizens who did not play video games were more likely to report negative emotions and had higher levels of depression.[11]

One well-documented hardship of aging is a decline in a wide range of cognitive abilities. Video games show great promise as a valuable tool for helping fight this effect of aging through their potential to offset or even reverse some of the negative effects of aging on senior citizens' brains. Researchers at UC San Francisco[12] utilized a video game called *NeuroRacer*, which combines driving a digital car through a serpentine course using left hand controls while simultaneously shooting targets using right hand controls. As players get better, the game gets harder, constantly pushing the player to improve rather than being able to take it easy with the progress they have already made. These researchers used *NeuroRacer* to measure cognitive control, which they define as "a set of neural processes that allow us to interact with our complex environment in a goal-directed manner." The processes of cognitive control are especially crucial for tasks that require multitasking. Playing *NeuroRacer* requires extensive multitasking: maintaining situational awareness, responding to certain stimuli with one hand while responding to different stimuli with the other, adapting to changing situations, and so on. These abilities naturally decline significantly with age. However, people ages sixty to eight-five who played *NeuroRacer* for twelve hours in a month improved their cognitive control so much that their cognitive control abilities surpassed those of the average twenty-year-old who had not trained with the game. Even after the senior citizens spent a six-month break from playing the game, they still maintained the improvements they had made in this area.

NeuroRacer was specifically designed and fine-tuned to produce these results, and as such, it is premature to assume that other games that merely have similar mechanics will benefit at the same level. Sadly, *NeuroRacer* is not available for purchase, but its creators are currently creating a mobile app called *Project: EVO* that will capitalize upon all they learned with *NeuroRacer* to provide a fine-tuned video game tool for enhancing cognitive control. Although one should not assume that video games in general will have this specific benefit, logically other games that use similar mechanics will likely have similar results (although possibly not as dramatic or focused because they only approximate the same mechanics), especially if they have a growing difficulty level as the player progresses to continuously challenge and promote the growth of their cognitive abilities. For example, Nintendo Wii games that require the player to use the Wii control in one hand and the nunchuck in the other for performing different gaming functions (such as steering and aiming in *The Legend of Zelda: Twilight Princess* or *Tron Evolution: Battle Grids)* would likely interface with the brain in a fashion at least somewhat similar to *NeuroRacer*. Thus, there is a good chance of them producing at least some of the same benefits, although the degree to which similar benefits will be reaped depends upon the degree to which specific gaming mechanics activate the same cognitive processes. More research is needed to back up these hypotheses before making any definitive statements, however.

Fortunately, *NeuroRacer* is not the "only show in town" when it comes to games that have been demonstrated to help maintain and even rejuvenate cognitive functions in older adults. There are a number of other specifically designed "brain trainer" games, including *Lumosity, CogniFit Brain Fitness, Brain Trainer Special, Brain Fitness Pro, Fit Brains Trainer,* and *Eidetic.*[13] The mounting research on the outcomes of these games is encouraging. For example, *Lumosity,* a web-based program that offers a personalized cognitive training program for improving memory and attention, has also conducted research on the effects of their games on older adults. In one study evaluating the effects of a memory training game, researchers found that older *Lumosity* players' baseline memory measures were 20 percent lower than younger people at the peak of their cognitive abilities. This is consistent with what we know about how attention and memory decline with age. After twenty-five rounds of *Lumosity's Memory Match* game, older users' post-training memory scores vastly improved and were much closer to the baseline measures for people in their cognitive prime. For example, the difference between a seventy-four-year-old who trained with *Lumosity* and a sixteen-year-old who did not train shrunk to only 7 percent, essentially rejuvenating their abilities by 13 percent.[14]

Developers of these specifically designed "brain training" video games frequently warn that people should not assume that all video games have similar benefits. After all, these video games were specifically designed based off of scientific principles about neuroplasticity and brain development. To be certain, it would be an error to assume that all other video games had similar results. However, it would also be premature to assume that at least some kinds of video games that are not specifically designed to promote positive brain development do not have similar results, or possibly even superior ones. For example, in the first study of its kind that I am aware of, Florida State University researchers[15] conducted a pilot study in which they compared the cognitive skills of problem solving, spatial perception, and emotional persistence for people who trained with *Lumosity* with the same outcomes from a commercial, noneducational video game named *Portal 2.* For those unfamiliar with the Portal series, they are a unique set of games involving truly mind-bending puzzles that must be solved with a wormhole-generating portal gun. They were designed to be cerebral and sophisticated video games and are probably the best of their kind on the market, but they are not necessarily purposefully designed to be neurologically enhancing games. The results were intriguing; study participants who played *Portal 2* scored higher in each measure and showed more improvement than people who trained with *Lumosity*.

Given what I have learned about the interface between games and brains, I do not consider this finding surprising. Neuronal paths are strengthened by repetition (the first rule of neuroscience is "brain cells that fire together wire together"), and brain growth is promoted by novel stimuli that require the brain to expand beyond its previous methods in order to solve new problems. Video games can create unique worlds and unusual circumstances that people would never encounter in real life, and thus playing such games can help enhance brain growth and development through making the brain expand beyond experiences it is likely to have in everyday life. (Incidentally, if your real life is at all like *Portal 2*, I'd love to know where you got your portal gun from. Those things could come in pretty handy!) Because of this, there is reason to believe that other games similar to the Portal series—such as *Braid*, *QUBE*, *Antichamber*, *The Swapper*, *Magrunner: Dark Pulse*, *The Ball*, *Fez*, *World of Goo*, *TAG: The Power of Paint*, *Perspective*, *Monument Valley*, *Quantum Conundrum*, the *Half Life* series, *The Talos Principle*, or other games that involve unique and unusual puzzle mechanics with increasing difficulty levels—can be beneficial in ways similar to dedicated brain trainers such as *Lumosity*.

Some noncomparative studies also demonstrate cognitive benefits emerging from other video game genres. Scientists at the University of Illinois[16] provided 23.5 hours of training for older adults with a nation-building strategy game known as *Rise of Nations*. The scientists compared them with a control group on executive functions such as being able to switch between tasks, reasoning skills, working memory, and short-term visual memory. They also included tests of memory recall, visual spatial reasoning, and response inhibition (self-control). The senior citizens who trained with *Rise of Nations* performed better than the control group in areas of working memory, switching between tasks, reasoning ability, and short-term visual memory. Their results suggest that including strategic video games such as *Rise of Nations* as a part of older adults' self-care routines has great promise in helping them retain and even regain important cognitive functions.

Rise of Nations falls in a category of games known as 4X strategy games (technically, it is a blend between 4X and Real Time Strategy). Logically, other 4X games that offer similar gaming mechanics will likely have the same benefits. Thus, encouraging senior citizens to play games in the genre of 4X—such as the *Civilization* series, the *Master of Orion* series, *Alpha Centauri*, the *Galactic Civilizations* series, *Endless Space*, the *Age of Wonders* series, the *Age of Empires* series, and so forth—is recommended. And because *Rise of Nations* is also partially a Real Time Strategy (RTS), logic would suggest that we should find similar benefits from other Real Time Strategy games such as the *Supreme Commander* series, the *Total War series*, the *StarCraft* series, the *Sins of a Solar Empire* series, and *Planetary Annihilation*. Future research is needed to determine if the blend of 4X and RTS genres gives greater benefit than either of these two genres may offer separately, or if the combination of both is needed for the benefits seen in this study of *Rise of Nations*. Until further research provides more insight, I believe there is enough evidence of the potential benefits of 4X/RTS games for the cognitive well-being of older adults to suggest that if you are concerned about the health of your grandparents and are wondering what to get them for their next birthday (I mean come on, how many pairs of golfing socks does grandpa really need?), these types of games may well be worth considering.

Gaming Benefit: Superior Math Teaching Abilities

Experienced teachers will testify that teaching and learning go much better in the classroom when students feel that the material they are learning is both fun and engaging. Teaching-focused games provide an opportunity for education to be just that, and as such provide opportunities for not only making learning easier but also more effective. For example, studies on one math teaching program, *Monkey Tales*, showed that children who played the game as a means of learning math improved their pre-test/post-test scores by 6 percent, compared to increases of 4 percent for students who used traditional math training exercises and 2 percent for students who received no training. In other words, the difference in score increases using *Monkey Tales* above standard math teaching methods was as large as the difference between standard math teaching methods and no instruction at all. Students who played *Monkey Tales* also showed better results in measures of engagement and learning efficiency, and they reported they found learning through *Monkey Tales* more enjoyable, engaging, and motivating than other methods.[17]

Gaming Benefit: Teaching Emotional Regulation

Just as games can be helpful in teaching math, "gamification" has been demonstrated to be helpful when teaching people a variety of academic subjects. Beyond academics, games can also be beneficial when it comes to teaching skills that help with emotional regulation and promote general mental and emotional health. One example of such a game is *Personal Zen*. This app is the result of collaboration between a professor of psychology and neuroscience and a game developer. An initial study has shown that it effectively reduces anxiety levels of those who play the game.[18] The game developer recommends playing the game for ten minutes daily to build up resilience to stress and anxiety over time and also encourages people to do a ten-minute gaming session to prepare themselves when entering anxiety-provoking situations.

Another app similar to *Personal Zen* is *Happify*, which is also based on a decade's worth of research in the fields of psychology and neuroscience. This app is designed to help people learn to cope with stress, overcome negative thought patterns, develop gratitude and empathy, and develop a community of positive supporters. Yet another app, *ReliefLink*, was primarily designed as a powerful tool to help with suicide prevention, but it has also proven useful as a general mood tracker and teaching method for various emotional coping skills.[19] These games, and those like them, provide an accessible and useful resource for people seeking help in developing emotional coping skills, increasing personal resilience, and coping through challenging personal experiences.

Gaming Benefit: Positive Outcomes for Girls

Other real-world benefits from playing video games include improved positive emotional and relational outcomes for girls. A study out of Brigham Young University found that daughters who play video games with their parents display a surprising range of benefits, including decreased levels of aggression, improved positive and pro-social behaviors, increased sense of connection to their families, and improved measures of mental health.[20] Of course, savvy consumers of research may point out that these apparent benefits may not actually be the results of playing video games but rather the result of these girls spending time with their parents. However, in this case, the statistical analysis controlled for these variables found that coplaying video games with a parent (as opposed to other activities) still accounted for 20 percent of the variation in these positive outcomes. In other words, girls playing video games with their parents showed added benefits above and beyond merely engaging in any other generic activity with their parents. Evidence suggests that these benefits were particularly manifest in father-daughter relationships, although that could partially be because fewer mothers reported playing video games with their daughters. Nonetheless, coplaying video games clearly helped produce a variety of positive outcomes that most people would love to see in their daughters.

However, there is one major caveat here: the age-appropriateness of the video games was an important factor in producing benefits for girls playing games with their parents. When girls played games such as *Mario Kart, Mario Brothers, Wii Sports, Rock Band,* and *Guitar Hero,* all of these benefits were present. Note that all of these examples are rated E or T and thus are age appropriate. On the other hand, when parents played rated M games with their daughters, it weakened the connection between playing video games together and the degree of family connectedness that was felt.

In contrast, boys playing video games with parents was not a statistically significant contributor to the positive outcomes these researchers examined. The researchers posited that this may be due to the fact that boys tend to play more video games with their friends, so the experience of gaming with parents didn't stand out as much. However, if we think critically about this situation, I think there is a more compelling explanation. We noted that with the girls, the benefits were present with age-appropriate games but not with M-rated games. The games the boys tended to play with their parents were from the *Call of Duty* and the *Halo* series, all of which are rated M.

The M rating was shown to be corrosive of the positive benefits for girls to the point that it negated the benefits. That could be a part of why the benefits aren't apparent with the boys in this study. In other words, boys may not have the same benefits because they tend to play M-rated games with their parents. To be fair, boys also tended to play *Wii Sports* with their parents, which is rated E, but the fact that this was factored in with rated M games seemed to cancel out the possible benefits. It appears that what you play matters when it comes to certain positive outcome.

Gaming Benefit: Improved Reading Skills for Dyslexic Children

In what I consider a very exciting finding, researchers discovered that time spent playing action video games can actually help children with dyslexia read better.[21] Specifically, dyslexic children who played twelve hours of action video games per week showed greater improvement in their reading skills than dyslexic children in a control group that had no intervention and also a group of dyslexic children that had demanding traditional reading treatments for dyslexia. In other words, action gaming as an intervention produced better results than the standard, time-tested reading interventions for dyslexic children.

It seems counterintuitive that playing video games that don't require reading skills improves reading for dyslexic children better than interventions focused on reading, yet that is exactly what the research demonstrates. The short answer to this apparently puzzling outcome is that recent research has begun to tie the root dynamics of dyslexia to problems with visual attention rather than problems with language skills. By building visual attention skills, the action-oriented video games were intervening upon what appears to be a key neurological element of dyslexia. The researchers stated, "Action video games enhance many aspects of visual attention, mainly improving the extraction of information from the environment. . . . Dyslexic children [who played action video games] learned to orient and focus their attention more efficiently to extract the relevant information of a written word more rapidly."[22] It should be noted that this effect was only seen in action-oriented video games but not in other types of games. Dyslexic children playing action video games were able to read faster without losing accuracy and also showed gains in other tests of attention.

Before anyone gets too carried away, this should not be taken as a *carte blanche* to have dyslexic children play as many action video games as they want for as long as they want. Note that the positive benefits were found in that "golden zone" of approximately two hours per day, assuming the gamers took a day off from gaming each week. You'll notice that specific number for time limits keeps showing up rather frequently when we talk about beneficial "doses" of video games.

Gaming Benefit: Enhancement of Medical Treatments

Researchers from the University of Utah reviewed the efficacy of various specially designed video games in helping promote positive health care behaviors, motivation, and emotional well-being for a variety of health concerns, including diabetes, asthma, obesity, autism, depression, stroke, Parkinson's disease, cancer, and injuries requiring physical rehabilitation.[23] In all of these areas, they noted that specifically designed video games have been effective in educating patients and effectively motivating them to actually follow through with important self-care items that help with their specific diseases or disabilities, which is a task that is often challenging for health care providers to accomplish.

One example of these kinds of games is the *Re-Mission* series (available free online at http://www.re-mission.net/), developed by HopeLab. These two games were designed for teens to help them virtually and literally fight cancer. Through the help of the games, cancer patients get to blast their cancer cells while learning skills and techniques that help them cope with the symptoms of cancer and its treatments. A study published in the scientific journal *Pediatrics* found that cancer patients who played *Re-Mission* maintained higher levels of chemotherapy in their blood and took their antibiotics more consistently than the control group that did not play the game.[24] These factors improve treatment outcomes and are directly related to survivorship. Cancer patients who played *Re-Mission* also showed faster acquisition of knowledge about their disease and its treatment and showed a faster increase in a feeling of self-efficacy and control over their disease process and its treatment.

These kinds of results suggest that video games have the potential to fulfill important functions in increasing positive healthcare outcomes for people suffering from a wide variety of diseases. (I should clarify that the classic *Dr. Mario* probably doesn't qualify as one of these types of games. No offense intended, Nintendo!)

Gaming Benefit: Fighting Cravings

While there are valid concerns about video games being a source of addiction, it turns out that a video game may actually be useful in recovering from addiction and overcoming impulsive cravings. Elaborated Intrusion Theory posits that visualization and imagery are central to cravings. People who have cravings often visualize the thing they are craving, be it nicotine, alcohol, or brownies. Marketing is based upon the idea that if you show me a (likely touched up) picture of a big, juicy hamburger, it will kick off a craving for a big, juicy hamburger. Go ahead and try it. Picture your favorite dessert. Imagine its color, its texture, the way it feels in your mouth. Notice anything going on yet? I don't know about you, but as I write this, I am now distracted by the thought of New York cheesecake with strawberry sauce. Luckily, there is help to be found in the form of *Tetris*.

Apparently, playing *Tetris*—a game that requires visuospatial attention and strategy—helps prevent the brain from forming enticing visual images of the things you are craving. By disrupting this process, the craving fades. Researchers found that playing *Tetris* in short, three-minute bursts was effective at reducing the strength, frequency, and vividness of various types of cravings by 24 percent.[25] Keep in mind, the research doesn't support the idea of long gaming marathons to avoid cravings but rather supports the idea of "surgical *Tetris* strikes" to break up the momentum of craving. Of course, this would also seem to suggest that engaging in other tasks that utilize visuospatial memory and skill, such as sketching, may also be helpful—provided the person is not sketching the thing they are craving. While further research into these other potential implications is needed, *Tetris* itself seems to be particularly effective at engaging visuospatial memory (possibly because the tempo and mechanics of the game are particularly effective at engaging visuospatial memory in a demanding fashion) and therefore has merit as a resource in addiction recovery.

Potential Future Gaming Benefit: Increased Social Skills

I want to take a few moments to explore the world of hypothetical gaming benefits that could be available in the near future. Consider, for a moment, a rising societal challenge. Currently, about one in sixty-eight children has been identified with an Autism Spectrum Disorder.[26] One common feature of Autism Spectrum Disorders (ASDs) is social anxiety, due in part to difficulties with reading noverbal language, picking up on social cues, and adequately imagining other people's thoughts, feelings, perspectives, and motives. This can make navigating relationships and important functions, such as school and work, very difficult. I believe it's quite possible, however, that a combination of the emerging trend of "wearable technology," advances in artificial intelligence, and good gaming design could become a very useful tool for those struggling with these difficulties.

The Affective Computing Group of MIT Media Lab has developed a rather interesting program known as MACH (My Automated Conversation coacH). It's essentially a human communication simulation game that performs accurate speech and nonverbal cues, and then evaluates the responses of the person using the program through a complicated process of behavior analysis and synthesis. This provides the user with active and specific feedback about if they are responding in an appropriate and effective manner and what they can do to improve their social responses.[27] MACH has already been demonstrated to improve job interviewing skills and is undergoing further development to help with social anxiety, PTSD, dating skills, and Autism Spectrum Disorders, such as Asperger's Disorder.

Imagine, for a moment, if the MACH technology was more fully developed and combined with wearable technology such as Google Glass. Such a device could offer real-time analysis of the verbal and nonverbal cues of people around the user, as well as providing in-the-moment feedback about how well the user is doing with appropriate responses and furnishing concrete options about what responses may be beneficial in their particular social circumstances. To avoid becoming merely a crutch, such a device could act as a game, providing points for positive social perception and responses and then gradually reducing the number of cues it provides as the user shows increases in his or her social proficiency. The learning curve could be calibrated to increase the user's reliance on his or her own abilities, similar to the science behind the *NeuroRacer* learning curve and how it promotes cognitive growth. The intention would be to eventually wean the player off the game entirely through reducing the "scaffolding" of assistance around social perception and responses. Such a game is not that far off from the technology that exists now and could be a potential boon for the growing population with ASD. However, I believe that users of such a game would have to avoid the temptation to constantly restart the game and perpetually use it on full scaffolding setting as a permanent social crutch. While there would certainly be some issues to be worked through, I believe the general concept is worth exploring.

That being said, there is room for concern about using wearable technology such as Google Glass. As we have discussed previously, smartphones and other technology that offer easy access to the Internet and social media have considerable potential for addiction. I believe that wearable technology has even greater potential for disruption and addiction. We have already witnessed the first documented case of a man being treated for Internet addiction using Google Glass. A man with a history of depression, anxiety, some features of social phobia, and obsessive compulsive disorder was admitted to a Navy Substance Abuse and Recovery program for alcoholism. While there, it became apparent to those treating him that his relationship with his Google Glass had also reached the threshold of an addiction. In the two months prior to his admission to the program, he had been using his Google Glass up to eighteen hours per day and would typically only remove it to sleep and to bathe. He reportedly would show "significant frustration and irritability related to not being able to use his Google Glass."[28] He showed a constant involuntary motion of bringing his hand to his temple, the same gesture used to access his Google Glass.

While going through treatment, this man experienced significant withdrawal symptoms and reported that the withdrawal from Google Glass was more intense and difficult than his withdrawal from alcohol had been. After thirty-five days without his Google Glass, he was showing decreases in irritability, improvements in short-term memory, greater clarity in thought processes, and a reduction in his involuntary gestures of touching his temple. However, he continued to report that in his dreams, he seemed to be looking through his Google Glass.[28]

A commentator on the CNN.com article that featured this story offered this opinion (I know, by reading this I broke rule number one for a happy life: never read the comments section on any story on the Internet. Ever. Really. Seriously. Don't ever do it.): "The device was obviously just the pacifier of the moment for an already unstable individual - though it's scary to think what an unstable stalker would do with these. Texting while driving, non-stop phone fidgeting, glassholes - at some point rational society needs to say 'Enough, put your toys away and grow up.' Technology needs to stop being an excuse for bad behavior."[29]

Part of this comment is on target and in part misses the point. First, the commentator points out that certain aspects of this man's background (mental health issues relative to depression and anxiety) might make him more vulnerable to this kind of dynamic. I believe this is on target because it is my understanding that problematic Internet and gaming use is a result of the interaction between our specific makeup—our genes, history, relationships, emotional coping, neurological hardwiring, and so on—and the specific dynamics of the particular piece of technology and programming that we are interfacing with. That is also why I believe the second part of the comment—which insists that this is merely a matter of maturity and that the solution is as simple as people growing up and putting their toys away—is an oversimplification and misses the point. The Google Glass was not "just the pacifier of the moment." Its dynamics interacted in a complex way with this particular man's physiological and psychological vulnerabilities to produce a powerful and entrenched addiction. If we don't understand that addiction is a relationship between everything that makes up who we are and some external stimulus that interacts with those various facets of our identity, we will find that our efforts to prevent or overcome addictions will be ineffective.

While the research on mental health and addiction supports the idea that people experiencing mental health challenges (which, by the way, makes up a significant fraction of the population) have an extra layer of vulnerability to addictions, the science on addiction is equally clear that simply not having mental health issues such as depression or anxiety does not make us invulnerable to addiction, be it chemical, digital, or otherwise. What is interesting about technology like Google Glass is how well suited it is to interact with us on multiple facets of who we are. Because it interacts with us more constantly and seamlessly, wearable tech such as Google Glass can be a powerful tool. But these same features give it the potential to be an equally powerful slave master. What can be so confusing about successfully navigating the cyber-scape is that many of the same factors that can be turned to benefits can be turned to detriments. I would submit that what makes the difference is how we relate to the various aspects of the cyber-scape, which then determines its effects on us.

Factors that Determine the Effects of Video Games

Based on his own extensive research and his analysis of the entire field of research on video games, Dr. Douglas Gentile identified five major factors that help explain the different ways in which video games can produce either positive or negative outcomes.[30] What can be confusing about this process is that positive and negative influences can be mixed based on the interaction between these various factors. Thus, to determine the likely impact of a specific game on an individual, we need to be aware of each of these factors and the way they impact each other. I will share his general findings and add my own insights and analysis.

Factor 1: Amount of Play

The simple measurement of the amount of time someone spends playing video games seems to be the factor that most people intuitively grasp. The general thought I hear expressed again and again is, *How much time playing video games is too much?* Or, *how much does someone have to play before it is considered an addiction?* We are right to take amount of play into consideration, although it is not the only important factor. Dr. Gentile observed, "Many studies found associations between amount of game play and negative outcomes, such as increased aggression."[31] However, he noted that it is not simply a matter of more play being directly proportionate to negative factors, such as aggression. "Some of these associations are not due to amount *per se*, but are artifacts of the relation between amount and the other dimensions." In other words, the amount of play in combination with a number of other factors explained the increase in negative outcomes.

Logically, this makes good sense. The more you play, the more exposure you have to the other influences of whatever specific game you are playing. Thus, increased game time simply gives more room for the other factors to "work their magic," so to speak. One way to think of it is this: amount of play is the beaker in which the other elements of gaming are mixed. If the elements mixed together are explosive, a larger beaker makes for a bigger bang and more damage. To stretch the metaphor a little further, some elements may not be explosive until they reach a certain volume or density, so a mixture that would not be explosive in smaller doses becomes explosive in larger doses. Furthermore, some elements are potentially explosive even in the smallest doses.

In case that metaphor just made things more confusing, let's take a look at an example. In his meta-analysis, Dr. Gentile observed that the total amount of time spent playing video games is independently related to school performance, risk of obesity, and other physical health outcomes.[32] In other words, you don't need any other factors to explain these specific relationships. The more you play, the more likely you are to be obese, have health problems, or struggle in school. This makes sense because it carves into the time that you might otherwise use for homework or physical activity. For these particular factors, a simple one-to-one, linear style of thinking works pretty well for making accurate predictions.

However, it gets more complicated than that, and the simple linear thinking breaks down as we look at other factors. If we separate the total amount of game time from violent content, game time predicts poorer school performance but not increased aggression. In fact, simply owning a gaming system actually serves as a predictor of declines in school performance for boys. A study found that boys who own a gaming system (or live in a house that has one) are more likely to have low scores in reading and writing compared to boys who live in a home without a gaming system.[33] Does that mean having a gaming system in the home automatically hurts grades? Certainly not, but having one in the home makes it more likely that someone could spend enough play time to have their grades suffer. After all, people tend to do what is convenient. The more accessible the games, the more likely someone is to play them, and the more a person plays video games, the more likely other areas in their life will suffer as a result of neglect.

The same set of data also indicates that although video games can cause increased levels of aggression, aggression is not a direct function of time spent playing. If we separate violent content from total time playing games, violent content directly predicts increased aggression but not school performance. Therefore, violent gameplay doesn't seem to have an impact on school performance, but a person doesn't have to play violent games a large amount of time in order for the violent content to contribute to increases in aggression.

Up to a certain point, more game play is not necessarily worse; it's just more. This could certainly mean that more game time results in more of the downsides. But, it can also mean more game time produces more benefits, at least within certain limits. There seems to be a pretty consistent point at which the amount of benefits from game time dissipates and the downsides start to mount, tipping the cost-benefit analysis of the situation into the red zone.

Let's consider a specific example of how this kind of balance point works. Playing video games has been found to help increase visual attention. At the same time, playing video games has been found to decrease impulse control.[34] (Incidentally, this is part of how violent video games can lead to greater aggression, both by rehearsing aggression in the mind while increasing the impulse control needed to suppress aggressive urges.) Playing video games can help someone focus more on visual tasks, but when the amount of game time has reached a certain point, people experience more and more declines in impulse control, which for all practical purposes negates the benefits of being able to focus more. After all, what good does it do to have to possess the cognitive ability to focus if we lack the impulse control needed to exercise that skill?

While time spent playing is not the only factor to be considered, it is a very important factor. Furthermore, it is the easiest factor to measure and the most obviously accessible when it comes to providing structure for ourselves. As mentioned previously, this golden balance point for gaining benefits without mounting downsides seems most likely to be found at somewhere between one to three hours maximum of non work- or school-related total screen time per day. The specific amount within that range is a function of the interaction between an individual person's biological, psychological, and social makeup, strengths, and vulnerabilities and the dynamics of the specific games they play.

If the golden mean is about one to three hours of screen time per day, how are we as a society doing with meeting that balance point? A recent study found that 31 percent of high school students report using computers for noneducational reasons for more than three hours per day, with boys self-reporting as being more likely to spend that time gaming and girls self-reporting as being more likely to spend time on social media.[35] That's not total screen time, that's just computers. Approximately one-third of us are maxing out with just one form of screen interaction. In examining total screen time, a study by the Council for Research Excellence indicated that in 2009, the average American adult tends to get about eight and one-half hours of screen exposure per day, with TV usage still the most dominant form of screen time, followed by computer usage as a close second.[36] In other words, the average American blows right by this golden balance point without even batting an eye as if it were some rundown, drive-by ghost town on Route 66. The most immediate implication is that most of us probably really need to reevaluate the sheer amount of time we are dedicating to screens and work on thoughtfully pruning back the time we invest in them. That's not a complete solution by itself, but it is an obvious starting point.

Factor 2: Content of Play

Dr. Douglas Gentile's second factor is content. Game content refers to what is actually going on in the game.[37] Is the game based on jumping from platform to platform and stomping on monsters? Does the gamer step into the role of an interstellar space trader? Does the gamer experience killing people as part of combat in a war? Is the central experience of the game raising vegetables and fruits to fend off zombies? What we experience in the game plays a significant role in how the game affects us. The general rule of thumb is whatever we do in the game acts as a close mental analogue for actually doing it in real life. The more realistic and immersive a game is, the less of a difference there is between experiencing something in real life and experiencing something in a game, as far as your brain is concerned.

To illustrate this principle, consider the following research. At Harvard Medical School, neuroscientist Alvaro Pascual-Leon conducted an experiment to see how learning and practicing new behaviors actually changed the structure of the brain. He had research participants practice the piano two hours daily for five days. Following their training time, he used a transcranial magnetic stimulation test to see how the portion of the motor cortex in the brain connected to the finger movements used in playing the piano had branched out and made multiple new structural connections. In a nutshell, the learning process actually changed the structure of their brains. Our choices, especially repeated ones, change the very instrument with which we perceive both the world and ourselves, the very cradle of our consciousness and identity.

So far, this finding is a confirmation of the basic fundamentals of neuroscience. While the idea that our choices and behaviors actually change our brain is the most fundamental principle of our understanding of the nature of human brains, I am struck by how many of us live so unaware of the implications of our constantly moldable neurological nature. Think about it: we mold our brains by our choices, and then we use that changed brain to make more choices. The circular causality of this dynamic is powerful. But do virtual choices and behaviors shape the brain in a manner similar to physical choices and behaviors? Here's where Dr. Pascual-Leon's research gets even more interesting: research participants who did not actually practice the piano but instead rehearsed the same movements mentally also showed the same kind of brain shaping and growth. The changes for those who actually played the piano and the changes for those who just rehearsed it mentally were, as far as could be discerned, functionally equivalent.[38] In other words, mental practice was the same to the brain as physical practice. Not just our behaviors, but our very thoughts actually work to alter our neurological "hardwiring." (Tangentially, this also means that there may actually be some validity to music teaching methods of the con man Harold Hill from the classic musical *The Music Man*.)

This idea lies at the very heart of visualization techniques in sports psychology. It is also an especially important principle in understanding the impact our gaming experiences have upon us. The actions we take in the games we play are mental rehearsals enhanced by complex and sophisticated computer technology. Thus, in gaming as in other areas, what we rehearse mentally through our game playing will influence our brain development similarly to the ways it would change our brains if we were to take those actions in real life.

Perhaps nowhere else is the potential impact of the content of games and their impact upon us of greater concern than in the content factor of violence in games. Violent game content tends to get a lot of attention in the public discourse, and rightfully so. While it is not my intention to get into all the nitty-gritty details of the research on violent video game content and its effects upon people, I do want to touch upon the general, overall outcomes of the research on this topic and provide a few examples I find to be the most important. There are dozens of studies about short- and long-term effects of video games demonstrating causal connections, real-world associations, and longitudinal accumulation of effects across time between violent video game content and actual real-world aggression. In other words, research tells us that violent video games do, in fact, contribute to and create aggression in those who play them, that this aggression does spill out into real-world situations, and that these effects accumulate over time.[39] That being said, the same is also true of pro-social themes. Game content that encourages problem solving, team work, nonviolent conflict resolution, or ways of addressing dangerous situations that still show respect for human life also help to actually create pro-social attitudes and behaviors. Thus, video games can actually be a source of personal growth and character development, and their potential for performing that function is probably underutilized and worthy of more discussion. For the purpose of this section, though, I'd like to go into detail about the potential darker side of video game content and its affects upon people.

A study out of Ohio State University found that people who played a violent video game for three consecutive days showed measurable increases in aggressive behavior and also showed significant increases in their hostile expectations from other people each day they played.[40]

In contrast, people who played nonviolent video games did not show any measurable changes in aggression or hostile expectations. The researchers noted that these increases in aggressive behavior (not just thoughts) and hostile expectations increased over time as a result of consistent participation in violent video game activities. This provides solid support for the idea that violent video game content, and not just video game playing in general, has a real-world influence on aggressive human behavior.

This idea is further supported by a study from Iowa State University, wherein researchers found that the frequency of playing violent video games was strongly linked with delinquent and violent behavior.[41] Of course, the question to be asked here is whether people who are already violent choose to play violent video games, or if the video games are helping to create and fuel their aggressive behaviors. Researchers were able to statistically isolate the influence of having a history of violence, and still found statistically significant results of violence and psychopathic traits and found that the connection between frequency of violent video game usage and actual violence held firm, even when factoring out the presence or absence of criminal psychology or a violent past. In other words, violent video games are not just a way that aggressive people "express themselves"; violent video games help people become aggressive and violent.

Part of this happens through a process of desensitization. Researchers from the University of Missouri conducted experiments utilizing the violent, action-oriented games *Killzone*, *Call of Duty*, *Hitman*, and *Grand Theft Auto* and discovered that "the brains of violent video game players become less responsive to violence, and this diminished brain response predicts an increase in aggression. . . . Playing a violent game in the lab caused a reduced brain response to the photos of violence—an indicator of desensitization. Moreover, this reduced brain response predicted participants' aggression levels: the smaller the brain response to violent photos, the more aggressive participants were."[42] I wish to emphasize that they found these increases in aggressive tendencies also resulted in an increase of measurable aggressive behaviors in the real world.

As I stated previously, the more realistic and immersive games become, the less of a difference there is for our brains between doing something in real life and doing something in a game. This idea is supported by the findings of researchers out of the University of Connecticut, who found that battling human-looking opponents in video games was more likely to produce aggression than fighting against monsters, aliens, robots, or otherwise less human-like enemies.[43] As we become accustomed to committing acts of violence and aggression against human-like computer characters in a game and feeling unempathetic and detached from the experience—partially due to desensitization from the constant repetition and partially due to the fact that there are no real consequences for that violence—we train our brains to be desensitized and detached from acts of aggression toward humans in the real world. In fact, heavy players of violent video games (playing three or more hours of violent games per day . . . there's that number again) showed blunted physical and emotional responses to playing a violent game. In other words, they display tolerance the same way a drug addict shows tolerance to their drug, leading them to have to increase their doses and branch out into more potent drugs to get the same level of high.[44] Given this information, it is no surprise to me that the violent content of video games is increasing year after year. Of course, this also indicates that violent video game players' sense of empathy is becoming less and less responsive. I find that very concerning. We train ourselves to neurologically separate aggression from consequences and to silence our internal sense of empathy toward other people. This reshaped brain, primed for aggression, is then what we are left with to process and respond to the other stimuli in our lives.

The impact of violent gaming content on human aggression is affected by the way the game can continue on in the mind of the player long after the gaming system has been shut off. Our brain has amazing visualizing abilities, and we are able to replay our gaming experiences or fantasize new ones, even when we are not able to physically interface with a video game. Thinking about a game after we play it is a bit like getting radiation treatments for cancer. When a cancer patient goes through radiation therapy, they get immediate effects from the dose of radiation they are exposed to. However, the residual radiation can keep a cancer patient "cooking" for a while after the treatment. Similarly, if we continue to think about and visualize the game after we are playing it, we continue to have its active effects, almost as if we were still playing it. The game lives on in the mind, even after the game itself is over. It is no surprise, then, that research has demonstrated that people who continue to think about the violent games after they are done playing show spikes in aggression that last significantly longer than people who do not ruminate over the game after it is over.[45]

Besides increasing aggression, violent video games have also been found to result in general declines in impulse control, resulting in behaviors such as cheating, overeating, lying, and stealing. Additionally, evidence suggests that regular participation in graphically violent video games contributes to a sense of moral disengagement, meaning that a person fails to believe that ethical standards apply to them in whatever situation they may find themselves in.[46] Combine the desensitization process (with its accompanying erosion of empathy and increased dehumanization of other people) and "brain training" aspects of violence in video games with moral disengagement and decreases in impulse control that tend to accompany extended amounts of game playing, and you have a pretty good recipe for aggressive, unethical, and otherwise destructive human behavior.[47] Because violent and dehumanizing content shapes people's brains in this manner, it is not surprising, then, that when people speak out publicly asking the video game industry to rethink the content it is producing, whether it be graphic violence, racism, sexism, and so forth, the response that is produced from gamers is utterly brutal.

Perhaps the setting in which this has been most starkly illustrated is in the recent #GamerGate controversy. For those unfamiliar with it, Jay Hathaway explains: "#GamerGate is an online movement ostensibly concerned with ethics in game journalism and with protecting the 'gamer' identity. . . . Even regarded generously, GamerGate isn't much more than a tone-deaf rabble of angry obsessives with a misguided understanding of journalistic ethics . . . #GamerGate actually began in August, [2014] as a pernicious attack on one female game developer, Zoe Quinn, and her sex life. . . . It's hard not to look at the last several weeks of chatter in the gaming community and not come to the conclusion that [#GamerGate's attack on Quinn are not about any flaws with the game she developed, but] about the fact that she's a woman."[48]

The members of #GamerGate have also made vicious attacks against other prominent gaming critics, including notable feminist scholar

Anita Sarkesian. These attacks consisted of the most brutal, misogynistic insults and death threats, to the point that several of the targets of #GamerGate assaults were forced to flee their own homes for safety. As I have observed #GamerGate, I have noticed a strong dynamic of groupthink. They operate like an angry lynch mob, emboldened by the fact that they feel invulnerable in their online form. A functional analysis of #GamerGate's behavior seems to indicate that they are outraged with anyone who suggests the necessity of rethinking the violent and sexual content of video games in the same way that an alcoholic lashes out at anyone who suggests they have a drinking problem and tries to cut off his or her supply of booze. Members of #GamerGate respond with all of the aggression one would expect to be brandished by individuals who have undergone regular and extensive "brain training" in aggression from graphically violent and sexually objectifying games. In my mind, the brutish way groups such as #GamerGate protest against people who express concerns about the aggression-producing effects of graphically violent and sexually objectifying game content actually proves their critics' point quite effectively. There is intense and bitter irony in their overall message, which can be summarized as follows: *I will rape and kill you and your family if you tell me that my video games are violent and sexist and that they make me violent and sexist!*

I have heard people dismiss the notion that violent video game content contributes to human aggression and violence with statements such as, "Look, if violent video games made people kill, then every teenage boy would become a Columbine-style school shooter." Let's be clear about something. The weight of the science is quite sufficient to state with great confidence that violent video game content has a direct causal influence on aggressive thoughts, feelings, and actions. However, it is not the only influential factor. The difference between one person screaming aggressively at his mother when she asks him to stop playing and another person shooting up a high school is caused by a number of other risk factors in combination with the effects of their violent video game playing activity. Research out of Ohio State University demonstrated that although violent video games are not the only determiner of actual violence, they are still a powerful influence even when factoring in other major contributors such as age, race, and the age at which someone was first referred to the juvenile justice system.[49] The magnitude of this influence is easily underestimated and often lost upon us because of how common the use of graphically violent video games is. The fact is that video games are fantastic teachers, and aggressive and morally detached video games excel at teaching aggression.

On the other hand, when the content of video games is educational in nature, they also excel in teaching a wide variety of subject matters.[50] Overall, video games teach in a way that our brains seem primed to learn from. We should not underestimate the degree to which their content will teach us and the degree to which our brains will readily integrate what is being taught. To me, this suggests that we should be very thoughtful about the content of our games because we will almost certainly learn from them, be shaped by them, and play out what we have learned in our thoughts, feelings, and actions in a wide variety of ways.

Factor 3: Context of Play

Douglas Gentile's third factor, context, refers to the goals and objectives of the game.[51] In combination with other, more quintessential factors, context helps create what I refer to as the game's "attitude" or "culture." For example, does the game have an attitude of valuing teamwork, or is its personality more rugged and individualistic? Does the game reward creativity, diplomacy, or brutality? What are the messages and values implied by the presentation of various aspects of the game? For example, are women respected or objectified? Is violence seen as something to be used with restraint and only when necessarily, or is it glorified and encouraged in its most extreme forms? This factor of context tends to be the least researched dimension, which I find unfortunate because I see it as having tremendous potential for shaping the impact a specific game has upon a person.

I especially find it interesting to see how the factor of context can interact with the factor of content to produce either moderating or magnifying effects. For example, in his review of the research, Dr. Gentile observed that games that have a context of pro-social teamwork (for example, fighting to protect innocent people, utilizing teamwork to achieve objectives, and so on) actually show potential for moderating the aggression-producing results of violent content.

On the other hand, ruthless, dehumanizing, senseless, or misogynistic tone or attitude in depictions of violence shows significant potential to actually increase the aggression-producing results of violent content.[53]

These kinds of factor interactions can produce some interesting variations in the way a specific game can impact people. An example of this is the *Deus Ex* series. This legendary game series is set in a cyberpunk future in which all of today's most common conspiracy theories are true. The gamer assumes the role of a number of cybernetically enhanced people, capable of performing tasks ranging from lifting heavy objects, becoming invisible, hacking into computer systems, and using pheromones to influence others in conversations. The player is given immense power and placed in morally confusing situations. While the player is fully capable of approaching each situation as a ruthless killing machine, the game provides alternatives to lethal force, including nonlethal force, stealth, and negotiation. Throughout the game, there is a continuous meta-narrative about the value of human life, even the lives of those considered enemies. Nonviolent solutions are often more difficult, but they are portrayed as superior and rewarded in a variety of ways, while easy, violent, lethal solutions to problems are often openly criticized. The game constantly invites the player to ask the following questions: Just because you can use force, should you? Just because someone has done terrible things, is killing them really the best answer? That being said, if the player does decide to resort to lethal force, it can be accomplished with bloody detail.

Thus, the *Deus Ex* series presents an interesting example in which another factor influences the way the game affects the player: the player's own choices. A player can end the series having participated in a constant bloodbath. If they have done so, the game chides them in a number of ways, but they do not lose the game. Perhaps they will hear the message and it will give them pause, or perhaps they will just simply move on and give it no thought. On the other hand, a player can finish the series having had an intriguing, thought-provoking experience that has challenged them to ponder deeply about their own sense of morality and how they might be falling for the trap of substituting what is easy for what they believe is right in their own lives. This one game can have these two very different outcomes based on how the player chooses to play it.

Let's contrast this with the context of another game, *Saints Row IV*. In this game, violence is encouraged and abounds in great variety, ranging from the absurd to the grotesque, including letting the player commit sodomy with a firearm. Besides that, the overall tone of the game is replete with racism, misogyny, crude sexuality, full nudity, and more. It's as if the shock jockey Howard Stern was milked for the essence of his radio show and transformed it into video game form. As a result of its highly edgy material, the game was banned in Australia. And yet, the review site Destructoid crowned it as one of the best open world sandbox games a player could ever hope to encounter. (A sandbox game provides an open world setting where the player can roam freely and interact with various parts of the world as they please.) I suppose that sounds better than "*Saints Row IV* is the best psychopathic, homicidal, sodomy simulation you will ever play." It's slightly less marketable that way, I suppose, but no less accurate. That fact didn't seem to faze consumers. *Saints Row IV* sold more than one million copies in its first week.[54]

Then there is the infamous *Grand Theft Auto* series, which is essentially an open world sociopathic sandbox in which the player is rewarded for all kinds of brutal crimes. They can run over innocent civilians, hire prostitutes and then kill them, carjack, break and enter, mug, ambush, commit drive-by shootings, mutilate, steal, and participate in virtually any kind of crime imaginable (except for tax fraud; maybe they will include that in the next one). All of this in the game is portrayed with a cold, hard, gritty veneer, devoid of remorse, empathy, or even basic human dignity. It sounds like the perfect holiday gift, wouldn't you say? "Merry Christmas, sweetheart! Peace on earth and goodwill toward all. Now, have fun pretending to be a scumbag thug!" If sales have anything to say about it, a lot of people bought in to that line of thinking. *Grand Theft Auto 5* has sold more than 33 million copies.[55]

With context, not only what we do but why we do it and how it is portrayed are all important factors in determining how a specific game will affect us. Everything discussed earlier in this book under the section "The Power of Context" applies to gaming context as well. As

I said, human beings are contextual beings, and we underestimate the degree to which context shapes us at our own peril. What we rehearse mentally, as well as the emotions attached to it in the rehearsal, has great power to influence our minds, feelings, and sense of ethics and humanity.

Factor 4: Informational Structure

Video games require gamers to interface with some kind of screen display to process information (hence the name "video game," I suppose). Dr. Douglas Gentile observed that as a result of this basic fact about video games, "Screen displays are therefore carefully structured to provide meaningful information."[56] A game's structure consists of the layout and methods used for displaying the game's information. The way that information is portrayed can affect how people interpret the information. Dr. Gentile gave the following example: "If a couple enters a bedroom and shut the door, and it fades to black, we take away a very specific meaning about what happened behind the door. If, however, we see the same couple shut the door and it cuts to the next scene, we do not assume the same thing." Thus, how a specific image or transition is presented on the screen influences how we interpret it. In this way, informational structure can affect game context in a variety of subtle ways.

The game's structure can also contribute to how games promote and develop specific cognitive abilities. For example, action-oriented video games that feature enemies or obstacles popping up at rapid speeds require the players to constantly visually scan all aspects of the screen if they do not wish to meet an untimely virtual death. As a result, action video game players develop greater visual attention skills by practicing and utilizing visual attention techniques that are adaptive to the way the game is portrayed on the screen. Furthermore, many modern games are presented graphically in three dimensions, while in reality they are two-dimensional images. Research indicates that playing three-dimensional video games improves 2D to 3D reasoning and promotes improved skills in navigation, orientation, and mental rotation.[57]

A phenomenon that is worthy of examination is the upcoming introduction of virtual reality headset displays as a replacement for flat screen displays. High resolution virtual reality, such as that offered by the upcoming Oculus Rift, will add significantly to the visual and overall sensory interface of video games. This promises to add a whole new dimension to the immersive quality of the video game experience. In fact, users of the Oculus Rift often report having the sensation of losing track of their own body while using the device. I hypothesize that as a result of the greater level of immersion offered by high fidelity virtual reality as opposed to flat screen interfaces, the effects of video games, both positive and negative, will be amplified. Thus, I am observing this emerging technology with both anticipation and concern.

Factor 5: Mechanics of Gameplay

Whereas informational structure is how the game presents its information to the user, the mechanics of gameplay refers to the method of input the gamer uses.[58] This can range from purely manual input focused on fine motor control using a classic game controller or keyboard and mouse combination, to a slightly more kinesthetic form of input using a motion controller such as the Wii remote, to a full-body kinesthetic form using a full-motion detection interface that relies on gross motor control such as the Kinect. In a video game, there is a continuous feedback loop occurring between the informational structure (what the game portrays to the gamer) and the mechanics of gameplay (the input the gamer gives to the game).

The interaction between mechanics of gameplay and informational structure of the game helps to explain a number of gaming outcomes. For example, laparoscopic surgeons who played video games for at least three hours each week were 27 percent faster and made 37 percent fewer errors on advanced surgical skills.[59] This was likely due to the way their video game playing developed a coordinated, transferable skillset between viewing 3D images on a 2D screen and manipulating the images using fine motor controls.

A factor interaction between amount of play and mechanics of gameplay can actually help to mitigate the connection between amount of gameplay and risk of obesity and other health problems. One commonly brought up criticism about video games is that they encourage a sedentary lifestyle. This valid criticism is a concerning one, given the connection between physical activity and both mental and physical health. Americans don't tend to do well with physical activity. Less than 15 percent of children and adolescents engage in regular physical activity. A study published in the scientific journal *Pediatrics* found that games that use motion controllers and use gross motor skills (such as *Dance Dance Revolution* or *Wii Sports*) help bring people closer to recommended daily physical activity levels.[60] This disrupts the otherwise linear relationship between amount of play and health issues relative to a sedentary lifestyle. Before we get too excited about that, though, notice the careful wording that such games merely "bring people closer" to the amount of exercise they need. They don't act as a substitute for other forms of physical activity. In fact, the same researchers found that the people who tend to use games for exercise the most tend to be teenage girls who are stressed about their weight, and they tend to use exercise games in fifty-minute sessions twice a week. While some games may help as a part of a solution for the epidemic of inactivity and obesity, they are not a full solution in and of themselves.

Factor Interactions: A Possible Mixed Bag

Are video games good or bad? Are they to be embraced or shunned? What's the verdict? Dr. Douglas Gentile stated,

> The irony is, both the critics and the proponents are correct about the effects that games can have. The flaw is that they extend their arguments to conclude that video games are ultimately harmful or beneficial . . . In fact, the same game can have both perceived positive and negative effects at the same time . . . Consider a hypothetical situation where a 12-year old boy spends a lot of time playing the violent game *Grand Theft Auto*:
>
> - Because he spends a lot of time playing, we might predict poorer school performance.
> - Because of the violent content, we might predict increased aggressive thoughts, feelings, and ultimately, behaviors.
> - If he plays with other friends online, [which provides various aspects of the context factor], this might enhance (or mitigate) the violence effect and could train teamwork skills.

- Because it is both a shooting and a driving game, we might predict improved 2D to 3D transfer skills and improved visual attention skills.
- If he plays with a joystick, we might predict improved joystick skills (and improved hand-eye coordination).[61]

To understand the impact of playing video games upon a person, we need to avoid the overly simplistic reasoning of *you play video games, so X will happen to you, which is good/bad.* We need to stop one-dimensional thinking and realize that this is a much more complex equation. Important questions to consider when examining the effects of video games include the following:

1. Which game is the person playing?
2. How much time is the person playing that game?
3. What other games is the person playing?
4. How much screen time is the person getting besides video games? What is the nature of that other screen time?
5. Does the person play single-player or multi-player modes?
6. What are they actually experiencing while they are playing the game?
7. What is the game's content?
8. Is there violence? If so, how graphic and realistic is it? What are the targets of the violence? Also, what is the attitude with which the violence is presented?
9. What choices are offered in gameplay? What choices does the person actually make?
10. Are their racist, sexist, or otherwise subversive themes in the game?
11. Does the game have pornographic content? If so, what is the exact nature of that content?
12. What input method is the person using?
13. What are the emotional states the person experiences while playing?
14. What is the specific neurological makeup of the person playing?
15. Besides video games, how are the other important areas of this person's life going at this time?

16. How else does the person meet needs for mental stimulation, social interaction, and stress relief besides playing video games?

This list could go on for quite a bit longer, but I think you probably get the point by now. In general, to understand the effects of a video game upon a person, we need to develop a good understanding of the characteristics of each specific video game that the person plays and place them in the context of the larger picture of that individual's biological, psychological, and social functioning. Video games as a whole are neither good nor bad. That being said, both good and bad effects certainly come from video games. Each specific video game provides a specific cluster of potential influences that interfaces with each individual based on their own unique factors.

Potential for Addiction

As with smartphones and social media, one particular area of concern for video games is the potential for the development of an addiction. When I speak of this, some people nod their heads and share with me stories they have seen in other people or experienced themselves with the phenomenon of video game addiction. Other people say, "Give me a break! People say everything is addictive these days." By being emotionally reactive about the way people overuse the word *addiction*, we run the risk of having addictions clearly playing themselves out in front of our very eyes without acknowledging them for what they are. Thus, we leave those struggling with such addictions without recourse or support.

While there is not yet an official diagnosis for video game addiction included in the *Diagnostic and Statistical Manual* for psychological professionals, there has been a mounting wall of evidence to clearly demonstrate that video game addictions are a real and pervasive phenomenon. They fall within the realm of process addictions, which were discussed extensively earlier in this book, and all of the different factors (such as brain chemistry, reinforcement patterns, and so on) that lead to process addictions with things such as gambling and social media apply to video games, as well. The evidence supporting the existence of video game addictions has grown to a point where Internet Gaming Disorder has now been included in the DSM-V as a "condition for further study." In general, this means that the evidence is compelling, although the weight of the research has not yet been sufficient for the American Psychological Association to grant it the status of a formalized diagnosis. In the DSM-V, the criteria for Internet Gaming Disorder are listed as follows:

> Repetitive use of Internet-based games, often with other players, that leads to significant issues with functioning. Five of the following criteria must be met within one year:
>
> 1. Preoccupation or obsession with Internet games.
> 2. Withdrawal symptoms when not playing Internet games.
> 3. A build-up of tolerance—more time needs to be spent playing the games.
> 4. The person has tried to stop or curb playing Internet games, but has failed to do so.
> 5. The person has had a loss of interest in other life activities, such as hobbies.
> 6. A person has had continued overuse of Internet games even with the knowledge of how much they impact a person's life.
> 7. The person lied to others about his or her Internet game usage.
> 8. The person uses Internet games to relieve anxiety or guilt—it's a way to escape.
> 9. The person has lost or put at risk an opportunity or relationship because of Internet games.[62]

Besides these specific diagnostic criteria, a number of associated features and warning signs alert us when someone has drifted into the seductive trap of video game addiction. For example, we may see the person downplaying the amount of time they spend playing or thinking about games. We will often observe that they are highly defensive when other people have concerns about their gaming or try to impose boundaries or guidelines for them. They will often avoid difficult emotions and can frequently be seen retreating into games to avoid feelings such as boredom, loneliness, stress, irritation, and so forth. They tend to show a lack of impulse control and often demonstrate a sense of social and/or emotional immaturity, including selfishness and short-sightedness. We would also likely observe a decline in important life functions, such as diet and exercise, school and/or work, and relationships. Other hobbies and interests not related to gaming tend to diminish or wither away entirely. People addicted to video games also tend to get more involved in arguments and physical fights. They show less patience and empathy for other people and are more likely to incorrectly attribute hostile intentions and motives to other people's actions. When forced to choose between allegiance to gaming and allegiance to other people or priorities, gaming increasingly wins.

Oftentimes, I hear people say, "Okay, so I'm addicted to video games. Big deal! It's not like I'm shooting up with heroin or snorting cocaine. I'm not hurting anyone, so why should anybody care?" I would actually question the validity of the statement that they are not hurting anyone. I rarely think categorical statements are true, but in this case I am willing to state categorically that there is no such thing as an addiction that only hurts the addicted person. Aside from the damage people addicted to video games do to themselves through having other aspects of their lives fall apart—not to mention increasing symptoms such as aggression, stress sensitivity, anxiety, and depression—there are also significant impacts on the people around them.

Let me illustrate my point with an excerpt from an article called "Things We've Learned from Xbox Live" from the online gaming site 1up.com. While this article was intended to be funny, it ended up telling a disturbing truth. Among other pithy pearls of wisdom the author shares about life lessons learned from participating in Xbox's online gaming service, the author notes he has learned that "babies do not require maintenance. They may scream endlessly in the background of your conversations with Arkansas [poser] gangstas, but given the inexhaustible multitude of children who've plagued you—and will continue to do so over the years— it's apparent that their feeding and upkeep is entirely optional." Translation: you hear a lot of neglected infants and children in the background of Xbox Live in the homes of problem gamers who are letting their gaming buzz interfere with their parental responsibilities and the needs of their children. Anyone who has suffered from neglect will certainly attest that it is a form of harm.

There are some forms of harm that come from video game addiction that are extreme. "Overdoses" can even lead to death. That's not an exaggeration. There are a growing number of documented cases of death as a result of video game binges. For example, in 2005 a twenty-eight-year-old South Korean man died after a fifty-hour long *StarCraft* gaming session led to heart failure from exhaustion.[63] Similarly, in 2011, a thirty-year-old Chinese man lost consciousness on a long gaming session due to not eating and drinking and then died. That same year, a young British man who often played his Xbox for twelve hours at a time died of a blood clot during one of his long gaming gluts. The list of examples goes on. In 2012, a teenager in Taiwan died after failing to eat or sleep throughout the course of a forty-hour-long *Diablo 3* binge. Authorities also suspected that he may have developed a fatal blood clot after so much time sitting while he played. In February of the same year, a twenty-three-year-old Taiwanese man died of heart failure in the course of playing *League of Legends* for twenty-three hours. When his body was found, his hands were still stretched out over his keyboard and mouse.[64] This is happening with increasing frequency, with the causes of death most often being heart failure due to exhaustion, heart attacks, or blood clots.

There are also cases of gaming-related homicides. One such case that caught the media's attention was the story of Daniel Petric. Daniel developed a pattern of playing video games up to eighteen hours per day after a health condition left him homebound. When his parents forbid him from playing *Halo 3* and confiscated the game from him after finding out he had snuck out at night to purchase it, he responded with frightening rage. He approached his parents a few days later, asking them to close their eyes because he had a surprise for them. Thinking he was going to do something special to apologize after responding to them so horribly, they complied with his request. It turned out that his surprise was a 9mm handgun loaded with hollow tip rounds. He shot his mother multiple times and then turned and shot his father in the head. Next he handed the gun to his father, attempting to make the crime scene look like a murder/suicide. His father survived to tell that tale, but his mother did not.[65] In another case in China, a gamer tracked down and killed another man for stealing a virtual sword from his character in a Massive Multiplayer Online Role Playing Game they both participated in. In fact, gaming-related incidents have become common enough in China that the government—which originally encouraged the growth of online gaming in China—has set up laws to deter Chinese citizens from playing video games for longer than three consecutive hours.[66] Other gaming-related deaths are similarly bone chilling. A man named Tyrone Spellman became so enraged when his seventeen-month-old daughter accidentally pulled the cords of his gaming system from the wall, thus disrupting his gaming session, that he flew into a violent rage and cracked her skull multiple times, which resulted in her death. There is also the case of teenager Devin Moore, a diehard fan of the *Grand Theft Auto* series. He was arrested on suspicion of trying to play out his gaming fantasies in real life by stealing a car. He took his gameplay mimicry to the next level by grabbing a gun and going on a shooting spree that resulted in the death of two police officers and a 911 dispatcher. After the bloodbath, he reportedly said, "Life is like a video game. Everybody's got to die sometime." Another case involved a thirteen-year-old boy who strangled and killed an eighty-one-year-old woman to steal money from her to buy video games.[67] I am still trying to decide if I find this story more disturbing than the 2010 case out of South Korea where a married couple was deeply immersed in raising a virtual child in an online gaming world, showering it with all kinds of gifts and attention to help it develop magic powers in the game. Their focus on this goal was so all-consuming that they ended up accidentally letting their real three-month-old baby—who was left unattended and alone in their apartment daily while they were away at an Internet café playing their game—starve to death.[68] As I said, one of the signs of a gaming addiction is that when the virtual world is pitted against the real world, the real world loses.

In talking about fatal gaming "overdoses" and gaming-related homicide as a result of video game addictions, I don't mean to be overly alarmist or sensationalistic. Most people who experience problems due to excessive, obsessive, or addictive patterns of gaming will not fall to these depths. However, it is important to understand the full breadth of the toll video game addictions can take. While such extremes in violence and aggression are relatively rare, parents, spouses, children, and other loved ones often experience significant verbal and physical aggression when they express concerns or attempt to set boundaries with people addicted to gaming. In the years I have been working with cases such as this, I frequently hear stories of both children and adults throwing fits, breaking property, yelling and screaming, pushing, shoving, hitting, kicking, biting, burning, disrupting family functions, and brandishing weapons at family members and other loved ones when they interrupt or threaten the addicted gamers' access to video games. These incidences are alarmingly common. Furthermore, video game addictions—like all other addictions—have significant opportunity costs in time, attention, allegiance, affection, service, support, and love. Again, I categorically challenge and discredit the assertion that having a video game addiction "isn't hurting anyone."

Prevalence of Video Game Addiction

Video game addictions are a growing problem across the globe. South Korea is known as the "most wired" nation in the world and therefore has had a tendency to lead out trends in cyber issues. South Korean government sources report that approximately 10 percent of South Korean Internet users (equaling about two million people or roughly 4 percent of their total population) meet the definition for online gaming addicts, with a considerable portion of that number spending almost every waking moment (and quite a few moments when they should probably be sleeping) playing games.[69] A study from Norway revealed that 4.1 percent of gamers studied self-reported problematic video game use, but that 6 percent actually met the criteria for video game addiction.[70]

In the United States, researchers found that 8.5 percent of gamers between the ages of eight and eighteen exhibit pathological gaming behavior. That means the average boy gamer clocks about 16.4 hours of gaming per week (averaging 2.3 hours per day, assuming the person is playing seven days per week), with the average girl getting in just over nine hours of gaming in a week (or approximately 1.2 hours per day). The average person who met the criteria for pathological gaming or gaming addiction put in about 24 hours per week, or about 3.4 hours per day. Twenty-five percent of the surveyed gamers (not just those in the "addicted" category) reported turning to video games in an attempt to escape problems, and nearly as many said they played instead of doing homework. Similarly, 20 percent of all of the gamers in this study said that their schoolwork had suffered because of the time they spent gaming.[71]

The lead author on this research, Dr. Douglas Gentile, points out that gaming addiction is about more than just how much a person plays video games. "What we mean by pathological use is that something someone is doing—in this case, playing video games —is damaging to their functioning. It's not simply doing it a lot." While it is true that dysfunction is more likely to be found over a certain number of gaming hours per week, time spent playing is not a complete indicator of addiction. Problems can exist at fewer hours per week than the average of 24 hours. In my own practice of working with people experiencing excessive, obsessive, and addictive patterns of gaming, I commonly see people who spend somewhere between 30 to 80 hours per week gaming. My current "record holder" in my personal practice was averaging about 100 hours per week.

Not the Predicted Singularity but a Singularity Nonetheless

Why are we seeing a spike in problematic video game use? It seems to me that one factor is simply the prevalence of video games has increased. They have ceased to be a niche market item and are now solidly entrenched in the mainstream of society. More people are playing them, and that by itself leads to an increased risk for pathological patterns to emerge and develop. But I believe there is a lot more to it than that. Video games themselves have evolved. The most obvious evolution has been in graphics technology, but this is also only the most superficial evolution. A lot has changed "under the hood" with video games in the mechanics of how they work and how they interact with the human brain. Many games today are complex masterworks that provide a highly coordinated, sensory rich, neurologically stimulating, and socially involved combination of compelling graphics, social connection, fantasy identity, escapism, constant novelty, accessibility, and psychological reinforcement. Each video game in this new breed creates a unique neuro-cyber interface, an ergonomic molding, meshing, and interweaving effect with the various aspects of the way the human brain works, including what stimulates it and what motivates it. While this new breed of video games can be more engaging and entertaining than some of their predecessors (no offense intended, *Pac-Man*, *Pong*, and *Space War*), they can also be more entrapping when our relationship with them becomes unhealthy.

Gaming Mechanics and Video Game Process Addiction

My clinical experiences have removed all doubt for me that video games are becoming increasingly addictive. Yet, I do not believe conspiracy theories that most game designers are purposefully making their games addictive. I believe there are exceptions to that rule, but I have found many game designers to be true artists with high integrity, such as Chris Roberts, Warren Spector, Lawrence Holland, and David Braben. Yet, designing and selling games is a business, and game designers and publishers must survive as businesses. Piracy has made making a living as a game developer very difficult. Game developers have had to get creative about making games that gamers will be willing to purchase once but then be willing to pay for repeatedly, even after they already own the game. This allows game developers to continue to increase their profits without having to spend much or any time at all, helping to offset a portion of the monetary losses to piracy. Gaming mechanics that produce circular, self-reinforcing sales have become more and more common because they produce economic results—results necessary for the survival of an industry that is at risk of collapsing under the greed and lack of moral and ethical self-regulation of its own consumer base. Therefore, game developers are strongly economically incentivized to create games with higher addictive potential, whether or not they know that is what they are doing.

Mechanics That Make Games Addictive

As I have spent several years working with people who have video game addictions and conducting qualitative analyses of my own, I have come upon several patterns that I have found very helpful in explaining why certain video games appear to have a higher addictive potential than others. These observations have held true in my clinical experience and have proven to be useful as both measures to prevent the development of video game addictions and guidelines to inform recovery from an addictive relationship with video games. I have been able to isolate several specific gaming mechanics that help explain the addictive potential of each game. I have found that the more these mechanics are present and the more prominent each mechanic is, the greater the addictive potential of a specific game.

Addictive Gaming Mechanic #1: Level Grinding

Level grinding, according to Cory Janssen, is what usually keeps a player involved in the game by completing the same boring tasks over and over again in order to gain things like "experience points or gold" necessary for developing new skills and abilities for their character. While this is a dull task, finally managing to level up provides a sense of achievement. And while level grinding may be uninteresting, gamers come to consider it a necessary evil to progress through the game to the fun parts.[72]

Here's the dirty little secret (hidden in plain sight) of a lot of modern video games: a large portion of the gameplay is not actually fun. Most gamers do not enjoy level grinding. But it keeps them playing in order to reach specific gaming goals, such as leveling up so they are not constantly getting stomped on by their competition. Overall, video games that require the player to engage in level grinding have them spend a large period of time in tedious tasks to qualify for brief but rewardingly fun gaming moments. It kind of feels like a racket or a con job. It's as if someone is saying, "Psst! Hey, kid! Why don't you go out there and beg from ornery businessmen all day long until you get fifty dollars? When you do that, come back here and give it to me, and I'll tell you a really funny knock-knock joke. It's a really good one, I swear." A lot of boring, mind-numbing work for a brief payoff doesn't feel like a fair trade or a fun game, does it? It sounds more like a job as a burger-flipper at a fast food joint, yet that's not that far off from the actual entertainment value of most level grinding.

If all of that is true, why is level grinding compelling and addictive? Level grinding has a few interesting psychological effects. First, it creates a sense of emotional investment in the game. At our core, most of us are motivated by what we feel. The more time, energy, and effort we put into something, the more it matters to us. The more that thing matters to us, the more it becomes a source of motivation for us. This is true of a spouse, a child, an education, a career, or an avatar in an online roleplaying game. One gamer described this kind of emotional investment in a video game through the tragic tale of the death of some cyber pets he spent years cultivating through level grinding:

New Year's Eve, 2002. My dating partner at the time was out of town, so I hunkered down to do some UO [Ultima Online]—a game I had put about four years into by that time. My little excursion out for the evening as a Tamer turned into an epic battle for both me and my irreplaceable pets—a Nightmare (fire breathing horse) and my Dragon. This was before pet summoning etc . . . you could spend hours finding the perfect beastie to tame, then spend hours more honing their skills. By hours, I mean weeks, months, etc. Once they died, they died.

And mine did. After about a two hour struggle (went down a bad tunnel into a spawn of Balrons then got flanked by another set) both pets went down. I ported out . . . confused, sad, befuddled as to what happened, distraught . . . those little pixels were under my watchful eye for two frigging years, and now they were gone. Gone! Emotional? Yup. Boring? Nope.[73]

Besides emotional investment, level grinding provides a strong intermittent reinforcement pattern. As we discussed previously in the section on process addictions, this is the same psychological reinforcement principle upon which slot machines and other gambling games are based. Just like those forms of gambling, the player puts in a great deal of time and effort without any real reward. However, when the rewards come, they tend to be large. The gamer may level up and gain new abilities. Now they can cast new spells, wear new armor, enter new realms, or finally kill that monster that has wiped them out dozens or even hundreds of times. The rewards feel like a game changer and provide a new sense of excitement about the game . . . only to plunge the player into a world where more is needed than they have achieved, setting off another long rigmarole of level grinding to repeat the process. Of course, this provides the game developer with another opportunity to make money by offering "micro-transactions" that allow the gamer to purchase their way up through levels or to buy virtual gear that assists in leveling up—all purchased with real money—thus relieving some of the grinding process for the gamer. The player invests time or money, but either way they invest, their motivation for playing the game is increased due to that investment.

Level grinding tends to be the backbone mechanic of every Massive Multiplayer Online Roleplaying Game that I know of, but it is not limited to them. Social media games often have a strong level grinding element to them, and game designers are integrating level grinding into first-person shooters and other action titles, most likely because it has become a very effective way to keep people playing the same game over and over again. Prominent examples of games with a heavy level-grinding mechanic include *World of Warcraft*, *Everquest*, *EVE Online*, and *Farmville*. While *World of Warcraft* seems to be the obvious king of the level grinding mechanic (and indeed, the very public poster child of online gaming addictions), my observations is that *Minecraft* performs this mechanic just as well, only much more subtly. The mining and crafting mechanics of *Minecraft* both rely heavily upon the mechanic of level grinding. It is just presented in a way that is experientially different than most other level grinding, giving it a fresh feeling. With this understanding, it is no surprise to me that others in my profession and I are seeing a huge surge in the number of people coming in for services who have an obsessive or addictive relationship with *Minecraft*.

Addictive Gaming Mechanic #2: Twitch

The second dynamic that can increase the addictive potential of a game is twitch. Technically, twitch refers to high-speed gameplay with constant micro-adjustments determining the difference between victory and defeat. In plain English, it means that the game tends to move along at a heart-pounding pace, and the gamer has to make rapid and accurate adjustments of the controls in order to survive. Twitch has been with video games from the beginning. Those who remember the original *Space Invaders* will recall that the twitch factor in that game started out low, with the rows of alien aggressors weaving back and forth and lobbing projectiles. As the game progressed, the aliens would speed up, ramping up the difficulty level and requiring the player to think faster and maneuver and fire with greater speed and accuracy. Of course, if I were an alien invader and I knew that earthlings had the ability to destroy hundreds of my ships with a single anti-aircraft unit, I would probably have considered invading a different planet instead. But, who am I to play Monday morning quarterback for highly pixelated extraterrestrials of yesteryear?

First-person shooters such as the *Halo* series are a prime example of twitch gameplay, as are high octane first-person puzzler/platformer games such as *Cloudbuilt*. Twitch gameplay is particularly effective at producing adrenaline and norepinephrine, which you may recall is one of the highly influential neurochemical "kingpins" discussed in the section on process addiction. Twitch gameplay keeps players highly stimulated with immediate, dramatic results of their actions and often involves a rapid sequence of player deaths and respawns. The buzz of simulated velocity and simulated danger make the player feel energized and alive, which makes playing the game an intrinsically rewarding experience, especially for people with ADHD.

To be fair, twitch is also a gaming mechanic that helps produce some of the gaming benefits we discussed, such as increased visual attention, increased speed of problem solving, improved spatial reasoning, and so forth. That being said, some interesting trends are happening with twitch gaming that have the effect of reducing the potential benefits of twitch while maximizing its addictive qualities. For example, some games are now altering their mechanics so that a player's shooting accuracy is not based on whether or not they are properly aligning their crosshairs with the target, but rather on that player's statistics based on leveling up, thus further encouraging level grinding. In other words, a player who is new to the game may be the reincarnation of Davey Crocket as far as his personal marksmanship is concerned, but the computer will calculate hits and misses based on his experience points. So, even when he is dead on target, his shot may be counted as a miss. On the other hand, a player with mediocre marksman skills may have his crosshairs misaligned for a hit, but because he has been spending a lot of time on the game, the computer counts it as a hit. The game rewards time spent on the game, not improved skills. Thus, learning curves are flattening, the requirement for strategy is decreasing, and spastic player input and long hours of gaming are increasingly rewarded. In this way, twitch has "gone bro" and dumbed itself down to the point where its benefits get watered down.

Many games involve some aspect of twitch, but it is most prominently displayed in first-person shooters (FPSs) such as the *Call of Duty* series, *Halo*, *Destiny*, racing games, and fighting games such as the *Mortal Kombat* series. The mere fact that a game has twitch is not necessarily reason to be alarmed, but when combined with a dumbed-down approach to the mechanic, level grinding, and online social guilds, it can be the "hook" that gets the other addictive pieces to sink in.

Addictive Gaming Mechanic #3: Guilds and Leagues

Humans, even introverted ones, are herd animals. We have social needs, and social isolation is traumatizing to the point it can literally drive us to psychosis. As a result, we are socially motivated. We find connection with other human beings rewarding, and many of us are willing to go to great lengths (and to commit considerably folly along the way) in order to feel like we belong, to feel like we matter, and to be a part of other people's lives. As games have moved online, they have explored various ways of tying social connections into the gameplay experience. Two major ways of doing this are creating leagues, in which gamers enter tiers of competition against each other, and guilds, in which gamers team up to achieve common goals.

The evolution of the culture surrounding guilds in online games has been fascinating to watch. They tend to mirror the organizational dynamics of mob families, gangs, or even cults. Groupthink tends to run fairly rampant, and there are often strong hierarchies in social structure. Guilds create and demand a strong sense of social obligation to attend guild activities and raids, and failure to do so can lead to expulsion from the guild. In the guild, it doesn't matter if it is two o' clock in the morning for you—if your guild needs you, then you must respond. Expulsion feels tragic to the expelled gamer, like being a digital leper cast out of a medieval colony, because many online role-playing games cannot be effectively played without being a member of a guild. I have worked with a number of clients who were so devastated by "banishment" from a guild that they attempted to commit suicide in real life.

A prominent example of the social pressure of guilds is the now infamous Battle of Asakai in the game *EVE Online*. In *EVE Online*, guilds are built at various levels, including federations, coalitions, and so forth, but the dynamics around them are the same. On January 7, 2013, the leader of a huge coalition was preparing for a medium-sized attack on an enemy position. However, by accidentally clicking his mouse at the wrong time, he ended up warping deep into the heart of a rival coalition without his support fleet to back him up, leaving his colossal warship (which was worth approximately $3,500 in real world money) completely vulnerable. The rival faction saw his weakness and began to close in for the kill. When he realized the situation he had gotten himself into, he sent out a red alert, marshaling every ally he could. The rival coalition responded in kind, calling in additional support from their own coalition members and any allies who would respond. The result was a colossal 3,000 player battle that stressed the servers so much that they had to dilate in-game time and distort in-game space in order to process the battle without crashing.[74] To have missed the call to battle would have been to subject oneself to intense social sanctions among guild members, regardless of whatever real life events might have been competing for the time and attention of the battle-hardened space warriors of *EVE Online*.

It was interesting to see the way some of their fellow gamers commented about the experience afterward. Alen on Slashdot.org poster queried, "How many were divorced the next day?" A fellow Slashdot poster replied, "Yeah, that was my thought, too. How many came out of the computer room sweating on their run to the fridge, uncommunicative, distracted, and wild eyed. Then crawled into bed late to a cold shoulder and a turned back. Then having to go to work/school the next day and not be able to explain it to anyone because, nobody would understand, and all the raised eyebrows, and looking askance, and rolling of eyes between workmates. Private little daydreams must be problematic when shared with 3000 other basement dwellers."[75] The nature of guilds in online games makes it extremely difficult—perhaps nearly impossible—to play a game in a moderate, reasonable manner that can be fit within the "golden mean" of one to three hours of total screen time per day. The time, energy, and commitment required to be a part of a guild is so substantial, it prompted one online commenter to state, "I still contend that EVE Online is simply a massive social experiment to see if you can get people to pay for the privilege of working a second full time job managing spreadsheets."[76] Guild membership and activities become a competing set of priorities for many players of such online games, and I frequently observe that it becomes gamers' predominant priority, hence the growth in the phenomenon known as World of Warcraft Widows or Game Widows. These people describe the degree of their gaming spouse or significant other's emotional and physical unavailability due to their gaming habits to be tantamount to them having an affair or even being dead, and have been observed to go through the same grieving process as people who have lost a spouse through infidelity or death.[77] The phenomenon of Game Widows has become so widespread they even have online support groups, such as gamerwidow.com.

Leagues, on the other hand, operate quite differently but exert no less of a social pull. I know of no game that has mastered the mechanic of leagues better than the *StarCraft* series (although it should be noted in the first *StarCraft* game, they were referred to as "ladders" rather than leagues). *StarCraft II* features seven hierarchical leagues, each with various divisions, as well as a practice league for newcomers to the multiplayer component of the game. Novices may play up to fifty practice matches in the practice league before they must face evaluation in the form of placement matches. After competing in five official placement matches, players are assigned to a league that fits their current skill level. However, regardless of how brilliantly a new player performs, they must work their way through the various leagues in order to reach the pinnacle Grandmaster League, which is limited to the top two hundred players in each region. A player's position in a league and division determines the matches they will be able to compete in. The matchmaking algorithm is designed to give each player an approximately 50 percent chance of winning each match. To keep players fully engaged, the matchmaking algorithm is also set to "decay"; if a player does not complete any matches in a two-week period, their ranking and status will gradually decrease.[78]

To add further incentive, highly accomplished *StarCraft II* players become international online celebrities and receive all of the trappings and attention that come with fame. One example of this is Choi Seong-Hun. He is currently considered the fourth best *StarCraft II* player in the world. Gaming has become his profession, and he pulls in more than $100,000 per year through his earning in competitions (there are now approximately 47,500 such competitions per year with more than 71 million spectators worldwide) and through money he makes from his online broadcasts.[79] Aspiring *StarCraft* warriors are known to spend countless hours studying the gameplay video of highly accomplished gamers, to the point that an excellent *StarCraft* player can pull in a good chunk of change from advertisers posting ads on the videos they place online.

This hearkens back to the way a casino works. One slot machine has addictive qualities, but put a thousand of them together in a room so each player can hear when one of them goes off, and those addictive qualities are amplified. Similarly, leagues provide tremendous rewards, both in a sense of accomplishment, status, social recognition, and even fame and money. However, they only provide those rewards for a small percentage of the people involved. Nonetheless, some people get huge payoffs that are prominently displayed to the whole gaming community. This incentivizes other players to sacrifice and strive to be among the few, the proud, the ones the gaming gods smile down upon. To climb the ladder, however, members of leagues must never stop. Besides the "decay" built into their rating if they do not constantly play, all of the other members of the leagues are constantly working to improve. Thus, trying to play moderately as a part of an online league is a significant challenge. If you are less excessive and obsessive than your competition, you will be left in the dust and remain a mere pawn in the social realm of the leagues.

The irony is this: I have many people who come to me and express concern about a loved one gaming in a way that seems excessive, obsessive, or addictive. Oftentimes, I will hear them say, "Well, at least they are playing with people online. That gives them some social interaction. That's a good thing, right?" The sad truth is that the online, social element of games—especially when guilds, leagues, or other similar dynamics are at play—actually significantly increase the addictive potential of a game.[80] In fact, I would say the vast majority of the people I have seen over the years who fit the criteria for an actual gaming addiction were not addicted to playing single player games but got hooked by the online multiplayer elements. I have found that one of the first things that needs to be considered with unhealthy patterns of gaming is whether trying to continue various aspects of online elements of gameplay is going to work. This is often a very emotionally painful piece of self-examination. Nonetheless, after working through much resistance, denial, and self-deception, many people find they have to let go of guilds and leagues in order to begin to form a healthy relationship with electronics.

Addictive Gaming Mechanic #4:
Social Status and Achievements

Guilds and leagues are not the only ways in which social status is worked into gamers' experiences. Gaming hubs such as Steam and Xbox Live have found ways to link players together in communities, even when they are not actively playing together online. This is often done in the form of ranking systems based on achievements each player has made in the games they are playing. Achievements can range from predictable tasks such as reaching a certain number of kills to random, mundane events such as bouncing a rock off a rooftop and down a chimney or falling in the water forty times. Some achievements are known ahead of time and placed as goals for players to strive for. Some are hidden, left to be stumbled upon by accident or by hours of endless experimentation to find hidden achievements. Achievements are used to encourage people to continue playing a game long after the game itself has run out of real content.

These achievements are then publicly tracked and displayed on gaming hubs and are considered a sort of status symbol among gamers. People who are particularly good at chalking up achievements can even become celebrities of a sort. One's prowess based on the achievements they have racked up is often referred to as their "e-penis," and it is made larger by playing more games and unlocking more achievements. (I am sorry if I offended anyone by using this term, but I'm just the messenger here. I didn't make it up). That being said, the term is instructive for understanding the culture that surrounds using gaming achievements as social status.

Let me illustrate my point. If you have the time and resources, consider trying the following sociological experiment. First, take a junior high school boys' locker room. Second, expand it to the size of the world. Third, provide all the boys with rewards and incentives for clawing their way to the top of the social hierarchy. Fourth, strongly promote narcissism as a social value. Last, provide the boys with weapons. Congratulations! You have just reproduced the culture of Xbox Live or the *DOTA 2* gaming community. The results tend to make *Lord of the Flies* positively green with envy. Yet by attaching gaming accomplishments to social status, publicly comparing status markers gained through gaming, and providing an oh-so-artificial link between one's gaming abilities and one's perceived sexual virility, gaming hubs that utilize achievements further incentivize excessive, obsessive, and addictive patterns of gaming when gamers choose to engage with this part of the gaming culture.

Addictive Gaming Mechanic #5: Fantasy Alter Egos

First, I want to acknowledge that escapism should not be viewed as inherently bad. Nor should escapism be seen as something that is unique to video games. People have found escapism for untold centuries through stories, and certainly it can be found in music, movies, and other forms of media. Fantasy can and does play a role in healthy lives. It can stimulate the mind to think more creatively. Fantasy play serves a role in the mental, social, and moral development of children. We can find relief and refreshment by connecting for a time with something that is separate from our own life. For these reasons and more, I believe fictional experiences are adaptive and beneficial.

On the other hand, when distraction becomes life and life becomes merely a distraction, people begin to fall into a rut in which their real lives begin to atrophy and rust. As important things in their lives decline, they feel a greater need for escapism and bury themselves in it more deeply, wrapping it around them more tightly so as not to let the decay of their real lives perturb them while they are in their fanciful cocoons. This is not a risk that comes solely with digital fantasies; people run the risk of getting lost in fantasy escapes in any kind of media, including books, television, and even their own purely internal daydreams. That being said, video games are a powerful tool for enhancing and experiencing fantasy. Thus, they have the potential to increase both the benefits and the pitfalls of escapism.

Some video games provide players with the ability to assume a pre-designed role, such as Mario, Link, Solid Snake, Colonel Christopher Blair, Master Chief, Michael de Santa, or Guybrush Threepwood. Other video games allow players to carefully craft their own character, determining their appearance, characteristics, abilities, allegiances, and so forth. This provides an interesting set of possibilities. Gamers can shape their character to be a sort of virtual compensation for the things they are not but wish they were. Gamers can try personas entirely different from their own. They can also play out fantasies of being the object of their own desire. All of these options provide numerous possibilities for psychological entanglement, and for the game to become more than just a game for the gamer, but an arena in which they are playing out important or vulnerable parts of their own psyche in a way that feels less threatening. There is potential for benefit from that kind of exploration, like the old psychological technique of psychodrama being played out in a digital realm. On the other hand, it can easily become a tool to enhance the debilitating psychological defense mechanisms of displacement or fantasy formation in which a person only dabbles with their own thoughts and emotions in the safety of fantasy and neglects taking healthy actions in their actual lives.

My clinical experience and qualitative analysis indicates that the deeper someone gets into fantasy elements of gaming and the more emotionally and mentally aligned he or she becomes with his or her gaming alter-egos, the greater the addictive potential is of a specific game, or any game that the person interacts with in the same manner. Thus, part of learning to have a healthy relationship with video games requires finding real-world ways of dealing with our thoughts and emotions besides just taking a break from them through fantasies.

Addictive Gaming Mechanic #6: Long Gaming Epochs and Persistent Universes

To describe this next mechanic, I had to invent some new terminology since I was unable to find any preexisting terms that accurately and parsimoniously describe the phenomenon I am talking about. One general definition of the word *epoch* from the Merriam-Webster dictionary is "an extended period of time usually characterized by a distinctive development or by a memorable series of events."[81] A "gaming epoch" refers to the amount of time needed to play before the status quo changes from the beginning of a particular gaming episode. One can begin to measure the length of a specific game's epoch by determining how much game time is required before the player is better off than when they started. Can a reasonable sense of progress or resolution be reached within five minutes, thirty minutes, or three hours?

Game universes can either be finite or persistent. A finite gaming universe is only active when the game is turned on and stops progressing in time, plot, and action when the game is turned off. Persistent gaming universes are always on and progressing, regardless of whether the gamer is playing or not. Whereas Mario doesn't either save the princess or die trying while you are away at work and not playing *Super Mario Galaxy 2*, the world and characters of *Everquest*, *Runescape*, or *World of Warcraft* continue to play while you are away. By definition, all Massive Multiplayer Online games have persistent universes. If you are not there, you literally miss out. (Incidentally, this is one of the dynamics that makes social media more addictive: the content of social media continues to evolve when the user is not engaged with it, and they can have a nagging sense that they are "missing out" by not checking in). In a game with a persistent online world, you are actually worse off by not playing, rather than just no better off—because you have fallen behind the development of the gaming world. So, interestingly enough, persistent universes can cause a sort of "negative gaming epoch" that creates a sense of deficit that the player then feels a need to make up for the next time they play.

An example of a game with short gaming epochs is *Rogue Legacy*. In this game, a player can select a character, venture into the dungeon, collect gold, die, and pass on their gold to the next character to be used to buy new equipment and abilities in gaming spurts ranging from a few seconds to a few minutes. In *Rogue Legacy*, an epoch is typically the length of a single "life." While completing the whole game takes time, a player experiencing one or several epochs will have more of a sense of fulfillment and is less likely to feel like they have been cut off "right in the middle," before they have been able to complete what they started off to experience. With *Rogue Legacy*, a player could possibly experience ten, twenty, perhaps even thirty or more epochs in an hour of play. Additionally, *Rogue Legacy* has a finite universe.

On the other hand, the game *Planetside 2* has very long gaming instances. This online, massively scaled, multiplayer first-person shooter creates a real-time, constantly evolving battlefield. Individual battles can stretch on for days, even weeks. And, of course, *Planetside 2* has a persistent gaming universe, combined with twitch gaming, guilds, social status markers, and fantasy identity elements. As you can see, *Planetside 2* is stacked pretty heavily with the addictive gaming mechanics we have discussed to this point.

Games that have a feature that allows the player to save at any time allow the player to artificially shorten gaming epochs. If the player has to save mid-game, they may not have completed their goal, but they have also not lost their progress. Thus, their game time was not as satisfying as if they had completed a natural epoch, but it is also not as frustrating as if they had been stopped short of an epoch and thus had lost all of their progress. It has been my experience that people are more likely to play excessively beyond reasonable time constraints (and thus end up missing things such as school, work, and important family events) for games that have long gaming epochs, persistent universes, or both. Therefore, gamers who are engrossed in these types of games are more likely to devolve into pathological patterns of gaming.

Addictive Gaming Mechanic #7: Interrupted Flow

The concept of flow in psychology was first put forth by Mihaly Csíkszentmihályi.[82] Flow is a state reached when a person becomes completely absorbed in an activity in a way that leads to a sense of heightened vitality, awareness, and fulfillment. It is a highly rewarding, resonating state that people experience through many experiences such as sports, education, work, service, and meaningful relationships. Flow experiences carry with them common factors, though not all of them need to be present to qualify as a flow experience. These include the following:

1. Having clear goals that are challenging, yet are still attainable.
2. Requiring strong concentration and focused attention.
3. Having aspects of the activity that feel intrinsically rewarding.
4. Providing a sense of serenity, and/or a loss of feelings of self-consciousness. This can be a very anxiety relieving experience.
5. Creating a sense of timelessness or a distorted sense of time. The person feels so focused on the present that they lose track of time passing.
6. Receiving immediate feedback from the experience.
7. Knowing that the task is doable but requires a significant amount of skill and effort.
8. Providing feelings of personal control over the situation and the outcome.

9. Creating a lack of awareness of physical needs. A person feels like they could continue without the need to sleep, eat, etc.
10. The experience allows for a complete focus on the activity itself.[83]

I believe that gamers can experience flow—or at least experiences close to flow or a functional facsimile thereof—in video games. A thoughtful game designer can engineer a game so that a gamer is just entering their state of flow (or pseudo-flow) when the game is interrupted and the gamer is required to do something to reengage the flow experience. At that point in time, the gamer is highly physiologically and psychologically motivated to do what it takes to get back to that state of flow, which means they are much more likely to be willing to pay in some way in order to continue their flow experience.

A specific example of how this is done is *Candy Crush Saga*. The game itself is fairly straightforward. Its goals are clear, and it provides an achievable challenge. Many people experience a sense of timelessness and loss of self-consciousness while they play it. *Candy Crush Saga* only allows gamers a set number of tries and failures on a specific level before the gamer must either wait a set amount of time to play again, invite other people to play, or pay to continue. In this way, the game designers have learned to interrupt flow at the most jarring, irritating moment, thus providing incentive for the gamer to either pay to continue, which means more money for the developers, or try to recruit others to the game, which also generates more money for the developers. The cost seems relatively small and worth the effort to the gamer in order to get immediately back to their flow experience.

This dynamic seems to have recently exploded in mobile apps and games such as the latest offerings by Rovio's *Angry Birds Go* and *Angry Birds Stella*. Why has this approach become so common? Because it works, plain and simple! It gets people to pay to continue to play. I have also observed that another, sort of backwards way of going about this is creating "free" games that include intrusive in-game ads. These ads tend to "harsh the mellow" the gamers get from the gaming experience. The game then innocently mentions that if they pay X amount of money, those flow-flubbing ads will disappear. Overall, by creating the sensation of flow, game developers increase the psychological appeal of the games, and by strategically interrupting flow at critical points, these games produce impulsive and compulsive behavior from game players, which plays an influential role in the development of excessive, obsessive, or addictive patterns of video game playing.

Addictive Gaming Mechanic #8: Infinity

A game's storyline and mission objectives help create a desire to play more. A well-crafted game can be like a well-written book, with pacing, tension, plot development, unfolding game elements, and drama weaved skillfully together (even in the absence of an actual story) to create an almost hypnotic influence over the reader or the gamer to find out what happens on the next page or after the next gaming epoch. Just as the most natural place to stop reading a book is at the end, the most natural time to stop playing a game is when you reach its completion. After all, it's the end; there's nothing left to be played. By that point in time, the objectives have been achieved, the story arch has been completed (or a setup has been made for a sequel), and there is a sense of satisfaction and "coming full circle" that accompanies reaching the end. However, what if the game literally has no end and is therefore a veritable *Neverending Story?* (If you lived through the eighties, you almost certainly have a certain song stuck in your head now.) Many games actually have become just that, using open-ended sandbox style gameplay to create games that literally have no end. I have come to refer to this gaming mechanic as "infinity."

Sandbox gameplay typically provides an open world setting, allowing the player freedom to roam and interact with various parts of the world as they please. Some sandbox style games literally have no real story or plot; they merely create a world and turn the player loose on it. Others provide a main storyline, usually consisting of specific mission objectives or a series of progressive quests or missions that a player can choose to engage in or ignore, as he or she pleases. But, even when the actual plot has come to a finish, the gamer still has full access to the gaming world and can continue playing the game with goals of his or her own choosing. Many developers will periodically release expansions (often in the form of DLC, or "downloadable content") that a player can purchase, adding additional quests, missions, characters, options, or areas in the gaming world. A savvy developer can keep a gamer playing and paying while putting a relatively small amount of work into periodic DLC expansions, thus helping make the developer's business more sustainable in the piracy-drenched environment in which they are trying to make a living.

The gaming mechanic of infinity is frequently combined with other mechanics such as a persistent online universe, level grinding, and multiplayer guilds or leagues. This provides a gaming experience wherein the gamer is incentivized to play frequently and for extended periods of time to invest in leveling up and being prepared for the next expansion of the game in order to avoid becoming an easy target for everyone else who plays more and therefore levels up more quickly.

Implications

While research on video game addiction is still developing, by combining the existing research and using deductive reasoning to apply current knowledge about the functions of the human brain, I believe that we can already draw the following conclusions with a high degree of confidence and accuracy. First, I think we are beyond a point of reasonable disputation about whether video game addiction is a real phenomenon. It has become quite clear that video games can indeed be addicting and that there is a significant portion of the population that experiences this phenomenon. Video game addictions, like all addictions, bring with them personal, familial, and societal costs. Second, not all video games have the same degree of addictive potential. Therefore, it is incorrect to lump them all together in the same category. Third, the addictive potential of each video game is a function of the interaction between the specific mechanics of a specific video game and the individual biological, psychological, and social makeup of a specific human being. Addiction is caused by the nature of the interaction between brain and program, something I have come to call the neuro-cyber interface. Fourth, while there is a great deal of individualization in the risk each person has to being addicted to specific games, there are also sufficient commonalities between human beings and also within various types of games for certain guidelines to be generally applicable.

Process Addiction and the Biopsychosocial-Cyber Interface

In general, the greater number of addictive gaming mechanics a specific game includes and the greater the magnitude of each of those mechanics, the greater degree of addictive potential of that specific video game. However, it should be noted that for these mechanics to have an effect of increasing addictive potential, the gamer in question has to actively engage with those mechanics. The mere fact that a game contains the dynamics is not what has the effect; it is the gamer engaging with those mechanics that has the addictive effect. The addiction is the result of the biopsychosocial-cyber interface, the connection and intermingling of the pieces of the person and the pieces of the program. For example, let's suppose I play *StarCraft II*. By simply not engaging in the multiplayer leagues, I have removed myself from three influential, addictive dynamics (leagues, social status, and achievements), and I have given myself more control over other addictive dynamics based on how I choose to interact with the game. I can artificially shorten gaming epochs by saving at any time, an option that is not available when playing online. I reduce social pressure by being able to play when it fits my life, rather than having to shape my life to be able to play when my matches are scheduled. Furthermore, I can use the ability to save at any time without losing progress in the game to manage the intensity of interrupted flow. It doesn't eliminate the sensation of interrupted flow, but it reduces its intensity by not penalizing me in the game for not continuing to play at that moment. I can also have longer gaps between when I play without feeling like I am falling behind relative to the other members of the league. The point is, the addictive potential of *StarCraft II* is different for me based on whether I play single player, in casual multiplayer matches with friends or family members, or as a part of the competitive *StarCraft II* leagues. I can help mitigate the addictive potential of *StarCraft II* by how I choose to play it.

On the other hand, some games are constructed in such a way that a person cannot really play them without engaging in all of the addictive mechanics. One example of this is *World of Warcraft*. By its very nature, the game is infused with the mechanic of infinity and includes a persistent online universe. It is impossible to play the game without those being present. Interrupted flow is virtually inevitable as the game itself will always continue when I log off. The game plays without me. It does not "ramp down" as my gaming session does, and therefore the separation is always going to be somewhat jarring. Fantasy identity is at the core of a player's experience with the game. The gameplay itself is entirely structured upon level grinding, and therefore one cannot play *World of Warcraft* without subjecting oneself to an extensive intermittent reinforcement pattern, with its accompanying addictive qualities. Leveling up takes a lot of time and investment, creating long gaming epochs. These long gaming epochs of leveling up help prepare a player for guild raids, which only compound the issue of long gaming epochs, given that it is not uncommon for a single raid to last three or more hours, depending on the raid objectives. Social status is heavily tied in with a player's level and affiliations. One has to structure his or her life to be present for guild activities. While I suppose someone could try to play *World of Warcraft* without being a part of a guild of some sort, it would make success in the game virtually impossible. When we take all of these factors into consideration, there is not really a practical way to play *World of Warcraft* that reduces its addictive potential. The structure of *World of Warcraft* makes all of its addictive mechanics inseparable from the experience of playing the game on any level. Therefore, the only move a person can really make to reduce his or her risk of addiction—or at the very least an unbalanced, excessive, or otherwise unhealthy relationship with the game—is not to play the game.

I am going to go on record as saying that there is no such thing as a game with absolutely no addictive potential. All games merit a degree of thoughtfulness in how we play them. But to fully evaluate the addictive potential of a game, I have to do more than understand the way the game is put together; I also have to understand how I am put together. Any number of things about me could make me more vulnerable to certain mechanics. For example, many people I know with ADHD resonate very powerfully to the gaming mechanic of twitch but are turned off by the gaming mechanic of level grinding. Thus, they are more likely to get addicted to high twitch games, such as the *Call of Duty* series. On the other hand, most of the people I know who have Asperger's Syndrome resonate powerfully to the level grinding mechanic, but their greater difficulty with fine motor coordination makes twitch less of a "fit" for the way they are put together neurologically. Thus, they are at lower risk for the twitch mechanics of *Call of Duty* but are at higher risk for the level grinding mechanics of Massive Multiplayer Online Roleplaying Games or *Minecraft*. In general, people who feel lonely or struggle with social connections are likely to be more vulnerable to fantasy identity, social status mechanics, and guilds. Our individual strengths and vulnerabilities, both neurologically and psychologically, help to determine our specific degree of vulnerability to the addictive nature of various gaming mechanics.

This fact can sometimes lead to surprising individual implications that can be hard to discern unless we are really paying attention. Let's examine a game widely considered to be an oldie but a goodie—*Wing Commander 3*. *Wing Commander 3* has no online element at all. It is a cinematic space flight simulator from the nineties and contains twitch gameplay and fantasy identity. The fantasy identity is fixed, as the player assumes the role of Colonel Christopher Blair. However, the player can shape Blair's relationships and fate through making various choices. Blair's wingmen are fleshed out with individual personalities and presented in a way to encourage the gamer to connect with them emotionally, so the game excels at creating some degree of emotional investment by the player. The game is divided into various missions, none of which are overly long, creating naturally short gaming epochs. There are no leagues or guilds, and the closest thing to social standing is a pilot's kill score. But this is not automatically shared with anyone. To share it, the player would have to overtly tell someone what it is. Overall, *Wing Commander 3* is pretty lightweight when it comes to the number and degree of addictive mechanics. So, just by evaluating the game itself, it would seem that there is little chance of addiction. That evaluation is correct: on its own merits, *Wing Commander 3* has a relatively low risk of addiction.

However, individual variations in people can create a situation where a person could create an addictive relationship with a game that only has low addictive potential. Let's suppose that a young adult male tends to have some difficulty with depression. He left home for college and is having a hard time connecting socially there. He's feeling lonely and depressed, and he is stressed out by his workload in his classes.

Let's suppose he starts to play *Wing Commander 3* as a way to blow off steam. So far, no harm and no foul. But there are some risks. By playing when he is depressed, he creates a sort of "slingshot" effect by elevating his crucial neurotransmitters. He goes from a low to a high, and the greater the magnitude of the change, the more the brain is motivated to repeat the experience. The characters he interacts with are well portrayed, and he can feel like he is getting some social interaction (even romance) out of his game playing experience. The twitch mechanic helps generate norepinephrine and can lead him to feel like he is the most alive and vital when playing *Wing Commander 3*. As he turns to this game more and more for his social needs and as a way to combat his depression, and as he reduces his efforts to meet those needs in other ways, he can create in himself a much higher risk of addiction from a low-risk game because his predispositions, lifestyle, and approach to his mental health and well-being is high-risk. The addictive potential of the game can be conceptualized as the following equation: $f(g + p) = ap$. High-risk factors of the game (g) plus the high-risk factors of the person (p) multiplied by the degree of "fit" between addictive mechanics (f) equals the addictive potential of the interface between the person and the game (ap).

Having a healthy relationship with video games is about much more than limiting screen time, as indispensable a step as that may be. First and foremost, having a healthy relationship with video games is about effective, adaptive self-care. To the degree that we are not creating and following purpose in our lives, developing and abiding by our code of ethics and values, building and maintaining good relationships, making meaningful contributions, stimulating and expanding our minds, taking care of our bodies, and engaging in other wholesome and effective forms of recreation, we increase our risk of forming any addiction, including a process addiction to video games. Who we are—our strengths, weaknesses, mindset, and approach to life—is an indispensable part of the equation of both health and addiction. If we find we are struggling with an excessive, obsessive, or addictive relationship with video games, we need to step back and examine how well we are doing with our self-care in all of the areas previously mentioned. While a process addiction is a problem in and of itself, it often also serves as a signal to call our attention to other important needs that are necessary to take care of ourselves, our relationships, and our lives. We neglect this call at our own peril, and failing to heed its warnings and attend to the matters it illuminates will make our efforts to have a healthier relationship with the cyberworld extremely difficult, prone to constant relapses, and have only superficial improvements.

Endnotes

1. Brightman, J. (2006). Women gamers outnumber men? *Business Week*. Retrieved November 24, 2014, from http://www.businessweek.com/stories/2006-04-18/women-gamers-outnumber-men.

2. Gentile, D. (2009). Pathological video game use among youth ages 8 to 18: A national study. *Psychological Science 20*(5), 594-602.

3. Association for Psychological Science (2009). Video games: Racing, shooting and zapping your way to better visual skills. *Science Daily*. Retrieved December 12, 2013, from http://www.sciencedaily.com/releases/2009/12/091217183448.htm.

4. Queen Mary, University of London (2013, August 21). Playing video games can boost brain power. *Science Daily*. Retrieved December 12, 2013, from http://www.sciencedaily.com/releases/2013/08/130821094924.htm.

5. Michigan State University (2011, November 9). Video game playing tied to creativity, research shows. *Science Daily*. Retrieved December 12, 2013, from http://www.sciencedaily.com/releases/2011/11/111102125355.htm.

6. University of Rochester (2014). Playing action video games can boost learning, study finds. *Science Daily*. Retrieved November 13, 2014, from http://www.sciencedaily.com/releases/2014/11/141110161036.htm?utm_source=feedburner&utm_medium=feed&utm_campaign=-Feed%3A+sciencedaily%2Ftop_news%2Ftop_science+%28Science-Daily%3A+Top+Science+News%29.

7. Bejjanki, V. R., Zhang, R., Li, R., Pouget, A., Green, C.S., Lu, Z., & Bavelier, D. (2014). Action video game play facilitates the development of better developmental templates. *Proceedings of the National Academy of Sciences of the United States of America*. Published ahead of print November 10, 2014, doi:10.1073/pnas.1417056111.

8. University of Texas Medical Branch at Galveston (2012). Using skills gleaned from video games, high school and college students outmatch medical residents in surgical simulations. *Science Daily*. Retrieved December 12, 2013, from http://www.sciencedaily.com/releases/2012/11/121115141642.htm.

9. American Academy of Pediatrics (2014). Media and children. Retrieved July 31, 2014, from http://www.aap.org/en-us/advocacy-and-policy/aap-health-initiatives/Pages/Media-and-Children.aspx.

10. Khatib, F., DiMaio, F., Fold.it Contenders Group, Fold.it Void Crushers Group, Cooper, S., Kazmierczyk, M., Gilski, M., Krzywda, S., Zabranska, H., Pichova, I., Thompson, J., Popovic, Z., Jaskolski, M., & Baker, D., (2011). Crystal structure of monomeric retroviral protease solved by protein folding game players. *Nature Structural and Molecular Biology, 18*, 1175-1177.

11. North Carolina State University (2013). Seniors who play video games report better sense of emotional well-being. *Science Daily*.

Retrieved December 12, 2013, from http://www.sciencedaily.com/releases/2013/03/130305131249.htm.

12. Anguera, J. A., Boccanfuso, J., Rintoul, J. L., Al-Hashimi, O., Faraji, F., Janowich, J., Kong, E., Larraburo, Y., Rolle, C., Johnston, E., & Gazzaley, A. (2013). Video game training enhances cognitive control in older adults. *Nature, 501,* 97-101. Retrieved September 5, 2014, from http://www.nature.com/nature/journal/v501/n7465/full/nature12486.html.

13. Santanachote, P. (2014). 10 best apps to train your brain. *Time.* Retrieved September 26, 2014, from http://www.cnn.com/2014/09/09/health/brain-training-apps/index.html?hpt=hp_c4.

14. Ballard, K., Sternberg, D. A., Hardy, J. L., & Scanlon, M. (2012). Training related improvements in cognitive performance persist over time but depend on age; An online study including > 140,000 participants. *Society for Neuroscience.* Retrieved September 26, 2014, from http://cdn-hcp.lumosity.com/uploads/completed_research_post/original_paper_file/10/ballard-et-al-2012-age-related-cognitive-decline.pdf.

15. Shute, V. J., Ventura, M., & Ke, F. (2015). The power of play: The effect of Portal 2 and Lumosity on cognitive and noncognitive skills. *Computers & Education, 80,* 58-67.

16. University of Illinois at Urbana-Champaign (2008, December 13). Strategic Video Game Improves Critical Cognitive Skills In Older Adults. *Science Daily.* Retrieved December 12, 2013, from http://www.sciencedaily.com/releases/2008/12/081211081442.htm.

17. Ghent University (2013, July 8). Math game more effective than paper exercises. *Science Daily.* Retrieved December 16, 2013, from http://www.sciencedaily.com/releases/2013/07/130708102921.htm.

18. Jaslow, R. (2014). Smartphone game designed to reduce anxiety shows promise in study. *CBS News.* Retrieved September 26, 2014, from http://www.cbsnews.com/news/smartphone-game-designed-to-reduce-anxiety-new-approach-in-mental-health-care/.

19. Santanachote, ibid.

20. Brigham Young University (2011). Video games are good for girls, if parents play along. *Science Daily.* Retrieved December 12, 2013, from http://www.sciencedaily.com/releases/2011/02/110201083341.htm.

21. Cell Press (2013). Action video games boost reading skills, study of children with dyslexia suggests. *Science Daily.* Retrieved December 12, 2013, from http://www.sciencedaily.com/releases/2013/02/130228124132.htm.

22. Ibid.

23. Bruggers, C. S., Alitzer, R. A., Kessler, R. R., Caldwell, C. B., Coppersmith, K., Warner, L., Davies, B., Paterson, W., Wilcken, J., D'Ambrosio, T. A., German, M. L., Hanson, G. R., Gershan, L. A., Korenberg, J. R., & Bulak, G. (2012). Patient empowerment interactive technologies. *Science Translational Medicine, 4*(152), 152-168.

24. Kato, P. M., Cole, S. W., Bradlyn, A. S., & Pollock, B. H. (2008). A video game improves behavioral outcomes in adolescent and young adults with cancer: A randomized trial. *Pediatrics, 122*(2), e305-e317.

25. Skorka-Brown, J., Andrade, J., & May, J. (2014). Playing "Tetris" reduces the strength, frequency, and vividness of naturally occurring cravings. *Appetite, 76*(1), 161-165.

26. Developmental Disabilities Monitoring Network (2014). Prevalence of Autism Spectrum Disorder among children aged 8 years. *Surveillance Summaries, 63*(SS02), 1-21. Retrieved October 8, 2014, from http://www.cdc.gov/mmwr/preview/mmwrhtml/ss6302a1.htm?s_cid=ss6302a1_w.

27. Gee, S. (2013). AI helps with social awkwardness. *I Programmer*. Retrieved October 8, 2014, from http://www.i-programmer.info/news/105-artificial-intelligence/6265-ai-helps-with-social-awkwardness.html.

28. Yung, K., Eichhoff, E., David, D. L., Klam, W. P., & Doan, A. P. (2014). Internet addiction disorder and problematic use of Google Glass in patient treated at a residential substance abuse program. *Addictive Behaviors, 41*, 58-60.

29. Fulghn (2014). Comment section from article Wilson, J. (2014). Man treated for Google Glass addiction. *CNN*. Retrieved October 24, 2014, from http://www.cnn.com/2014/10/15/health/google-glass-addiction/.

30. Gentile, ibid.

31. Ibid.

32. Ibid.

33. Association for Psychological Science (2010). Game on? Video-game ownership may interfere with young boys' academic functioning. *Science Daily*. Retrieved December 17, 2013, from http://www.sciencedaily.com/releases/2010/03/100310162835.htm.

34. Society for Personality and Social Psychology (2013, August 4). Video games boost visual attention but reduce impulse control. *Science Daily*. Retrieved December 31, 2013, from http://www.sciencedaily.com/releases/2013/08/130804081115.htm.

35. American Academy of Pediatrics (2013). Cyberbullying rampant among high school students: Nearly one-third of youths also report playing video/computer games for more than 3 hours a day. *Science Daily*. Retrieved December 12, 2013, from http://www.sciencedaily.com/releases/2013/05/130505073738.htm.

36. Stelter, B. (2009). 8 hours a day spent on screens, study finds. *The New York Times*. Retrieved November 13, 2014, from http://www.nytimes.com/2009/03/27/business/media/27adco.html?_r=1&.

37. Gentile, ibid.

38. Begley, S. (2007). The brain: How the brain rewires itself. *Time*. Retrieved November 17, 2014, from http://content.time.com/time/magazine/article/0,9171,1580438,00.html.

39. Gentile, ibid.

40. Ohio State University (2012). Violent video games: More playing time equals more aggression. *Science Daily*. Retrieved December 17, 2013, from http://www.sciencedaily.com/releases/2012/12/121210101344.htm.

41. Iowa State University (2013). Violent video games are a risk factor for criminal behavior and aggression, new evidence shows. *Science Daily*. Retrieved December 17, 2013, from http://www.sciencedaily.com/releases/2013/03/130326121605.htm.

42. University of Missouri (2011). Violent video games reduce brain response to violence and increase aggressive behavior, study suggests. *Science Daily*. Retrieved December 17, 2013, from http://www.sciencedaily.com/releases/2011/05/110525151059.htm.

43. University of Connecticut (2013, May 20). Human-like opponents lead to more aggression in video game players. *Science Daily*. Retrieved December 30, 2013, from http://www.sciencedaily.com/releases/2013/05/130520163904.htm.

44. Lippincott, Williams, & Wilkins (2013). Violent video games have lower effects on highly-exposed teens. *Science Daily*. Retrieved December 17, 2013, from http://www.sciencedaily.com/releases/2013/05/130503105027.htm.

45. SAGE Publications (2010). Violent video games increase aggression long after the game is turned off, study finds. *Science Daily*. Retrieved December 17, 2013, from http://www.sciencedaily.com/releases/2010/09/100920094620.htm.

46. Ohio State University (2013). Teens eat more, cheat more after playing violent video games. *Science Daily*. Retrieved December 17, 2013, from http://www.sciencedaily.com/releases/2013/11/131125101013.htm.

47. Society for Personality and Social Psychology (2013, August 4). Video games boost visual attention but reduce impulse control. *Science Daily*. Retrieved December 31, 2013, from http://www.sciencedaily.com/releases/2013/08/130804081115.htm.

48. Hathaway, J. (2014). What is Gamergate and why? An explainer for non-geeks. *Gawker*. Retrieved November 19, 2014, from http://gawker.com/what-is-gamergate-and-why-an-explainer-for-non-geeks-1642909080.

49. Ohio State University, ibid.

50. Murphy, R.F., Penuel, W.R., Means, B., Korbak, C., Whaley, A., & Allen, J.E. (2002). A review of recent evidence on the effectiveness of discrete educational software. Washington, D.C.: Planning and Evaluation Service, U.S. Department of Education.

51. Gentile, ibid.

52. Ibid.

53. Ibid.

54. Yin-Poole, W. (2013). Saints Row 4 sells one million copies in first week. *Eurogamer*. Retrieved November 19, 2014, from http://www.eurogamer.net/articles/2013-08-29-saints-row-4-sells-one-million-copies-in-first-week.

55. Macy, S. (2014). Grand Theft Auto 5 sells 33 million copies. *IGN*. Retrieved November 19, 2014, from http://www.ign.com/articles/2014/05/13/grand-theft-auto-five-sells-33-million-copies.

56. Gentile, ibid.

57. Ibid.

58. Ibid.

59. Rosser, J.C., Jr., Lynch, P. J., Cuddihy, L., Gentile, D.A., Klonsky, J., & Merrell, R., (2007). The impact of video games on training surgeons in the 21st century. *Archives of Surgery, 142*, 181-186.

60. O'Loughlin, E. K., Dugas, E. N., Sabiston, C. M., & O'Loughlin, J. L. (2012). Prevalence and correlates of exergaming in youth. *Pediatrics, 130*(5), 806-814.

61. Gentile, ibid.

62. Sarkis, S. (2014). Internet gaming disorder in DSM-5. *Psychology Today*. Retrieved January 27, 2015, from https://www.psychologytoday.com/blog/here-there-and-everywhere/201407/internet-gaming-disorder-in-dsm-5.

63. BBC News (2005). South Korean dies after games session. Retrieved November 21, 2014, from http://news.bbc.co.uk/2/hi/technology/4137782.stm.

64. Rudd, A. (2012). Diablo death: Teenager dies after playing video game for 40 hours without eating or sleeping. *Mirror*. Retrieved November 21, 2014, from http://www.mirror.co.uk/news/world-news/diablo-iii-death-teenager-dies-1147472.

65. Zurowski, C. (2014). Daniel Petric assassinates mom, shoots pastor dad in the head over video games. *True Crime Report*. Retrieved November 21, 2014, from http://www.truecrimereport.com/2011/06/teen_daniel_petric_murders_mom.php.

66. BBC News (2005). China imposes online gaming curbs. Retrieved November 21, 2014, from http://news.bbc.co.uk/2/hi/technology/4183340.stm.

67. Criminal Justice Degrees Guide (2014). 10 deaths caused by video games. Retrieved November 21, 2014, from http://www.criminaljusticedegreesguide.com/features/10-deaths-caused-by-video-games.html.

68. McCurry, J. (2010). Internet addiction driving South Koreans into realms of fantasy. *The Guardian*. Retrieved November 24, 2014, from http://www.theguardian.com/world/2010/jul/13/internet-addiction-south-korea.

69. Ibid.

70. Mentzoni, R.A., Brunborg, G.S., Molde, H., Myrseth, H., Skouveroe, K.J., Hetland, J., & Pallesen, S. (2011). Problematic video game use: estimated prevalence and associations with mental and physical health. *Cyberpsychology, Behavior, and Social Networking 14*(10), 591-596.

71. Gentile, D. (2009). Pathological video game use among youth ages 8 to 18: A national study. *Psychological Science 20*(5), 594-602.

72. Janssen, C. (2014). Grinding. *Technopedia*. Retrieved November 24, 2014, from http://www.techopedia.com/definition/27527/grinding.

73. Deekin_Scalesinger, (2013). *Slashdot*. Retrieved May 18, 2017 from https://games.slashdot.org/story/13/01/29/2157234/how-eve-online-dealt-with-a-3000-player-battle.

74. Pettite, O. (2013). EVE Online's battle of Asakai: Who was involved, the stakes, and the aftermath. *PC Gamer*. Retrieved November 25, 2014, from http://www.pcgamer.com/eve-online-battle-asakai/.

75. Icebike, (2013). Comment in the comments section of Soulskill (2013). How EVE Online dealt with a 3,000 player battle. *Slashdot*. Retrieved November 25, 2014, from http://games.slashdot.org/story/13/01/29/2157234/how-eve-online-dealt-with-a-3000-player-battle.

76. C-Bol, J. (2013). Comment in the comments section of Soulskill (2013). How EVE Online dealt with a 3,000 player battle. *Slashdot*. Retrieved November 25, 2014, from http://games.slashdot.org/story/13/01/29/2157234/how-eve-online-dealt-with-a-3000-player-battle.

77. Benedetti, W. (2007). Game widows grieve "lost" spouses. *NBC News*. Retrieved November 26, 2014, from http://www.nbcnews.com/id/20397322/ns/technology_and_science-games/t/game-widows-grieve-lost-spouses/#.VHX6y9LF-So.

78. Liquipedia (2014). *Battle.net leagues*. Retrieved November 26, 2014, from http://wiki.teamliquid.net/starcraft2/Battle.net_Leagues.

79. Fink, E. (2014). I make six figures playing video games. *CNN*. Retrieved November 26, 2014, from http://money.cnn.com/2014/10/09/technology/six-figures-to-play-video-games/.

80. Leung, L. (2004). Net-generation attributes and seductive properties of the internet of predictors of online activities and internet addiction. *CyberPsychology & Behavior, 7*(3), 333-348.

81. Epoch (2014). In *Merriam-Webster.com*. Retrieved November 26, 2014, from http://www.merriam-webster.com/dictionary/epoch.

82. Csikszentmihalyi, M. (1997) *Finding flow: The psychology of engagement with everyday life*. New York: Basic Books.

83. Cherry, K. (2014). What is flow? Understanding the psychology of flow. *About.com*. Retrieved November 24, 2014, from http://psychology.about.com/od/PositivePsychology/a/flow.htm.

CHAPTER 7

GENERAL RECOMMENDATIONS

Recommendations for Social Media

Fire is not inherently good or bad. It just is. There are ways in which our relationship with it can benefit us greatly. It can keep us warm and dry, cook our food, keep predators away, and soothe our inherent fear of the dark. It can cauterize wounds and refine materials. It can serve as a gathering place for forging the bonds of family and community. Outside of those bounds, though, fire can be a source of unbelievable destruction and suffering. Ancient cultures learned this about fire, and they learned to have a respectful relationship with fire and have a clear understanding of the parameters of what a beneficial relationship with fire looked like.

I believe the same could be said about social media. It is not inherently good or bad, it just is, and has great potential to benefit us. Used in one way, it can be a place where we connect with others, learn, share, and make a difference. Used in a different way, it can also contribute to us being distracted, mindless, shallow, and utterly ignorant of how we are atrophying. Because of this, I would like to make some general recommendations for how we can create a healthy relationship with social media.

Recommendation #1: Abandon the Illusion of Online Privacy and Anonymity

In spite of people's best efforts to guard the idea of online privacy, I think that the best advice for all of us is to accept the fact that our online activities are neither private nor anonymous. The data about the way the Internet works overwhelmingly supports these two facts. I do not foresee these facts ever really changing. People will try to change these facts and find ways to create privacy and anonymity, but the entities on the Internet will evolve in response to such efforts, and the current homeostasis will always likely remain, or even tilt further away from the ideal of privacy. The Serenity Prayer, popularized in 12 step recovery, states, "Grant me the serenity to accept the things I cannot change, the courage to change the things I can change, and the wisdom to know the difference."[1] As much as we may want it to be different, by and large, the ideals of online privacy and anonymity are, and likely will always be, merely a mirage. Insisting it should be otherwise will not change it. The only truly rational response to this fact, then, is acceptance.

In everything we post online in social media, in everything we text, and even in everything we send through email accounts that we do not pay for (like Gmail or Yahoo) we should be aware that there are other eyes watching. Some of those eyes exercise restraint in what they choose to watch, and some do not. Some of those eyes have morals that constrain what they do with the information they observe, and some do not. I would recommend that you conduct your online conversations in social media like you would handle having a conversation in a public place such as a mall or a restaurant, because that is exactly what social media is: public places. In fact, I think there may be reason to say that there is no place more public in the world than social media. How odd, then, that we have come to see it as private.

As a part of this acknowledgment, and perhaps most importantly, I think we also need to fully accept the fact that our online life is not isolated and compartmentalized from our offline life. I think this is most important because of the psychological and ethical effects of the belief that we can compartmentalize a part of our lives. When we hold on to the idea that there is a part of our life that is insulated and immune from the cause-and-effect world of our choices and their consequences, it appears to be common in human nature to use that secret realm as a place to indulge in appetites and impulses that can be destructive to our lives, our relationships, and all of the things that really matter to us most.

I believe it can be helpful to intentionally carry an internal model of other people and parts of our lives with us everywhere we go. In psychology, this internal construct of a real relationship is often referred to as an "internalized other."[2] Think about what matters to you most. It could include your spouse, children, employer, health, reputation, present and future opportunities, and freedoms. When we fully understand the implications of cause and effect, choice and accountability, then we can see that in a very real way, we carry these things and people with us at all times, whether we are aware of it or not. Just as their actions affect us even when they are away from us, our actions affect them even when we are away from them and even when we believe that our actions are private. I believe NCAA basketball player Jabari Parker gave excellent advice on this topic when he stated, "Just be the same person in the dark that you are in the light."[3] This approach will help you avoid the trap of the Gollum/Gyges effect.

I suggest we purposefully build our awareness of how we carry around the people and parts of our lives with us at all times and make a conscious effort to "keep them on our radar" and keep in harmony with them, even with the things we do in the pseudo-privacy of our online activities. When I explained this idea to someone, he replied, "Oh, I get it. You mean post like your mom is watching." Yes, I suppose that's the general idea, but besides just identifying your mother, you can plug anyone and anything that is important to you into that equation.

In application, this means that when I go to post, text, tweet, or private message, I think about my wife, sons, parents, siblings, friends, employer, the opportunities I want to have in the future, and my own moral compass. I try to align what I write, read, like, and search in such a way that they are compatible with these other things that matter the most to me. I try to think about how it would affect them if they could see what I was doing, and I try to keep in mind that what I am doing will, in some way or other, spill over onto them. It is ours to choose whether that spillover will be constructive or destructive of that relationship, person, or opportunity. We play a losing game when we choose incompatible actions between our online lives and what matters to us most and then try to compartmentalize them through walls of secrecy. The dams we build in this manner are leaky at best, and when they fail, they bring with them floods of regret. In 2005, Hurricane Katrina illustrated how building on the high ground is a better strategy than staying on the low ground and building even the strongest protective walls.

Recommendation #2: Assume That Everything You Transmit Online Is Permanent, Even If You Delete It

In a 2010 interview with the Wall Street Journal, Google CEO Eric Schmidt stated, "I don't believe society understands what happens when everything is available, knowable and recorded by everyone all the time."[4] In discussing the permanency of what happens on the web, he went on to predict that in the near future, children will have to legally change their names to escape being constantly and deleteriously tied to the indiscretions of their past that are recorded on the cyber-scape in a myriad of ways. Time will tell if that prediction comes true to the extent he predicted, but Mr. Schmidt was certainly in a position to understand the degree to what goes on the web stays on the web. It is as difficult to permanently erase one of your footprints in the cyber-scape as it is to leave a permanent physical footprint while walking through a river or through the waves on a sandy beach. Never assume you can do it. Do not plant something in the cyber-scape in the present if you would not be okay with it shadowing you forever.

Recommendation #3: Be Intentional in How You Use Social Media

There are so many areas in our lives where it is easy to go on autopilot, simply cruising forward with whatever seems to pop up that seems interesting, entertaining, gratifying, convenient, or easy. When we go on autopilot, we tend to live life on accident. We are merely responding—frequently in a simplistic and impulsive way—to whatever happens to flow into our lives. As a result, we tend to end up acting like Cookie Monster strolling through a bakery. "Mmm, that look good. Me just have a nibble. Oh, wait! Is that macadamia nut cookie? Oh, boy! So many cookies! Me in cookie paradise! Cowabunga! Nom nom nom! Uh oh. Me think me just spoil me dinner." The opposite of going on autopilot is being intentional: being deliberate about our lives, having our lives guided by what we value, being mindful of what is going on both inside and outside of us, and in general living life on purpose.

I have observed that it is especially easy to slip into living life on autopilot in social media, browsing our way through an endless stream of posts, pins, tweets, and memes without ever really getting much of any value or meaning out of it. In some ways, many people fall into the trap of consuming social media the way they may consume an endless supply of substandard carnival cotton candy. It's not particularly good or filling, but it was cheap, and it's right there in front of them, and because the supply is endless they lose track of how much they have consumed, so they just tend to keep munching away at it to occupy their time and their hands. How easy it is to do the same on social media, just consuming endlessly whatever comes down the digital stream without any thought as to why or what we are actually getting out of the experience.

This, for me, is one of the areas in which the previously discussed concept of opportunity cost really comes into play. Time is the ultimate nonrenewable resource. While rest and relaxation are worthy and healthy parts of life and there is room for some nonsense and drivel, we run the risk of letting the nonsense and drivel displace and disrupt things in our life that are of greater value to us unless we are intentional.

Take a moment and consider the following questions.

- What matters in your life?
- Does the way you are distributing your time, energy, attention, and resources—especially in your use of social media—match your actual values and priorities?

- If your social media use was cutting into things that matter in your life, how would you know?
- Is there any evidence at all that your social media use may be contributing to you not putting your priorities straight, or perhaps adjusting your priorities to fit your social media usage?
- Who would be the first person to notice if social media usage was beginning to take an unhealthy chunk out of your life? (Hint: the answer is not you! You are wrapped inside your own defenses, making it harder for you to perceive your mistakes in this area. Your shift in this area will be more noticeable from the outside, from someone who knows you well and from someone who is not wrapped up in their own unhealthy and unbalanced relationship with social media.)
- What do you spend your time thinking about when you are not on social media? How much time do you spend mentally on social media when you are not on it physically?
- How much time do you spend planning or anticipating what you will do when you access your social media next?
- Do you feel angry, agitated, distressed, or somehow wronged when you are not able to access social media?
- Do your actions ever indicate that you are ever choosing social media over the people and circumstances around you in the physical world?
- How often do you tell a loved one, "Not right now," or "Just give me a minute," to delay their attempt to engage you or get your attention because you are using social media? You may be surprised by how often it is happening without you realizing it.
- Is there any evidence that you are participating in groupthink on social media? Do you get riled up by stories and posts that you read there? Whatever your political or ideological views may be, is there evidence that your views have gotten more extreme as you have engaged in social media use? Are you really thinking critically about what you read, or are you merely joining the hive mind online?
- Is there any evidence that you are experiencing the shallowing effect from social media? How much time do you spend

thinking about superficial and frivolous things? How much of your social media use is about frivolous and superficial things?

- Are you actually accomplishing what you think you are accomplishing on social media? For example, if your purpose is activism, is there any evidence at all that your online activism is having any real-world impact whatsoever? Or, if your purpose is connecting with your family, what percentage of your time is spent actually connecting with family members in a conversation online versus all your other online activity?

I recommend that you take some time to actively, intentionally think about what your social media usage is about for you. Have a purpose for why you are using social media. Are you there to connect with family and friends? Are you there to get access to news? When you use it, actively seek to fulfill your purpose, then shift to something else. Don't just stick around because there is more to see. There will always be more to see on the cyber-scape; you will never see it all. Consider doing an experiment: for two weeks, only allow yourself 10–20 minutes of social media use per day (assuming that is a reduction in time for you). Then, for the next two weeks, only give yourself 10–20 minutes of social media use every other day (don't reduce it to five per day, skip an entire day in between using). With those 10–20 minutes, how do you prioritize what you do? If you hold tight to the parameters of this experiment, you will have many opportunities to begin to discover what really matters to you in social media, and what is merely superfluous fluff and filler. By the way, if the thought of doing this experiment sends you into an emotional death spiral, you've just proven to yourself that your relationship with social media is somewhere between obsessively codependent and addictive.

Set standards for yourself. Does posting cat memes on your mother's Facebook wall really count as fulfilling the purpose of connecting with her? Doing it occasionally may, if it is combined with other, more meaningful interaction. Doing it constantly becomes a poor substitute for connection of substance. Make sure that what you are doing actually fulfills your purpose. For example, if your purpose is political involvement, are you really being involved in something meaningful, or are you just on a bunch of social media outlets where people bash on the president, support each other in their mutual preconceptions, and encourage each other to go to greater ideological extremes without really accomplishing anything besides increasing polarization and a sense of self-righteousness? Don't just reassure yourself that you are meeting your purposes. Look for evidence. Look from a perspective outside of your own. What evidence is there that your social media usage is serving the purposes you have set for it? If you can't point to real evidence to this effect, it is definitely time to rethink your relationship with social media.

Set limits on how much, when, and where you use social media, and hold to those limits. Yes, even adults need limits! Inevitably, the question comes up of what these time limits should be. Dr. Hilarie Cash and Kim McDaniel recommend limiting total screen time (which includes television, computer games, handheld gaming devices, smartphones, and social media) to two to three hours per day for children, excluding computer use for school work.[5] The American Academy of Pediatrics recommends limiting total screen time to one to two hours per day, not counting computer time used for work or homework.[6] This is in contrast to the current average of seven daily hours of screen time for children in the United States. The Academy further recommends that families should create "screen free times," such as meal times, and that televisions, computers, and gaming systems should not be located in a child's bedroom. I believe these are sound recommendations for both children and adults.

However, I think there is a way of answering the question of "What should my time limits on social media be?" that can provide even greater clarity. I believe that when we are asking ourselves, "How much time can I save for social media?" we are actually asking the wrong question. I think the more important questions are:

- What really matters in my life?
- How will I know that I am investing enough time, energy, and investment into those things to help them go well now and in the future?
- How much time and effort do I need to put into taking care of my physical health, mental well-being, and relationships with people and my community?

- Do the people around me feel they are getting enough of my undivided time and attention?
- How much time would be healthy to dedicate to doing things that help me stretch and grow so I don't stagnate?
- Am I investing enough in other forms of recreation?
- Then, after all that, how much room is left in my life for social media?

What this means is that you will have to accept some limitations on exactly how much social media you can participate in. You may learn that you have to trim down how many social media outlets you use, how many accounts you manage, how many blogs you follow, etc. In fact, this will almost certainly be the case. That is why it can be helpful to go through the process of not just learning what you enjoy on social media, but what you enjoy and benefit from the most. There is too much of it to take it all in without it getting out of balance. It's like ordering a desert at the Cheesecake Factory: if you are taking good care of yourself physically, you can order one from time to time without harm. But you probably shouldn't order one all the time, nor should you order them all at once. You will have to make choices. Weep for that unordered slice of Oreo cheesecake if you must, but remember you can't have them all, or at least you can't have them all without serious health repercussions. The same is true of social media. So when you trim your social media use to a healthy size, keep what is most important and most beneficial to you, and let the other parts go, no matter how entertaining or appealing they may be.

Recommendation #4: Make a Place for It and Keep It in Its Place

As mentioned previously, time limits are an important part of keeping our relationship with social media—and screen time in general—healthy. But there are significant difficulties in maintaining time limits when you have your access to social media in your pocket or purse, integrated into the same devices that you use for making phone calls, keeping your calendar appointments, tracking your diet, keeping your budget, and so on. This difficulty is only amplified by the invention of wearable technology and augmented reality. It can be all too easy to just take one quick peek, (which invariably lasts longer than you intended or you realize) and have those incidences add up to an enormous sum. Like the old saying goes, the only way to eat a whale is one bite at a time. If you constantly chew at it, you will manage to eat the whole thing. Similarly, our tendency to constantly browse and nibble at social media often means we have consumed a whale's worth of it by the end of the day without even realizing it.

My general recommendation is *be where you are*. When you are with people physically, be with those people. Remember that texts, notifications, and phone calls are requests, not demands. Give preference and priority to the people you are with and the situation you are in. Set aside a time for yourself to engage in your social media, the way people might set aside a time to read a book or a newspaper. But, when that time is over, put it down until the next time. It will wait. The cyberworld is a permanent record; it's not going anywhere. Posts from last week and last year can be accessed with equal ease in real time today. The same is not true of the physical world of real life. Each moment is fleeting and unrecoverable; it shines for a brief instant and moves on into the past where it can only be accessed in memories. Because of this reality, I advise us all to avoid the impulsive temptation to be constantly plugged into the digital stream to catch each little morsel of information just as it hits the newsfeeds. If you try to multitask by being plugged in to the cyber-scape while being with people, one of the two realms will lose. My experience has been that it is the real world around you that loses. Just as it has been said that no person on their deathbed wishes they had spent more time at the office, I believe no person on their deathbed will mourn because they didn't spend more time on social media.

Recommendation #5: Increase Your Self-Awareness

Remember, in this entire discussion we are not just talking about social media; we are talking about your relationship with social media, and that means we are talking about you. Who you are—your abilities, strengths, vulnerabilities, genetics, coping strategies, patterns of learned behavior, other relationships, etc.—is just as much a part of the equation as the nature of social media is. Thus, in evaluating what a healthy relationship with social media looks like, you must do more than ask questions about time limits and what you use; you must be willing to ask questions about yourself. What does a healthy you look like? Understanding the answer to that question is the first step to solving the larger equation. From there, we need to develop the ability to see both ourselves and our relationship with social media more clearly. Consider the following questions:

1. How do you know when you are doing a good job of taking care of yourself, your relationships, and your future? What things do you do that are a part of being healthy in that way? What things do you refrain from doing that are a part of being healthy in that way?

2. How would you be able to recognize if your relationship with social media is healthy? (Hint: it's not healthy if you feel it's about the same as everyone else around you is doing.)

3. How would you be able to recognize if your relationship with social media is unhealthy?

4. Can you recognize when you are being defensive? Can you recognize when you are locked in self-justification? If so, can you see any signs that you are being defensive or self-justifying your current pattern of using social media? Are there any signs that you are rationalizing away any negative effects of your social media use so you don't have to think of them?

5. Can you recognize what your points of vulnerability around social media are? Where specifically do your temptations for having an unhealthy relationship with social media lie? Remember, temptations are things that you like, things that you don't want to resist, but things that ultimately are unhealthy for you. If you can't recognize any, then there is a good chance this means you have already given in to them and are currently in a state of self-deception.

6. How well do you take input from other people? Can you be open to their perspectives, especially when they are different from your own? Have you developed enough humility to allow yourself to hear observations from other people that imply you may need to change some of your choices?

7. If you are already aware of a gap between how you use social media and what healthy use would look like for you, how have you been keeping yourself from closing that gap?

A good place to start building this awareness is to simply track your time. Write down when you get on and when you get off. Record what you spent your time doing. If you want to take it to the next level, record how you were feeling and what you were thinking about before and after you got on. For extra self-awareness brownie points, track your thoughts and feelings while you are on as well. What you will find in this process will likely be very illuminating, and that awareness will be the starting point for you to make some evaluations about how healthy your relationship with social media is and which changes might be the most beneficial to you. I also strongly recommend that you gather other people's impressions and observations about you and your relationship with social media. If you do this, though, be aware that they may underreport your problems to you as a way of soothing themselves about their own problems with social media. So take any glowing accolades you receive for your perfection in this area with a grain of salt.

Recommendation #6: Have Allies and Wingmen and Take Feedback

When I work with various clients who use drugs, I often ask them the question, "Do you know anyone you think is addicted to drugs?" They invariably answer, "Yes." I like to follow up by asking, "How far into their addiction did they get before they realized they were addicted?" The answer is almost always either, "Pretty far," or "I don't think they even realize it yet." This leads me to ask, "Do other people know that person is addicted?" The answer is typically in the affirmative. By the time we are done with this conversation, we have almost always come to an agreement that the person with an addiction is usually about the last person to know they are addicted; everyone else can see it happening much sooner.

I think the same can be said about our relationship with social media. When our interaction with social media begins to drift into the realm of being excessive, obsessive, codependent, or addictive, we are poorly equipped to notice it by ourselves. This type of vision problem just seems to be part of human nature. Our hedonism and our defensiveness are two major barriers to this kind of self-awareness. Other people around us, especially those who know us well, are prone to notice that we have a problem long before we are willing to let ourselves see the evidence that our relationship with social media is either teetering on unstable ground or has already plunged off the precipice.

Therefore, I recommend that each of us have allies in our relationship with social media. I refer to these allies as wingmen. In the Air Force, the pilot in command of a mission—the wing leader—is tasked with making sure the mission objective is completed. It is his or her job to deliver the payload to the primary target. However, piloting a jet fighter is a very difficult task, requiring 720 degrees of situational awareness to avoid becoming a casualty. A wing leader cannot effectively focus on the mission objective while simultaneously maintaining a high degree of situational awareness. Therefore, the wing leader flies with at least one wingman, a pilot who is tasked with watching and protecting the wing leader. The wing leader knows that his or her wingmen have a better vantage point and a superior perspective on the wing leader's situation, so when a wingman calls out, "Incoming SAM. Break right and deploy countermeasures!" the wing leader doesn't hesitate or look around to try to identify the incoming threat; he or she acts immediately, trusting in the wingman's observation.

In our use of social media, we have a tendency to be so absorbed in our own experience that we do a poor job of monitoring ourselves. We stand to benefit greatly from having someone with a different perspective as an ally in our path through the cyber-scape, someone who can help us be aware of our situation and how we are navigating within it. Knowing that others who know you, love you, will look out for you are, and are aware of what is going on in your social media use can be a powerful force in helping you avoid the Gollum/Gyges syndrome discussed previously.

If you are married, I suggest that you allow your spouse full access to your email and social media. Friend your spouse on Facebook, have him or her follow you on Twitter, etc. So many marriages have been damaged by one or both spouses creating a secret life on social media that leads to temptations and reckless decisions. Be loyal to the dignity of your spouse, children, and other family members in what you post online and what you send via private messages.

For everyone married or single, ask a parent, sibling, or someone who you see regularly in the physical world to check in with you regularly with what they observe about you in your social media. Be open to the feedback they give you—even if it is hard or even if you don't see it yourself—keeping in mind that their perspective is frequently going to be more accurate than yours about your patterns of interaction with the Internet because you are constrained by your own defenses. Also, remember that just because your wingman doesn't see a problem, that doesn't mean there absolutely isn't one—there just isn't one they have detected yet, or they may be reluctant to tell you about it for fear of what your reaction might be. If they do see a problem that you don't see, don't dismiss it. Remember, a wingman's perspective allows him or her to see a threat against you before you can see it.

Parents, establish with your children the expectation that you will be able to have access to their social media. This expectation will be best received if you make it an expectation from the beginning of the time you allow your children access to social media. Don't allow your child to lie about their age to get onto social media sites early. Also, be mindful of your child's level of maturity; just because they are the age the website says is required does not necessarily mean they are emotionally mature enough to begin. When your children start using social media, walk them through it in person. Have them start small; don't simply allow them to sign up for a bunch of social media all at once. Help them learn to navigate one site, and when they can handle that well, you can explore the possibility of using another, keeping in mind that it is not realistic to have them join all sites and still maintain any kind of healthy balance. Talk with your children regularly about the online part of their lives, just like a good parent talks to them regularly about the other aspect of their lives. Be equally open to feedback from your children about your own social media use. Sometimes, children speak truths that adults would never say. A truly wise person can take good feedback regardless of who gives it or how skillfully it is given.

Recommendation #7: Evaluate Your Relationship with Social Media on Its Own Merits

It can be easy to insist that you should be able to have and handle what everyone else around you seems to have and handle. When it comes down to it, though, it does not matter what anyone else can "handle." This is about you. This is about the interface of your genes, thoughts, feelings, strengths, weaknesses, personality, and everything that makes up you as an individual with the specifics of the cyberscape that you are engaging with. While there are generalities to what does and does not work, there is also a piece of your healthy relationship with social media that is very individualized.

One person may be able to handle having the Facebook app on their smart phone. Yet, for another person, having it loaded on their phone overpowers the limits of their impulse control and makes it nearly impossible to maintain healthy patterns and limits. You have to develop an awareness and honesty about what you are capable of and how each aspect of social media affects you as an individual. Keep in mind that if this line of thought leads you to the conclusion, *That means I can handle a lot more than most people can*, you are probably deceiving yourself.

Can you have a Facebook account without it taking over your life? For example, can you go through your day without constantly seeing everything through the filter of what you could post next? Can you go for a good chunk of time without checking Facebook without a sense that you are missing out on something? Can you receive a Facebook message without feeling anxious until you have read it and responded to it? Can your mind be at peace when you don't have access to your smart phone? Can you say that your offline relationships receive the lion's share of your time and attention? If the answer to any of these is no, then you very likely have a problem. Don't excuse your problem because other people have the same problem, and don't ignore your problem because it is common and apparently normal.

You may have to find that you change the way you interface with certain apps. For example, you may find that there are certain apps or sites that are the most problematic for you, and that you may have to give them up. Dr. Kimberly Young suggests that as you evaluate your Internet habits, you consider giving up the ones that are the most unbalanced and out of control.[7] If you do what you have done, you will get what you have already got—and more of it. For you, that might mean you can have a healthy relationship with Facebook, but *Candy Crush Saga* has got to go. Not everything needs to be eliminated. However, you do need to keep the option of elimination on the table for each app and site if you find that there isn't a way at present for you to have a healthy, balanced relationship with them.

Recommendation #8: Slow Down the Sequence and Think

In a conversation I had with one of my sisters, she shared with me that she had deleted the Facebook app from her smartphone. That doesn't mean that she never visits Facebook on her phone, rather, she found that she could have a healthier, more balanced relationship with Facebook if she had to actually visit the web page and enter her user name and password before proceeding. By reducing the ease of simply popping onto Facebook, this helps her to be more thoughtful and mindful about whether it is a good time for her to use it or whether she is just getting online because she has a spare second and it is easy to do so (which always ends up taking more than the spare second she has). I thought this was a brilliant move on her part as she evaluated her personal relationship with social media on its own merits, while at the same time illuminating another important strategy: slowing down the automatic process of accessing social media.

In family therapy, a common technique for helping to break up an unhealthy interaction cycle is to insert something into the pattern to break up the flow. This can sometimes be something that seems extremely trivial, like asking a husband and a wife to open and then softly close their bedroom door when they are beginning to have an argument. The intervention has nothing to do with solving the problem; after all, opening and closing doors is not a conflict resolution skill. But, adding a step—almost any step, actually, it doesn't necessarily matter exactly what it is—helps break up the pattern that has been placed on autopilot through the process of sequence learning and opens up the possibility for conscious, rational thought. For each of us, finding something that helps us slow down the process of just simply whipping out our phone or popping onto a website—something that helps us stop and think, *Okay, is this a good time for this? How much time have I spent on this today? What else needs my attention?*—has great potential for getting us off autopilot and back in the captain's chair regarding our social media use.

Recommendation #9: Actively Cultivate and Prioritize Your Life outside of Social Media

If the only approach you take to trying to create a healthy relationship with social media is to limit your social media use, you can reasonably anticipate that your efforts will be unsuccessful. That approach is like digging a hole in the sand and expecting it to remain there. If all you do is create an empty space in the sand, the wind and the rain will combine together to fill that hole with sand again in a relatively brief span of time. If all we do is create a hole, we feel it in a very real, very visceral manner. It gnaws at us, and the larger the chunk of our lives that was previously devoted to social media, the more appealing it will feel to simply return to it as a way to fill the void. Nature truly does abhor a vacuum.

Our excessive, obsessive, codependent, or addictive use of social media can create quite a quandary and quagmire for us. As it consumes more and more of our lives, we have less substance in our lives to rely upon once we realize that something in our interaction with social media needs to change. Social media is so quick and easy and offers such immediate rewards that our dependence upon it for instant gratification can turn us into wimps when it comes to our ability to put some effort into relationships and activities and to be patient while we wait for the benefits of our efforts to blossom. On social media, we don't really push ourselves outside of our comfort zones. We may drift to the least common denominator of socially acceptable behavior, but that is not the same as pushing our limits and expanding ourselves. We can become unaccustomed to what real effort feels like in recreation, learning, and relationships, and thus we are likely to be discouraged when we have to come face-to-face with the real world in a larger sense again, like someone trying to start up an exercise routine again after years of slacking off. Atrophy is a daunting enemy to overcome.

Part of the challenge of reengaging our offline life is that in the beginning, it will often feel fairly uninteresting to us. The effort and delayed gratification that the real world requires can lead us to pine away for the constant and immediate buzz of the digital current. We may grudgingly push ourselves through the paces of a different activity, all the while secretly (or not so secretly) longing for the moment we can plug ourselves back in to the cyber-scape. It takes time to retrain ourselves neurologically and emotionally. It also takes time to build up enough substance in our real-world life to reach a critical mass where things start to click and our real life can be rewarding. To get there, many people pass through a challenging period of working through boredom and feeling that their life is merely *meh*, and our constant use of social media has subtly trained us to self-medicate feelings such as malaise, boredom, uncertainty, and dissatisfaction. In that way, the experience is not at all dissimilar from a drug addict going through withdrawal.

To help us get through this period, it can help to cast a broad net in reinvigorating our real-world life, looking for physical activities, mental stimulation, emotional coping skills, positive social interaction, and ways to engage with our sense of meaning and purpose in life. In doing so, it is important not to throw so many ideas at ourselves that none of them stick. Rather, it can be helpful to start with picking one item from each category: biological, mental, emotional, social, and spiritual/purpose. Start small, and give things time to develop. Don't expect to be blown away by instant, amazing results. Be persistent, discipline yourself to engage in these things daily, push your comfort zone a bit, and you will notice the balance start to shift.

Recommendation #10: Actively Cultivate Effective Coping Skills

Another thing I frequently hear in my work with clients who use drugs is, "Well, I don't smoke/drink for emotional reasons." That line is a classic. I usually respond, "Well, why do you smoke, then?" They often reply, "For fun." I then tend to respond, "Okay. I'll buy that. While you are having fun, are you experiencing an emotion?" As we dig into that, they may identify that they experience happiness, excitement, or relief from stress or boredom, and pretty soon we recognize that those are all emotions. So it seems that smoking or drinking for fun is actually smoking or drinking for emotional reasons after all. Usually as this discussion progresses, we hit upon the idea that they may not have started using drugs for emotional reasons, but they developed a pattern of using drugs for emotional reasons. After all, why one begins an addiction and why one continues are frequently different reasons, although the reasons for beginning never really go away, they are just added upon as the addiction progresses. Addressing any addiction requires enhancing our toolbox of emotional coping skills.

I believe this is also true of making our relationship with social media healthy, whether it is excessive, obsessive, codependent, or addictive. There are a lot of emotions that were a part of why we got involved; after all, curiosity, boredom, a desire to fit in, fear of being left out, and a desire to have friends and connections are all emotions. While we may think we did not start our relationship with social media for emotional reasons (and for the most part, I think our claims about that are on very shaky ground), it certainly continues for emotional reasons, among others. I believe that making sure we are addressing our emotional and relationship needs effectively is an indispensable part of helping make and keep our relationship with social media healthy. Otherwise, we are at high risk of using social media in an unhealthy psychologically compensatory fashion.

While it is not my intention to go into great detail about how to develop healthy emotional coping skills, I do want to share a few thoughts about the process of doing so. When we have negative emotions, most of us have the same immediate reaction: we want the negative emotions to go away! There are many ways we can try to do this. We can distract ourselves. We can try to numb ourselves. We can blame others. We can blow up and vent our emotions. We can bottle them up and pretend we don't have them. The problem is, we spend so much time running away from negative emotions that we put ourselves in a position where we never learn from these emotions. By doing this, we never actually get around to doing anything that will help to fix the cause of the negative emotions, and although we may feel better in the moment by running away from the negative emotions, we actually make ourselves more vulnerable to those emotions repeating themselves in the future.

When we have negative emotions, we often think that they are the result of things that are going on outside of us. It is true that events around us impact the way we feel. Our situation may serve as a stimulus for fear, excitement, loneliness, sadness, and any number of emotions. However, we must remember that our emotions are *our reaction* to the things around us, not things that our circumstances give us. Emotions are something we do. This means that because emotions aren't just something that happens to us, or something that other people cause in us, they are something that we can actually do something about.

How, then, do we get stuck in negative emotions? How can we get out of them? One way is to listen to them, learn from them, and grow from them. While distracting ourselves from our emotions is sometimes effective and appropriate, it is important to learn to go beyond that simple strategy and find ways to address our emotions directly. There are some questions we can ask ourselves to help us in this process:

1. What is the cause of the negative emotion? Can I see any ways that I am contributing in its creation?
2. What does the negative emotion mean? What can it teach me?
3. What needs does the negative emotion suggest I have?
4. What are some specific, constructive ways (that are in my control) that I can go about meeting the needs that this emotion indicates I have?

I won't go into further detail on this at the moment (perhaps I will write another book on it some other time), but hopefully these thoughts can serve as a good starting place.

Recommendation #11: Be Aware of the Temptation to Rationalize and Justify

I think there are many conundrums that come along with being human. Among them is this: oddly, many things that are a bad idea or are unhealthy still feel satisfying and good, at least in the moment. This fact tends to make our lives harder until we get a handle on things like impulse control, delayed gratification, taking a big picture perspective, and so forth. If our relationship with the Internet, smartphones, and social media is unhealthy, then it almost certainly falls within this conundrum. The fact that our excessive, obsessive, codependent, or addictive relationship with the Internet feels good and satisfying in the moment means that we are going to be reluctant to admit that the relationship is unhealthy.

Furthermore, since an unhealthy relationship with the Internet tends to take up a large portion of our lives, we are probably struck with a sense of emptiness and demotivation at the thought of cutting back on the amount of time we spend on it.

So we have two major barriers to getting healthy in this relationship. First, we are going to be prone to intellectualize, justify, and rationalize the problem right out of our consciousness. If we manage to make it through that barrier, we run into the obstacle of low motivation to change. Even when we begin to recognize we need to make some changes, many of us will run into the problem that we don't really want to change very much. Why would we, after all, if the way things are right now feels good and stimulating? The truth is, we often won't feel the desire to change—at least not as powerfully as we feel the desire to maintain the status quo—until we are well into the process of change. Therefore, we need to learn to be on guard against our tendency to rationalize and justify our way into forgetting the reasons change may be necessary.

As a part of this, it helps considerably to develop the ability to take your own thoughts with a grain of salt, so to speak. Learn to consider your own thoughts as subjective. Recognize that your thoughts and feelings are real, but that they don't always tell the whole truth, nor do they always give you good advice. Become familiar with the common rationalizing arguments you tend to use on yourself, such as "There are certainly worse things I could be doing now. It's not like I'm using drugs or doing anything illegal." Anytime you hear yourself think that way, train yourself to identify that you are stuck in self-justification. Learn to label that kind of thinking for what it is when it happens, and do it consistently every time you have those thoughts (for example, *Uh oh. I'm thinking like a net junkie again!*). Recognize that whatever course of action those thoughts try to lead you to or excuse you from is something for you to steer away from. When you know you are rationalizing and justifying, don't take your own advice! This is a difficult skill that does not come naturally to many of us, but it can be learned if practiced consistently. Indeed, the ability to refrain from obeying your own rationalized thoughts may be one of the most powerful coping skills a person can develop.

Recommendation #12: Regularly Engage in Practices That Sharpen Your Ability to Think Deeply

If, as Douglas Carr concluded, our Internet usage is channeling us both neurologically and psychologically into shallow thought and shallow priorities, it makes sense to purposefully and actively engage in practices that help us expand our abilities to think deeply and critically and to broaden our view when it comes to setting and keeping priorities.[8] There are many things that fall within this category:

- Read an actual physical book.
- Research both sides of a controversial topic and try to come to an accurate understanding of the opposing perspectives.
- Practice slowing down and questioning your own assumptions and conclusions.
- Sacrifice some of your own time to do something uplifting for someone else.
- Practice waiting without having to distract yourself with something.
- Take the time to watch a sunset and notice the progression of colors throughout the experience.
- Focus on what other people say to you and learn to listen deeply.
- Make something with your hands.
- Sketch or paint.
- Keep a journal about things you learn and things you are thankful for.
- Make a practice of thanking other people for their contributions to your life.
- Learn to tolerate and even appreciate imperfection.
- Cook something from scratch.
- Meditate and/or pray.
- Pay attention to others' needs and do something to help without being asked.
- Connect with something bigger than yourself.

- Make amends for your mistakes.
- Actively engage in problem solving with the challenges in your life rather than avoiding your problems.

The possibilities for helping deepen our minds, priorities, and values are virtually endless. However, they are very easy to miss when we spend our lives perpetually plugged in to cyberspace.

Recommendation #13: Be Vigilant and Recognize That Having a Healthy Relationship with Social Media Is an Ongoing Process

Moving from an unhealthy to a healthy relationship with social media, smartphones, and the Internet in general will take time and effort. There will be many times along that path when we will need to take inventory of how far we have come and honestly evaluate how much farther we need to go. Once we reach a healthy spot, we need to be careful to not simply congratulate ourselves and relax. The same dynamics that sucked us into an unhealthy relationship with cyberspace in the first place can just as easily pull us in again. We can all benefit from having periodic check-ins with ourselves and with trusted friends and allies about our relationship with social media and smartphones. Any human relationship takes effort to establish in the beginning and then ongoing effort to maintain it over time. Healthy relationships are ones in which people make constant efforts to nurture the relationship and maintain helpful boundaries. The same is true of our relationship with social media and the Internet. If we allow ourselves to go on cruise control, we very likely will find the health of this relationship slowly eroding with time.

The question, "Is my relationship with the Internet healthy?" cannot be fully answered in isolation. We can only truly get a full answer to the question when we pair it with the question, "Am I investing sufficiently in all the important aspects of my life?" We will do well to consider our relationships, health, goals, dreams, values, and all things of worth in our lives as we evaluate the ongoing health of our relationship with the Internet. The things that matter in your life require your time and attention. Ask yourself, "What have I done today to invest in those things that matter most to me?" Let that question be your guide in maintaining a healthy relationship with the Internet.

Recommendation #14: If It isn't Working, Learn from It and Try Differently

My grandfather is a skilled woodworker. I have a childhood memory of him teasing me once by saying, "You know, Ryan, I've cut this board three times now and it's still too short!" Clearly, when you cut the board too short to begin with, continuing to cut the board is not going to solve the problem. As painfully self-evident as this fact may be, my experience has taught me that many people make this very same kind of mistake when they try to improve the health of their relationship with the Internet.

For example, someone may try setting a timer to keep track of how much time they are online to keep Pinterest from being a giant black hole, sucking in all their time and attention. They may try this and fail many times. It is true that often times we do not succeed in efforts to change on the first, second, or even third try, and it is wise to continue trying even when we have been unsuccessful to work up enough momentum to be successful. Sometimes, though, our efforts aren't working because what we are trying just isn't going to work for us. After multiple attempts with the same approach, it is probably time to ask what else we may need to do differently to make success possible.

In all of this, there is a possibility that we need to be open to. We may need to consider that our past interactions with specific problematic apps have shaped us in such a way that for us, individually, there is not a realistic expectation of interacting with that specific app in a healthy way. Again, we return to the research findings of Dr. Kimberly Young when she noted that people with unhealthy patterns of Internet use often find they have to eliminate the use of the apps, programs, or websites that were most problematic for them.[9] This is often a very difficult truth for people to accept, but I have found that difficult truths are often the most helpful kinds of truth if we can embrace them rather than wrestle with them. So our hypothetical Pinterest user may find that he or she can develop a healthy relationship with other forms of social media, but may have to leave Pinterest behind. This is not a foregone conclusion for everyone, but it is one I believe we must all be willing to be open to.

Recommendations for Video Games

Rather than rehashing them all, I will simply point out that every recommendation I made about creating a healthy relationship with social media also applies to creating a healthy relationship with video games. I especially think this is true when it comes to the recommendation to have allies and wingmen to help you monitor yourself and give you feedback. When our relationship with something is unhealthy, we should expect to have poor insight. As much as Western culture values independence, most of us need others to help us overcome addiction and other pathological relationships. We are often too mired in our own self-deception to navigate our way out of addiction and unhealthy relationships without an outside perspective. Please review the social media recommendations and apply them to gaming. That being said, there are also some unique considerations to be taken into account when making informed and mindful decisions about video games.

Recommendation #1: Educate Yourself about the Potentially Addictive Mechanics in Games You Are Playing or Considering Playing

I am an advocate of being an informed consumer. One of the nice things about the cyber-scape is that it provides wonderful opportunities to be quickly and easily informed (although we should not forget the risk of being just as quickly and easily misinformed). I recommend we find out what we are getting into with a game before we play it. Several excellent sites provide content review for games, such as commonsensemedia.org, jorimslist.com, and parentstv.org. While these usually do a good job of letting consumers know vital data about game content issues, I am not yet aware of any site that reviews the addictive potential of games. Maybe someday there will be, but until then, it takes a little more consumer research to determine the presence and magnitude of various gaming mechanics. In the meantime, resources such as YouTube gameplay videos or *Let's Play* series can be helpful in extracting enough information to make reasonably informed decisions.

Online forums about specific games offer many clues about the experiences gamers are having while they play simply from reading the titles of threads posted there. And, as much as it is a highly questionable source of reliable information on many sources, even Wikipedia can usually tell enough about a game for a relatively informed consumer to extrapolate information about the presence of various potentially addictive gaming mechanics. As I mentioned before, we can use the equation $f(g + p) = ap$ to estimate the addictive potential of a game, where "g" is the degree of addictive mechanics in a game, "p" is the degree of our personal vulnerabilities, "f" is the degree of fit between our vulnerabilities and the specific gaming mechanics, and "ap" is addictive potential. Notice in this equation that the most influential factor is the degree of fit; its influence is so large that it is multiplied instead of added in the process of determining the addictive potential of a game. We need to understand each part of this equation to be an informed gaming consumer, and that starts with being able to identify addictive gaming mechanics when they are present in a game.

In my experience, once people become aware of what potentially addictive gaming mechanics are, they usually begin to be able to pick up on them in games they have played or seen. Some are instantly recognizable. Twitch is probably the easiest to discern, and a consumer can get a read on it from watching gameplay videos on YouTube. The faster the pace of the twitch-style gameplay, the greater its magnitude and influence. Thus, a casual search of gameplay videos on YouTube could reveal to the average consumer that *Mario Kart Wii* has a moderate degree of twitch, but *Nexuiz* and *Cloudbuilt* have an extreme degree of twitch. Just because a game has a high amount of twitch in it doesn't mean we should run away screaming, but it is important for us to note its presence and magnitude as a part of the equation.

Games don't tend to advertise level grinding. As I mentioned previously, level grinding tends not to be a lot of fun, so a game that overtly advertised itself as having more level grinding than any other game would be like asking to be tarred and feathered by mobs of angry gamers. Level grinding can take many forms. Games that include things like XP (experience points) and character classes and levels often include a level grinding mechanic. Most Role Playing Games (RPGs)—online or otherwise—have significant level grinding. *Space*

Pirates and Zombies includes level grinding in the form of having more difficult enemies guard jump gates to other sectors and crucial plot-related mission objectives, requiring the player to battle previously defeated classes over and over again to gain enough power to move forward. *Minecraft* packages its level grinding in a different form with the player chipping away at pixelated blocks with pixelated pick axes to mine and craft pixelated objects. Online games often rely heavily upon level grinding to provide content to keep gamers busy. In general, any game that makes the player spend a lot of time doing minor, repetitive actions has a level grinding mechanic. I often have parents tell me, "I watch my child play their game, and it just looks like they are running around a lot." Chances are, they were observing level grinding. Like I said, level grinding is not usually that fun or interesting to watch. That is why it is easy to underestimate the addictive potential of the emotional investment it requires and the intermittent reinforcement pattern it builds upon. Who in their right mind would think the boring part of the game was potentially addictive? Then again, a critical thinker might point out that if people persist in doing something apparently quite boring to an outside observer, that might be the very most overt sign of its addictive potential.

Most games are fairly overt about whether they contain persistent gaming worlds and involve guilds or leagues. In fact, whereas level grinding is usually kept on the down low, persistent gaming worlds (or universes, as the case may be) are usually proudly advertised. As far as I know, every Massive Multiplayer Online game will feature a persistent online gaming world. When online content of a game does not involve a persistent gaming world, it most often utilizes some kind of competitive league to flesh out a multiplayer experience. Many Real Time Strategy (RTS) games have an online element that involves leagues. Online leaderboards in games, including mobile gaming apps, also fulfill the role of this same mechanic.

Things like gaming epoch lengths tend to be harder to discern from watching gameplay videos or visiting gaming forums. One general rule of thumb is that Massive Multiplayer Online games tend to have long gaming epochs. Single player games that can be saved at any time have the ability to have either long or short gaming epochs, depending on how the gamer uses this feature and the degree to which he or she is capable of simply saving and walking away. Mission based games such as *FreeSpace 2*, *Sol: Exodus*, or *Strike Suit Zero* tend to have short gaming epochs, unless, that is, the missions are a part of a larger sandbox or open world gaming mode. "Rogue-like" games such as *The Binding of Isaac*, *Rogue Legacy*, *Spelunky*, and *Teleglitch: Die More Addition* tend to have very short gaming epochs (however, the character's tendency to die frequently may produce a counterbalancing interrupted flow gaming mechanic).

Interrupted flow has become incredibly common in gaming apps for mobile devices. When considering purchasing an app, look to see if it has in-app purchases. This can be a sign that the game is put together to interrupt flow in such a way as to compel the gamer to spend money to reengage flow. In addition, games that require a player to wait a set amount of time before playing again after a certain number of tries or levels, but simultaneously provide the means to purchase immediate continuance of gameplay, are often heavily built upon the mechanic of interrupted flow. Perhaps one of the most prolific examples of this kind of game is *Candy Crush Saga*.

Because all this research can be a lot of work, I will endeavor to provide a few rules of thumb:

1. In general, almost all online play increases the number and magnitude of addictive gaming mechanics.
2. Massive Multiplayer Games tend to have a high mixture of addictive gaming mechanics.
3. When a game has both single player and online multi-player options, the online multi-player mode will almost always have greater addictive potential.
4. Social media games and social mobile games in general tend to have a fairly high degree of addictive potential.
5. Games that cannot be saved at any time have a higher addictive potential than games that can be saved at any time.
6. Open world or sandbox games have higher addictive potential than mission-based games.

The most common "problem games" that I see in my professional practice at present conform to these rules of thumb and should be considered high-risk for addiction. This is not an exhaustive list of games with a high risk of addiction. These are currently the most common problem games for people I work with who have problems with gaming. They include (in no particular order):

- *World of Warcraft*
- *Runescape*
- *EVE Online*
- Massive Multiplayer Online Role Playing Games in general (MMORPGs)
- *DOTA 2*
- *Destiny*
- *Grand Theft Auto V*
- *League of Legends*
- *Minecraft* online multiplayer survival mode
- *Call of Duty* series online multiplayer
- *Halo* series online multiplayer
- First-Person Shooter (FPS) games in general, online multiplayer
- *StarCraft* series online competition ladders/leagues
- Real Time Strategy (RTS) online game leagues in general
- Social media games in general (*Farmville*, *Candy Crush Saga*, and so on)

To understand why these games are my current "frequent flyers" in the world of problem gaming and gaming addiction, let's dissect the one at the top of the list—*World of Warcraft*. First off, *World of Warcraft* (or *World of War*crack as it is known in many circles), has expertly designed and implemented level grinding woven deep into the very heart of the gameplay experience. It has masterfully paced the balance between level grinding and sufficient rewards through leveling up to hit the "sweet spot" of the intermittent reinforcement pattern. Second, *World of Warcraft* is arguably one of the best MMORPGs at building, promoting, and sustaining guilds into its culture and gameplay. There is a high degree of insularity within guilds and with significant demands of time and loyalty placed upon guild members. Third, the gaming mechanic of grinding to level up is tightly dovetailed with social status within guilds and between guilds. Fourth, the game not only provides fantasy alter egos but also allows a high degree of customization of these characters, allowing the player to shape their online avatar in the way that is most psychologically compelling for them. When the game designers throw in the ability to make these characters sexy and clad them in revealing attire, they add the additional allure of activating the innate sexual drives as a gaming motivator. The fact that the average player will intermittently encounter a wide variety of such sexy characters throughout the game provides fairly constant novelty to this particular stimulus, keeping it fresh, powerful, and innately motivating. Fifth, level grinding and raids both involve very long gaming epochs, requiring gamers to invest a lot of time and energy before the status quo has been satisfyingly altered. Sixth, its persistent online gaming world, constant release of new quests, and self-directed objectives make it a textbook example of the infinity gaming mechanic. Seventh, the nature of the infinity, guilds, and long gaming epochs is highly adept at making stopping playing both socially sanctioned and a significant visceral experience of interrupted flow.

The only addictive gaming dynamic for which *World of Warcraft* does not receive a high rating for is twitch. Thus, by understanding how *World of Warcraft* combines almost every addictive gaming mechanic in carefully orchestrated plentitude, we should no longer be surprised that it has won a position of dubious honor in the annals of *Who's Who in Gaming Addiction*. In other words, its "g" value is so high that the other values in the equation $f(g + p) = ap$ can be very small and the sum will still equal a very high level of addictive potential.

Recommendation #2: Build an Awareness of Your Specific Vulnerabilities to Specific Gaming Mechanics

Individual variations will give specific gaming mechanics a higher degree of addictive potential to some specific individuals than to others. In the equation $f(g + p) = ap$, we must learn to understand the value of our personal vulnerabilities (p). Who you are and how you manage yourself is an important part in the equation of addiction. As I mentioned previously, people who have ADHD or are drawn to adrenaline rushes are likely to be at much higher risk for twitch mechanics but may find level grinding so dreary that the degree of risk from that particular mechanic is reduced. Therefore, having ADHD increases the value of "p" but also means that if a person is playing with a twitch game, the influential factor of the fit between his or her vulnerability and the game's mechanics (f) is also increased. It's a double whammy in increasing the person's risk of addiction, especially since the degree of fit is the most influential factor in the equation. That being said, it also means that the addictive potential of a level grinding is lower because of a poor degree of fit between the gaming mechanics and the person's vulnerabilities.

On the other hand, people on the autism spectrum tend to take greater interest in small parts of objects or experiences and tend to enjoy repetitive actions more than people who are not on the autism spectrum. Therefore, level grinding is likely to be much more interesting and compelling for them than it is for other people. Having an autism spectrum disorder by itself increases the value of "p" but also increases the value of "f" when that person is playing a game with level grinding. Remember, the degree of fit between your vulnerabilities and specific gaming mechanics is the most influential part of the equation $f(g + p) = ap$. Even if a game has relatively few addictive gaming mechanics, if the degree of fit between your personal vulnerabilities and the addictive mechanics in the game are high enough, it can still push you over the edge.

In general, certain personal vulnerabilities tend to lead to a high degree of fit with specific gaming mechanics. While this is not an exhaustive list, I have observed the following general patterns:

- People with social anxiety tend to be more vulnerable to fantasy identity, guilds and leagues, and social status and achievements.
- People with ADHD and impulse control issues tend to be more vulnerable to twitch and interrupted flow.
- People who struggle with delaying gratification also are more vulnerable to twitch and interrupted flow, as well as infinity.
- People with compulsive, perfectionistic, or obsessive tendencies tend to be more vulnerable to long gaming epochs, interrupted flow, and level grinding.
- People with Autism Spectrum Disorders (such as Asperger's) tend to be more vulnerable to level grinding, fantasy identity,

infinity, social status and achievements, guilds and leagues, and long gaming epochs.

- People with disrupted sleep patterns tend to be more vulnerable to twitch, level grinding, infinity, and interrupted flow.
- People with depression are more vulnerable to level grinding, long gaming epochs, and interrupted flow.
- People who have a sense of emptiness and lack of fulfillment or meaning in their lives are more vulnerable to fantasy identity, guilds and leagues, social status and achievements, and infinity.
- People who spend a lot of time thinking about and socializing about video games when not playing them tend to be more vulnerable to all potentially addictive gaming mechanics.
- People who play video games as their first line of defense for stress and/or as their primary coping skill tend to be more vulnerable to all potentially addictive gaming mechanics.

One question we all need to ask ourselves is, What kinds of games hit our "f" value hard enough to be unacceptably high risk for us? Ask yourself, *What kinds of games are so compelling to me that I never feel satisfied? I could always play more; I would never really want to turn it off.* Consider this: What game can you not stop thinking about for a long time after you have stopped playing? What kinds of games have you become obsessive over? While games should be fun and compelling, are there types of games that you become infatuated and obsessed with? What kinds of games do you end up spending more time on than you intended? What kinds of games do you make sacrifices for? The problem with addiction is that it will feel very good to us. We tend to be defensive about it. The first place to start looking for our vulnerabilities are the types of games that we enjoy the very most and thus tend to have a hard time regulating.

It is also a good idea to build awareness of just how well you are taking care of yourself. While some of your "p" values are fixed (such as personal developmental issues), others vary based on your self-care behaviors (having a mental health issue increases the risk factor; having a mental health issue that we are not managing effectively increases the risk factor even more). The factors that change based on our self-care are ones we have some control over, and therefore we can make specific choices that either increase or decrease our level of personal vulnerability.

Consider the following: How is your physical health? How well are you attending to your physical needs for nutrition, exercise, and sleep? How is your emotional health? Do you have effective ways of dealing with stress, solving problems, and functioning at home and in school and work environments besides gaming? Are you making meaningful investments in your future? How is your relational health? Do you have healthy, reciprocal relationships? Do you spend meaningful time in face-to-face activities with other people? To the degree that you are struggling in any of these areas, you are increasing your vulnerability to video game addiction.

For example, if you have trouble with depression and you don't really have any effective way of dealing with it besides holing up and gaming, then you are at increased risk for developing an addiction or at the very least an unhealthy and counterproductive relationship with games. The better you are at taking care of each of these crucial areas in your life, the lower your basic risk level is for developing a gaming addiction. However, don't fall into the trap of thinking that if you are just well enough, you can make yourself immune to the effects of addictive gaming mechanics. Again, we are talking about increasing and decreasing risk, and it is important to always remember that there is no such thing as being invulnerable to risk.

Recommendation #3: Reduce Risk by Carefully Choosing What Games You Play and Do Not Play

Once we have become relatively skilled at identifying addictive gaming mechanics and we have developed some insight into our own specific vulnerabilities, we are now in a position to begin making some educated choices. The first and obvious strategy is to choose not to play games that contain a large number of addictive gaming mechanics. For example, if I know I need to be concerned about potential gaming addiction, it would be wise for me to refrain from *World of Warcraft* and other MMORPGs and MMOs, since they tend to have high levels of addictive mechanics virtually across the board by their very nature. The second obvious strategy is to be specifically aware of what gaming mechanics we are most vulnerable to and thus be very cautious about playing any games that may be low on other potentially addictive gaming mechanics but high on the ones that we are most vulnerable to. Thus, if I am particularly vulnerable to twitch gameplay, I may really need to rethink whether playing high-speed first-person shooter games is the right choice for me. Sometimes, as the old saying goes, the only winning move is not to play. Chances are, there are some games that you cannot play without it becoming a problem. This can be a very hard thing to accept. But at the very core of addiction recovery is the understanding that there are some things that you cannot try to interact with while remaining in control. In fact, the first step of the famous twelve-step process is to acknowledge that you are facing something that you cannot control yourself with. Therefore, the only logical step in that case is to cease trying to control it. If in the equation $f(g + p) = ap$ the value of the addictive potential of the game (g) and the fit between the game and my vulnerabilities (f) is already so high that the sum of the addictive potential (ap) is already in the range that would be an addiction before even factoring in the value of my personal vulnerabilities (p), then it is unrealistic to expect to play without becoming addicted.

Recommendation #4: Reduce Risk by Carefully Choosing How and When to Play Games

Whereas completely refraining from a specific game will likely sometimes be necessary, there are other circumstances where changing how we play can be an effective strategy. Depending on the way certain games are constructed, a person may be able to choose what parts of the game they interact with in order to reduce the addictive potential of it. For example, *StarCraft II* is constructed in a way that I can play it at various levels: single player, simple multiplayer, or organized competitive online multiplayer in leagues. It is possible that I can be successful in having a controlled and balanced relationship with *StarCraft II* by engaging in the game modes with fewer potentially addictive gaming mechanics. Therefore, rather than playing *StarCraft II* in leagues, I can choose to only play single player. That reduces the risk significantly. Or I may find that with only a little more risk, I could try to play online multiplayer with specific friends or family members in one-on-one matches outside of the league structure.

So in the previously mentioned equation $f(g + p) = ap$, by reducing some of the risk factors of the game (g) by not playing in a way that exposes us to certain addictive factors such as leagues, we also likely reduces some of the fit between the game's addictive mechanics and the person's vulnerability (f). Thus, we reduce the value of two influential parts of the equation, and we can often significantly reduce the addictive potential of a specific game for a person. So, maybe I can't play *StarCraft II* multiplayer without it becoming a problem, but I can play it single player, especially if I work at increasing my general self-care and investment in my real-world life (p).

There is another important principle to keep in mind: it is easier to start our relationship with a specific game by making risk-reducing alterations in how we engage with it to begin with than it is to take a relationship with a game and make it healthy after it has become excessive, obsessive, or addictive. If our relationship with a game has become truly addictive, we may find that we can't dial it back to being something balanced and healthy by changing how and when we play, whereas we may have been able to have a balanced relationship with it if we had started more cautiously and thoughtfully to begin with.

My wife also found that by changing the schedule of how my children play video games, she can reduce the amount of rumination they have over their games. Our children are not allowed to play the same game two consecutive times. For example, if they decided to play *Conquest: Frontier Wars* today, tomorrow they have to choose a different game. We have found that to be an effective and helpful strategy.

Tech Time Tetris

As a part of an overall strategy for creating a sustainable relationship with technology, I've developed a technique I call Tech Time Tetris. This technique is designed to help people make choices about logically arranging their tech time in a way that maximizes satisfaction and reduces the risk of using tech longer than intended. For those unfamiliar with *Tetris*—the game upon which this strategy is based—it is one of the most popular video games of all time. It involves a randomized assortment of four-tiled shapes falling from the top of the screen. The player is tasked with rotating the pieces to make them fit in complete lines. When the player makes a complete line, the line disappears. But if the player does not clear lines, the pieces eventually stack up to the top of the screen and the player loses.

Same Game, Different Context

Managing your tech time so it is both fun and balanced can be a lot like playing *Tetris*. For example:

- There is a limited amount of space you can fill. So you have to get creative and strategic about how to make the pieces fit.
- If you don't plan ahead strategically, it can be very easy to let the pieces stack up in a way that doesn't work and lose the game.
- Sometimes a piece won't fit if you have it turned one direction, but if you turn it another way, you can make it fit.
- When you do it well, you can have a lot of fun.

There are also some differences:

- Unlike *Tetris*, not all tech time items are the same size. For example, it only takes about five minutes to play a round of *Rogue Legacy*, but the average length of time of a *World of Warcraft* raid is four hours. If a healthy amount of screen time is between one to three hours per day (and science says that it is), there is no way to make a four-hour gaming experience that cannot be saved part way through fit into the equation.
- Unlike *Tetris*, some pieces have the potential to hypnotize you and make you obsess over them, thus distracting you from the game's objectives of trying to make things fit.

The Rules of the Game

When you are trying to balance out a satisfying and sustainable relationship with tech, the game you are playing has a few objectives for you.

1. You must keep your total screen time within the time limit.
2. You must have fun.
3. You must be able to walk away feeling like you had a satisfying experience.
4. When you are done, you must be able to shift your time and attention to other things.

5. When you are not playing, you can't just wait around for tech time to show up again.

Some Winning Strategies

There are some individual variations in how people can achieve all five of those objectives. That being said, there are some strategies that tend to be helpful for most people.

1. Whenever possible, pick games that can be saved at any time, rather than having to reach checkpoints or finish rounds.
2. If you are playing a round or mission-based game, try to pick ones where you can play at least two rounds within your tech time. For example, if I have an hour to play, and the average mission on a specific game takes 15–20 minutes to complete, I could conceivably fit between 2–4 missions in a playing session. So even if I only manage to pass one of the missions, I'll have had the experience of feeling like I accomplished something and progressed in the game.
3. If an average round takes 15–25 minutes to play and you only have 15 minutes left, don't try to start another round. Odds are that you will go over. Choose another tech activity to do with your final 15 minutes.
4. Give yourself less tech time on week days then on weekends.
5. On weekends when you have more tech time, don't use it all in one block. If you have two hours, consider breaking it into two one-hour blocks. If you have three hours, consider breaking it into two hour-and-a-half-long blocks.
6. Every 15–20 minutes of playing, take a break to get up and stretch. This reduces the stress on your body and also helps prevent you from getting in that hypnotic, timeless state.
7. Have more than one game you are playing at a time. If you have one game with long mission rounds/turns, have a second game with short rounds/turns. That way, if you can't fit in another round of your longer game, but you still have some extra time, you can still play your shorter game with less of a chance of going over the limits.

8. If you have a portable gaming system, don't carry it around with you. You'll be tempted to turn to tech whenever you have an empty moment. Treat portable gaming systems as if they weren't portable.

9. Don't use tech time first thing in the morning or as the last thing you do before you go to sleep. No screen use in the last 30–45 minutes before you go to bed.

10. Whenever possible, play games with your friends in person rather than over the Internet.

11. Tell your friends your boundaries so they can be supportive, rather than constantly tempting you to break them.

12. When tech time is over, it's over. Your other recreation needs to be about something other than video games, so spending hours poring over game manuals or planning out gaming strategies doesn't really count as working on balance.

13. Have at least one day every month where you don't use tech recreationally. Don't just sit around on this day, actively go out and work on engaging in satisfying, nontech activities and relationships.

14. Have a set time and place for tech time. Don't just pick it up for a bit whenever you have spare time. If you are constantly nibbling at it here or there, you are virtually guaranteed to go over, and it keeps you constantly thinking about it even when you're not playing. That's not a winning strategy.

Recommendation #5: Be Open and Nondefensive about Your Limitations

I am going to say something that might offend you: you have limitations. Hate me if you must, but it's true. You have limitations, I have limitations, your mom has limitations. Everyone has limitations, yet we don't like to think about them. Limitations don't have to be harmful. In fact, I would contend that understanding one's limitations and living in accordance with that understanding is a part of how people thrive. It is our refusal to acknowledge them that often leads to them being damaging. Ignorance of our limitations is far from bliss; it's a recipe for unremitting self-sabotage.

You have limitations in what you can "handle" with games and social media. I would go so far as to say everyone does. Conceptually, I think most people can accept that fact—especially when they think about how it may apply to people other than themselves—but it gets obfuscated by emotions when it comes down to applying this idea to ourselves in real life. That's where this truth gets hard.

For example, let's say you have a game that you really enjoy playing, but your relationship with it has clearly grown into something that is excessive, obsessive, or addictive. Let's also say that you get to a point where you realize it's a problem, and you try to do something about it. You increase your general self-care and involvement in real life to decrease your "p" value. You change from playing multiplayer to single player to reduce the "g" and "f" values. You make an effort to minimize the amount of time you spend thinking about the game in between gaming sessions. You structure your life and your time, you make rules and boundaries for yourself, and you genuinely intend to follow them. Overall, you go through a lot of effort to find a way to make a specific game work in your life without it becoming unhealthy, but it always seems to drift back into something that is absorbing and disruptive. Of course, you don't see that fact as clearly as other people do. That's part of how it works. If that is the case, it is time to really consider whether you have run into one of your limitations, because you have. With this game, you can't make the math of $f(g + p) = ap$ add up to something healthy and sustainable because it just simply doesn't for you, and in some cases, there is nothing you can do about it. Maybe the "g," the "p," or the "f" values have a minimum value that is just too high to begin with, and there is nothing you can do about making that equation work so it doesn't add up to excessiveness, obsession, or addiction. When this is the case, you can bang your head up against the facts in stubborn frustration for decades, but it won't change them. It's time to accept that you have found one of your limitations and let go. The ability to do this is crucial in order to follow recommendation number 3.

I have noticed that when people do this, they go through a grieving process that is very much like what people experience when they break up with a codependent boyfriend or girlfriend. They know it's good for them, but it feels like the end of the world in some ways, and it's only after they have put some time and distance between themselves and the experience that they can really feel good about it. I'm not going to sugarcoat it; it tends to be an emotionally challenging transition for most people. But once they are in a more balanced spot in their lives, people tend to come to a point of genuinely understanding why it was necessary and how their lives have improved as a result of this action. In fact, looking back on the type of grieving they did for their game often provides greater illumination for people about just how unhealthy their relationship with that game had become. Nonetheless, in spite of the old saying, hindsight is not automatically 20/20. It is only after we have changed and gone through the work of maturing (and it is work; it doesn't just happen magically) that our vision into the past is any clearer than our self-deceiving vision at that time was for us in that moment. While you are going through the process of accepting one of your limitations, remember that just because you can't yet see the light and be happy about it does not mean that you won't come to feel that way if you continue to move forward. You have to work for it, but it will come. Accepting and adapting to our limitations is a key to personal freedom.

Endnotes

1. *The Essential Reinhold Niebuhr: Selected Essays and Addresses*, Reinhold Niebuhr, edited by Robert McAfee Brown, page 251, Yale University Press; New Ed edition (September 10, 1987).

2. Tomm, K., Hoyt, M., & Madigan, S. (1998). Honoring our internalized others and the ethics of caring: A conversation with Karl Tomm. *The Handbook of Constructive Therapies*, 198-218. California: Jossey-Bass.

3. Luscombe, B. (2014). 10 questions with Jabari Parker. *Time*. Retrieved July 24, 2014, from http://time.com/13807/10-questions-with-jabari-parker/.

4. Jenkins, H. W. (2010). Google and the search for the future. *The Wall Street Journal*. Retrieved August 15, 2014, from http://online.wsj.com/news/articles/SB10001424052748704901104575423294099527212?mg=reno64-wsj&url=http%3A%2F%2Fonline.wsj.com%2Farticle%2FSB10001424052748704901104575423294099527212.html.

5. Cash, H., & McDaniel, K. (2008). Video games and your kids: How parents stay in control. Washington: Idyll Arbor.

6. American Academy of Pediatrics (2014). Media and children. Retrieved July 31, 2014, from http://www.aap.org/en-us/advocacy-and-policy/aap-health-initiatives/Pages/Media-and-Children.aspx.

7. Young, K. S. (1998). *Caught in the net: How to recognize the signs of internet addiction—and a winning strategy for recovery*. New York: John Wiley & Sons, Inc.

8. Carr, N. (2011). *The shallows: What the internet is doing to our brains*. New York: W. W. Norton and Company.

9. Young, K. S., & de Abreu, C. N. (2011). Clinical assessment of internet-addicted clients. *Internet addiction: A handbook and guide to evaluation and treatment*. New Jersey: John Wiley & Sons, Inc.

CHAPTER 8

CLOSING THOUGHTS:
PLATO'S CAVE REBORN

The ancient Greek philosopher Plato, whose thoughts still help mold and shape the world we live into a significant degree, wrote an allegory that I find is particularly applicable to our time and to our relationship with the cyber-scape. It is known as Plato's "Allegory of the Cave" and can be found in his book *The Republic*. In this allegory, Plato imagines a society of prisoners that live out their lives in a cave, facing a blank wall, restrained in a manner that removes their ability to look away. Rather than interacting with real objects, all of the people stare at one wall that is illuminated by a fire behind them (like a projector at the back of a movie theater) and watch the shadows of objects that pass in front of the fire. With their imprisonment, the inhabitants of the cave have come to think of the shadow figures as reality. When they see a shadow in the shape of an elephant, they think they are seeing an elephant. If they see a shadow of a crescent, they think they are seeing the moon. They come to accept the shadows as their reality, and thus they do not feel like they are missing out on anything.

Plato speaks of a person who is freed from his bonds and leaves the confines of the cave. In doing so, he experiences real objects for the first time. Imagine, if you can, the contrast of looking at the shadow of a tree and then finally coming face-to-face with one and listening to its leaves rustling in the wind, feeling the complex texture of its bark, cooling yourself in its shade, and plucking, smelling, and tasting the fruit from its branches. In that moment, I imagine you would be profoundly struck by just how different a real tree is from a mere projected shadow of a tree. You may wonder how you ever accepted the shadow as the real thing. Plato writes about the freed prisoner's experience of seeing the stars and the moon and watching the sunrise for the first time. At first, because he is unaccustomed to the light, it is blinding and painful, but once he adjusts to it, he beholds it with a profound sense of wonder. This ex-captive quickly concludes that reality is far superior to shadows, and he feels a deep sense of pity for the other prisoners still in the cave who have no way of understanding what they are missing. He realizes that as a prisoner, he himself didn't have the mental tools to even consider what he now saw before him and was only just beginning to understand. The ex-prisoner is filled with a desire to bring the other cave dwellers out into the world to experience it for themselves.

He is frustrated in this desire. Upon returning to the cave with eyes now accustomed to sunlight, he is blinded by the darkness and the smoke from the weak fire. The other prisoners take this as a sign that his time outside of the cave has harmed him, and they conclude it is foolish to venture out. His tales of the outside world sound like madness to them, and his efforts to get them to leave and experience what is out there feel like he is seeking to do them harm. In fact, Plato goes so far as to conjecture that the prisoners would seek to kill anyone who tried to forcibly remove them from their cave. They reject the message of the now-enlightened prisoner who journeyed to the real world, and they return to their shadows, more determined than ever to never to be removed from their dim and dismal realm.

I imagine that as I share a message encouraging all of us to reconsider how we collectively approach our relationship with the cyber-scape, my words may sound as crazy to some as the words of the prisoner who ventured out of the cave sounded to those who remained in it. When I encourage all of us to not make the mistake of thinking that being a part of an online community is the same as being part of an actual community, I may sound narrow-minded. When I contend that there is a very big difference between being able to actually reach out and touch someone rather than just "poking," "liking," or "retweeting" someone, I may sound old-fashioned. When I speak critically of the difference between a gaming achievement and a real-life achievement, I may sound condescending. When I talk about limits and boundaries and even consider giving certain things up, I may sound oppressive, controlling, and extreme. I understand all that. But how would you know if I'm right? In fact, if I am right, and if you are in an unhealthy relationship with the cyber-scape, all of those things are exactly how we would expect my message to sound. We end with the same question we began with as we return to the question of epistemology: how do you know what you think you know about your relationship with the cyber-scape? The cyber-scape is such a sensory-rich experience that it can leave us feeling like we aren't missing out on anything by our complete and constant immersion in the digital realm. However, that is not the same as not missing out on anything; it merely means we do not perceive what we are missing. Therefore, if we are immersed in an unhealthy manner in the digital world, how would we know? Furthermore, what would we do about it? I hope by now you can honestly ask yourself these questions and come up with some accurate and helpful answers.

I am a big fan of the cyber-scape. I think the world is a better place because it exists, and I think it has the potential to enrich our lives in a multitude of ways. I truly believe we can all benefit from it. However, I am also greatly concerned about what happens when the digital realm becomes our lives. I believe the cyber-scape has a place in our lives if we will keep it in its place. However, if we allow the cyber-scape to overflow the bounds of its place in our lives—as is happening for many of us—then we face the very real danger of having nothing in our lives hold the place it actually deserves, especially for those people and things that matter most. That is why the question of the healthiness of our relationship with the cyber-scape matters. I wish you clear vision as you consider this question in your own life, and I wish you the courage needed to act upon what you discover.

Endnote

1. For updated news, tips, and strategies, reviews, and ideas about having a healthy relationship with electronics, follow Navigating the Cyber-scape on Facebook at https://www.facebook.com/pages/Navigating-the-Cyber-scape/842173335850399?ref=hl.

ACKNOWLEDGMENTS

A thought unspoken doesn't go very far to benefit the world. A thought unwritten has no greater reach than the strength of the speaker's voice. Thus, I would like to thank Dr. Tim Thayne for encouraging me to go beyond thinking and talking about these ideas with small groups of people to writing them for a larger audience. Hopefully my thoughts can be of help to some who read them, and hopefully my thoughts will stir ideas far greater than those contained in these pages in the hearts and minds of others.

Every soul needs something to commit to. I am lucky enough that the woman of my dreams decided to commit to sharing her life and her heart with me, just as I am committed to her. There is nothing I accomplish that is not equally her accomplishment. There is no mind that strengthens mine like hers does.

Every heart needs a dream for the future. My dream has taken human form in two bright, intelligent, and energetic sons. The challenges they face inspired me to write these words so that I may be of service to them and to their future children, that while they enjoy the amazing cyberworld of their future, they may be firmly rooted in the physical world of their past and present.

Every man needs an anchor. I am blessed to have parents who have nurtured me and believed in me all my life. I could not ask for a better foundation than what they have provided me. The only gratitude I know how to express is to humbly and bravely build upon all they have given me.

Every person needs friends. I am blessed to work with the most intelligent and dynamic collection of friends I could imagine having at Telos. Their excellence inspires me to stretch myself. To all of you, thank you.

ABOUT THE AUTHOR

RYAN J. ANDERSON received his BS degree in marriage, family, and human development and his MS degree in marriage and family therapy from Brigham Young University. He received his PhD in medical family therapy from East Carolina University and completed his internship at the Duke Comprehensive Cancer Center. He has worked as a family therapist in outpatient practice, inpatient psychiatric settings, cancer care, and several other medical settings. He has also been a wilderness therapist, the assistant clinical director at Outback Therapeutic Expeditions, and a therapist at Telos Residential Treatment. His teaching experience includes undergraduate university courses, first-year medical students, and community outreach and education programs. He has also been a speaker at various conferences and continuing education events.

In addition to his work in the social sciences, Ryan spent nearly a decade dabbling to various degrees in video game design and production, working as a voice actor, writer, and designer for numerous mods and several independent games. He is also excited to be a part of the development team and the clinical director for Telos U, an upcoming treatment program designed to help young adults in the "failure to launch" category. Ryan has a variety of other interests including martial arts, history, cooking, music, language, physics, astronomy, hiking, and European board games. Most of all, Ryan enjoys spending time with his family.

SCAN TO VISIT

WWW.TELOSU.COM